Truly a *sociology* of social problems, Professor Green's text provides not just the descriptive catalogue of facts contained in so many others, but also an important glimpse of social problem development within a society. The outstanding quality of the book is the novel theoretical approach taken. The author proposes that social problems are created by differing attitudes which have a cultural and historical context. He argues that an ideological struggle between polarized extremes over what constitutes social problems and what should be done about them is the main arena of conflict on the contemporary scene.

Although many social problems are considered, five—crime, race relations, poverty, ecology, and population growth—are given major treatment, viewed in terms of an integrated social context, and examined from different aspects throughout the text. Professor Green examines how these problems came to be defined as problems and how processes that lead to their definition also influence attempts at their resolution. Throughout, he is excruciatingly objective, with a willingness to treat the ideologies of competing sociologies and to present a frame of reference and a mode of analysis that is theoretically based, and sociological rather than politically ideological.

oblems:

of Conflict

Social Problems:
Arena of Conflict

Arnold W. Green

Lecturer in Sociology
Humboldt State University

McGraw-Hill Book Company

New York
St. Louis
San Francisco
Düsseldorf
Johannesburg
Kuala Lumpur
London
Mexico
Montreal
New Delhi
Panama
Paris
São Paulo
Singapore
Sydney
Tokyo
Toronto

Library of Congress Cataloging in Publication Data

Green, Arnold Wilfred, date
  Social problems.

  Includes bibliographical references.
    1. Social problems. 2. Attitude (Psychology)
I. Title. [DNLM: 1. Social problems. HN18 G795s]
HN18.G675   362′.042   74-11481
ISBN 0-07-024310-7

Social Problems:
Arena of Conflict

  234567890MUBP798765

This book was set in Times Roman by National ShareGraphics, Inc.
The editors were Lyle Linder and John M. Morriss;
the cover was designed by Anne Canevari Green;
the production supervisor was Thomas J. LoPinto.
The printer was The Murray Printing Company; the binder, The Book Press, Inc.

For Colleen and Gregory

About the author
Author of many journal and magazine articles, Professor Arnold W. Green received his Ph.D. from the University of Pennsylvania. He has since taught at the University of New Hampshire, American University, and Humboldt State University where he is currently Lecturer in Sociology. His three other books are: **Sociology,** Sixth Edition; **Recreation, Leisure & Politics;** and **Henry Charles Carey.**

Contents

Preface

Textbooks about social problems are generally devoted to descriptions of them, usually preceded by an initial chapter on "theory" which may apply in some degree to the separate narrative and statistical accounts which follow. The format of this book differs. Historical and sociological analysis takes precedence over description. Each problem is also viewed as part of a forest rather than a separate tree, and various aspects of the same problems are examined in all the chapters.

Treatment of specific social problems is thus in some ways more intensive than in other books of this kind, but less so in other ways. No attempt has been made to catalog everything which has ever been labeled a social problem. To be sure, many social problems are discussed, but for various reasons of assumed priority five have been singled out for major consideration: crime, race relations, poverty, "ecology," and population growth.

The numbered chapters can be reduced to as many propositions. First, social problems are the result of attitudes and not the comparative seriousness of deplored conditions. Second, the attitudes which create social problems have a cultural and historic context. Third, the "same" social problems nevertheless are redefined in time. Fourth, social-problem definitions and programs incorporate a clash of interests, a power struggle, and images and their manipulation. Fifth, the ideological struggle between hip extremists and militant squares over what social problems are and what should be done about them is the main arena of conflict on the contemporary domestic scene. Sixth, in part as a result of this struggle, neither "deviance" nor "social disorganization" is of much aid in classifying or analyzing social problems. Seventh, attempts to solve social problems do not proceed along a straight line. And finally, eighth, as an exercise in speculation and conjecture, if certain trends should continue or combine in specified ways, if certain ascendant attitudes wax or wane, if attempts are made to push given values to their logical conclusion, then, cautiously, this or that intermediate outcome is possible.

The approach and development of this book owe much to Max Weber's thought. The concept of attitude, the central one employed, meets Weber's chief requirement for sociology. He said that interpretive understanding of social action requires assessment of the actors' subjective meanings. This concept is combined with that of conflict, especially status struggle, within a society viewed as being in flux and not as a rigid system.

Weber is assumed to be correct in his judgment that no sociologist in his role as sociologist can tell others what goals they should pursue, what values they should adopt. Nevertheless, no more than he did can any other sociologist avoid ultimate value postulates of his own in the selection and ordering of his materials. What informs this book is a concern for the values of historical liberalism. The desirability of preserving what is loosely called "democracy" is taken for granted. That admission made, it is hoped that Weber's "scientific" ideal of ensuring that private wish does not intrude upon objective analysis has been fulfilled.

A device has been employed to distinguish references which are merely bibliographical from those which elaborate a point. The numbers of the latter references have been italicized in the text. The reader is urged to review all the italicized references carefully. They are situated at the end of each chapter to avoid disrupting the main flow of presentation. But they are essential to a full understanding of it.

Arnold W. Green

Social Problems

Arena of Conflict

The Concept of Social Problems

Like a newspaper, any description of modern social problems commands high reader interest. The reader is offered immediacy, drama, conflict, oftentimes identifiable good guys and bad guys, and always the satisfaction of being posted on what is going on in the world. But a study of social problems—as distinct from a description of them—must be something more, and less, than a newspaper. The best and really the only way to study social problems is to approach the who, what, and where of the cub reporter obliquely rather than directly. Otherwise, what social problems are and how they got to be what they are will remain unanswered questions.

Little could be learned about crime, for example, by merely studying the details of a hundred or even a thousand crimes. Such a morass of particulars would inform as much about that subject as inspections of a thousand isolated sand dunes would reveal about the structure of a shoreline. Sheer description tells nothing about how crime, or any other social problem, became a social problem. About any social problem we need to know whether it is the "same" problem here as it is there, now as it was then. Who conceived and defined it, and for what purposes? Why do some social problems arouse more controversy and social conflict than others? Can this or that one be solved? Who will benefit from and who will pay for measures adopted to solve it?

SCIENCE AND SOCIAL PROBLEMS

Like all other social phenomena, social problems can be scientifically formulated and investigated. They offer no insuperable obstacle to rigorous analysis. There is, however, one peculiarity about social problems that is virtually unique among social phenomena. While the sociologist on his own can readily identify, say, social institutions and social processes, he cannot identify a social problem until the attitudes and beliefs of nonsociologists so determine it. The *identity* of any given problem is and can only be a matter of belated recognition on his part.

Sociologists are faced by a constantly shifting consensus about this or that matter of concern expressed by various groups and factions who are involved in a social struggle to impose their own ideas about what is wrong in the world and what should be done about it (1). This situation is the sociologist's primary focus of attention and analysis. As a scientist he cannot settle questions about whether this or that expressed concern is valid or invalid, correct or incorrect, or whether this social problem *should* take precedence over that social problem.

What he can do, as a scientist, is to assess the technical adequacy of the means that are being adopted by others to achieve the goal which they themselves have set. For example, sociologists have reviewed programs of birth control in the United States and abroad, and evaluated the effectiveness of these programs. What they cannot do, as sociologists, is prove that resistance to the use of birth control devices on, say, religious grounds, is wrong, because questions about the ultimate meaning of life cannot be settled by any scientific procedure now available or ever to be devised.

What Science Is and Is Not

Although science may be defined in many ways, as a sheerly technical enterprise it is simply a method of inquiry within one or another severely delimited area of experience. Within sociology, inquiry is limited to what men believe and how and why they act as they do in their social behavior. No scientific method of inquiry, in or outside sociology, can determine which goals men *should* pursue and how they *should* pursue them. These issues are continuously redefined within the social struggle itself, as cooperating factions compete with other cooperating factions to make their own attitudes decisive.

Many people, some of them scientists, view science as a sort of deity; for them, "science says" has the crushing authority of a Delphic oracle. Such a transcendental view of science, a *faith* in science, a belief that science can tell us how to live and answer all ultimate questions of being, arose within a larger value complex which is peculiar to the modern West *(2)*. But science, whether viewed narrowly as a method of inquiry or broadly and mistakenly as a means to achieve unity of social purpose, can never inform and direct how men should live. This theme is of considerable importance in our present approach, and it is expanded upon in subsequent chapters.

With that approach the emergence of certain social problems in one time and place can be explained, and so can the interrelationships among them. What it fails to do, a deficiency shared with all other known approaches to the subject, is reduce the *descriptive content* of several concurrent social problems to interchangeable propositions of common explanation. The scatter of social problems severally recognized by modern students of the subject—a scatter which includes war, alcoholism, poverty, automation and leisure, environmental pollution, male dominance, aggression, materialism and success, dope addiction, suicide, homosexuality, marriage or divorce, sterility or population expansion, conformity or alienation or conformity *and* alienation, and so on and on—makes any such effort futile.

Such a multitude of particulars prevents any attempt to focus upon all of the conditions variously described. There is, however, one factor common to all social problems, and this factor provides the only available single focus. All social problems are viewed as conditions which merit some kind and degree of moral disapproval. The only common identification of social problems stems, then, not from an objective but from a subjective factor. The scientific study of social problems is thus a study of attitudes.

THE PRIMACY OF ATTITUDES

The evidence of environmental pollution convincingly assails our eyes and nostrils. The danger of recurrent war constantly threatens the wishes and goals of most of the people who live in any modern state. Some people have much less income than others and thus are often said to be part of the "social problem of poverty."

These conditions all exist, but their "reality," apart from disapproving attention, remains ambiguous. If such conditions are ignored, or by a heavy weight of effective opinion are thought to be right and essential, they simply remain the way things are. They do not become social problems *(3)*. The subjective criterion, or the intensity and spread of attitudes, thus becomes of sovereign importance.

For our purposes, the term "attitude" is defined as an acquired predisposition to *respond* in relatively consistent ways to objects and other people. Some writers use the term in this sense, but also apply it to mental pictures of the self and others. For the latter usage, the term "image" is employed here. The place of images in social life, and their relationship to attitudes, is discussed in Chapter 4.

Place and Time

Attitudes, not conditions, determine social problems. It would be erroneous to assume that even a combination of attitudes and conditions creates social problems, for conditions can and do vary independently of attitudes adopted toward them. That is made clear when different societies or when different periods of time in the same society are compared.

Prostitution was no social problem in ancient Greece. At that time and place attitudes generally held sex for hire to be one of many acceptable commercial transactions. The practice was taxed by the various city-states to bring in what was regarded as indispensable revenue. At least in Corinth, prostitution and religious worship fused. The earnings of priestess-prostitutes built and maintained the temples dedicated to Aphrodite (4). On the other hand, prostitution in modern Greece, as well as in all other industrialized nations *is* a social problem, because sex for hire is generally held in ill repute.

Poverty was no social problem in medieval Europe, even though living conditions among the vast majority of the population were incalculably worse than anything in the experience of the poorest modern American. That most people should be poor remained unquestioned, an uncontested reality about the human condition, even though that reality doubtless occasioned more complacency among the rich than the poor. Almsgiving, to be sure, found approval in popular sentiment and sanction by the church. But no schemes for any real income redistribution can be found in the record. The rich were not charged with guilt, nor did they feel guilty, about their wealth. The injunction to distribute alms stressed not the need of the poor but an opportunity for the rich to assure themselves of a secure place in heaven *(5)*.

In old India the Hindu caste system was no social problem. The several castes accepted their hereditary status as fixed from the beginning of time, and their religion sanctioned acceptance of that status. Caste went unquestioned because it was deemed to serve real religious goals. The Hindu theory of karma, for example, portrays a man's moral deeds as automatically determining the fate of his soul in the next life. Dharma, another ancient principle, assigns ritual-magical duties appropriate to each caste which transcend in importance religious beliefs themselves; dereliction of these duties is synonymous with expulsion from Hinduism. The proper fulfillment of karma and dharma ensure a favorable transmigration of souls, and ultimate attainment of the absolute, the negation of ego, which for centuries has been the supreme goal of Hinduism.

War was no social problem in the old Comanche and Crow cultures. Warfare was the towering institution which dwarfed all others. Heralding the exploits of warriors, and preparation for war—this was their way of life *(6)*. Rudimentary levels of sociotechnological development, however, do not ensure that war will be celebrated as a natural part of the human condition. The Hopi Indians were in their own phrase the Peaceful People (they still are) who abhorred violent conflict. When the Comanche occasionally showed up to fight them, they faded from sight and left their possessions for the invaders to collect.

By the same token, the conditions of modern Western civilization have not created the social problem of war. Under the jingoistic Nazi regime war ceased to be the social problem that it had been during the Weimar Republic, when there was no armed conflict. Although the German populace remained indeterminately ambivalent, any general yearning for peace was reconstituted with propaganda and a paramilitary organization which covered every phase of social life. What the people were offered, and by and large came to accept, in Hitler's own words was "Peace, supported not by the palm branches of tearful, pacifist female mourners, but based on the victorious sword of a master people, putting the world into the service of a higher culture" *(7)*.

Attitudes and Deplored Conditions
There is no discernible relationship between expression of attitudes and comparative severity of conditions. Under conditions of diffused affluence in modern America, poverty commands more attention than it ever did during the Great Depression of the thirties, when the major social problem was not poverty but unemployment. Interestingly enough, there was no gradual transition in the sociological literature. Poverty "disappeared" there during the forties and fifties, as it waned in public consciousness; during the sixties and seventies poverty became widely publicized among, first, nonsociologists, and then sociologists (8).

An extensive 1962 Gallup-Hill survey reported that only a trifling proportion of married American women were discontented with the housewife-and-mother role; a majority declared they *wanted* to be subordinate to their husbands (9). No similar findings are available for the situation a decade later, but one may reasonably assume that the 1972 figures would fall off from those of 1962. That an intensified condition of "male dominance" was responsible for the assumed change seems quite implausible. In either event, the wholesale rejection of historic female roles by a militant minority of American women which occurred in the latter part of the intervening decade was strikingly disproportionate to any conceivable change in the "balance of power" between the sexes.

That rejection accompanied the civil rights movement of the sixties, as the earlier feminist movement had accompanied the movement to emancipate the slaves. Excited expectation of some that old barriers might fall, fearful intimation of others that such collapse might not be preventable, suffused the social atmosphere. Whether old grievances were at last permitted expression, or new grievances encroached upon a failure of will to defend preexisting limits, is a question that cannot be answered. At any rate, what did happen was a sudden intensification of emancipatory attitudes that cannot be securely traced to any worsening of "female servitude" since 1962.

Oftentimes, "objective conditions regarding the problem are far worse during the preproblem stage than they are by the time the public becomes interested in it" (10). Actually, in the contemporary setting a more extreme generalization seems justifiable. The attitudes which create a social problem tend to intensify when the disparaged conditions improve. Thus poverty, or female "inequality," or racial exploitation and discrimination, becomes in a sense a "worse" social problem as the conditions addressed are modified and in statistical measure are "improved" *(11)*.

Successful attempts to change conditions like these foster expectations of and demands for further change. As gains are made, attitudes of dissatisfaction and rebellion harden, at least in the short term. This generalization more clearly applies to social problems which involve role change, as in the case of Women's Liberation, than to those in which no role change is involved, as in the case of ecology. In history, however, no trend ever continues indefinitely in one direction. Reaction sets in, the enthusiasm of reformers slackens, new issues command public attention and oftentimes a temporary plateau of compromise between tradition and reform is reached, as happened when the feminist crusade of the nineteenth century achieved the voting privilege.

Concern about What?

The attitudes which create social problems are always matters of concern to the definers, and for that matter to those who in one way or another contest their definitions. But concern alone, even widespread and deep concern, will not by itself define a social problem. Those matters about which individuals are most concerned, and many about which people are collectively, and gravely, concerned, never attain the status of social problems.

First: individual concerns. Several polls and studies have consistently shown that people are primarily concerned about themselves and their immediate families. Financial worries predominate, and health ranks high, followed by marriage and children, and sex. When people are asked not which social problems bother them but "what kind of things" they worry about, social problems trail off in rapidly descending order with distance from the respondent's personal life (12). Income, race, education, sex, occupation, age—none of these factors affect the balance appreciably. An original study which compared American responses with those gathered in several foreign countries, including some Third World countries, disclosed that an overriding concern about self and immediate associates is not peculiar to this country (13).

Second: collective concerns. In the social action of expressing concern about some public issue, motives grounded in an individual's private personality will largely govern what he reveals to others with his public personality. In his private personality he is concerned about self and whatever in the outer world might enhance his own satisfaction, whether that be stealing money or dramatizing the self with noble self-sacrifice. Very few people care to reveal the central place which self holds in their public actions, and most of them, when they comply with the wishes and expectations of their associates, remain unaware of how much their expressions of public concern serve idealized self-interest. The reality of concern about public issues is not being questioned, only being placed in perspective. On the other hand, the line which separates "genuine" concern about social problems from attempts to secure public recognition for that concern cannot be drawn, as is shown in a later chapter.

In any event, the severe restrictions of the public forum do not allow the private personality free expression of its hopes and fears. Within the public forum the fate of others' private personalities is a matter of indifference. Only through identification with a group, a cause, a social problem, can an individual achieve recognition there. That is why—despite the universal predominance of self-concern—the expression of concern about social issues is critically important for personal reasons. For the most part, we *must* communicate with others at the outer periphery of personality. There is no other accepted way to become a recognized part of the larger society beyond the circle of intimates.

Social problems thus deal only with public issues. And these public issues must receive the expressed concern of a large segment of the general public. This subjective factor, attitudes of concern about a public issue expressed by a large segment of the general public, nevertheless by itself will not raise the status of that concern to a social problem.

To become a social problem some publicly expressed concern must have a narrow focus and lend some hope of specific remedial action. Many paramount public concerns are diffused in focus, and there is no foreseen way that social action could mitigate the conditions deplored. For example, when 1,000 Boston homeowners were asked to name "the most serious urban problem," their common response was a theme of "improper behavior in public places." What bothered them most was "a sense of the failure of community" (14). But purpose and action cannot be mobilized against an assumed decline of morals, no matter how widespread and deep the concern about it may be, and thus it is not a social problem.

Likewise, criticism of an assumed drift toward concentration of power and control in the federal government, denounced with equal fervor by young militants and old mossback conservatives, does not create a social problem. In this instance, the defined condition which arouses concern is too diffused to grapple with and organize against. Also the majority clearly favor the drift. Still others, including some ambivalent young militants and old mossback conservatives, define at least some of their own interests as being in harmony with this or that government program.

Events and Trends
No social problem is ever defined in terms of a single event. A social problem is always conceived as an undesired *established* trend to which deliberative and long-range remedial action can be applied. The attitudes which create a social problem are never addressed to a particular historic circumstance. Thus while war, war in general, qualifies as a social problem in modern America, the war in Vietnam, the most divisive, unpopular, detested conflict in American history, did not.

A social problem is always conceived as a *trend* of events which calls for a correction projected into the future. On the other hand, the war in Vietnam or any other historic event does affect the way in which the related social problem is viewed as becoming better or worse; and an event can arouse emotions which directly affect action taken about the related social problem. Although, as another instance, no specific crime can ever become the crime problem, the connection is drawn in a later chapter between public demands for a reinstitution of the death penalty and particular murders which arouse popular revulsion.

THE RANGE OF CONCERN AND PROBLEM DEFINERS

Only a shared concern, an expression of attitude about some matter which apparently transcends narrow self-interest, can lay legitimate claim to the attention of others in their limited roles as public personalities. Characteristically, a shared concern is expressed by either a majority of a population or a political-intellectual minority within it. Either source of a declared social problem invokes combinations of ends and means which are characteristically distinct, a subject left for later exploration.

Problem Definers

In broadest overview, however, social problems defined by a majority and those defined by political-intellectual minorities differ in one basic dimension *(15)*. Political-intellectual minorities invariably seek to change social institutions for the benefit of distant others. Political-intellectual minorities also usually insist that the majority should improve themselves, change their habits and outlook, become less selfish and adopt the standards of right and just behavior formulated for them by the political-intellectual minorities. The majority, on the other hand, usually want to see distant others change their ways or be forced to change their ways for the sake of the majority's convenience, safety, and pocketbook.

That is why crime is a very popular social problem with the majority; they see other people being controlled and punished, people who threaten them. Conversely, the "problem of leisure" is met with total indifference by the majority, as was "physical fitness," promoted during the sixties with vigorous and idealistic enthusiasm by professional recreationists and the executive branch of the federal government (16). In one case the majority are told they have too much time on their hands by experts who volunteer to help them fill their empty hours with worthwhile projects; in the other the majority are presented a nonflattering portrait of themselves as the flabby American. So long as exhortation of this kind is unaccompanied by power to issue orders, it is harmless enough, but the number of converts made is modest.

Whenever a political-intellectual minority designates as a social problem that which would require the majority to shape up in one way or another, propaganda—it is called "educating the public" —is always either hopefully invoked or vigorously exploited. As a matter of fact, use of such means positively identifies a given social problem as one which a minority is attempting to define about the majority, for the majority. And when maximum public indifference or even hostility is encountered, as with Zero Population Growth, propaganda keens to shrill heights.

Range of Concern

This is not to say that the majority lack concern about all social problems. When the results of several recent public-opinion polls are combined, a fairly consistent profile emerges of how much concern the majority feel about the five social problems to be examined intensively. Crime ranks first, followed in order by race relations, "ecology," poverty, and finally population growth. There is, of course, no assurance that these relative positions will continue unchanged, even in the immediate future (17).

The range of concern expressed by political-intellectual minorities cannot be so treated for two reasons. First, in some, though not all, cases a given minority may center attention upon one issue, and crusade in its behalf with a passionate zeal which will brook no distraction to other issues. Second, while a minority may be even more concerned about a "popular" social problem than the majority, their definition of it will be somewhat distinctive and include the majority as part if not most of the problem.

Like the majority, certain minorities have expressed grave concern about crime. The aims pursued, the rhetoric employed, so differ, though, that the "crime problem" becomes a somewhat distinctive phenomenon according to which perspective is employed.

Viewed as an entirety, the "crime problem" displays a severe and persisting conflict of attitudes.

The majority want protection from criminals, whom they want apprehended and incarcerated. Certain intellectual minorities want the "underlying causes of crime" to be explored and mitigated; they tend to locate responsibility for crime in "society," to view punishment procedures as an obvious failure, and they seek to educate the public in more enlightened attitudes. Both sides possess considerable knowledge about crime, but in each case selective indignation forms a distinctive image of what the "problem" is and what should be done about it. Very little communication is taking place across the barrier, or at this time seems possible.

The majority-minority gap is much narrower in the case of race relations. Since World War II there has been a phenomenal shift in attitudes in all sections of the country, which has been fully documented in periodic opinion polls. Erstwhile definition and rationalization of second-class citizenship for, especially, black citizens, have been replaced by endorsement of equal rights. The idea of racial equality, as fact and ideal, is virtually unchallenged by a majority that has been constantly growing. How much self-generated voluntarism was involved would be impossible to assess. Surely the force of law and executive decree, as well as mounting pressure from the mass-communications media, have done much to persuade or dragoon the recalcitrant and even the reluctant. In any event, except in a few backwater enclaves, there is no remaining supportive comradeship which will sanction blatant racist attitudes.

The main goal, that of ideological racial equality, is no longer a bone of contention between majority and various political- intellectual minorities. Only certain means of achieving it survive in dispute, such as the busing of schoolchildren and politically enforced job quotas for racial minorities in the name of compensatory treatment for past injustices. The majority have come to accept the principle of individual equal opportunity for all racial and ethnic minorities. What they tend to reject is official favoritism. Some individuals take such a stand on principle; others oppose official favors only when they are not themselves the beneficiaries.

Of the five social problems, "ecology" stands at the midpoint of majority concern *(18)*. As a social problem ecology for some time has been moving from a minority definition to one which growing numbers in the majority accept. The terms of their acquiescence, however, are both limited and special.

No available evidence suggests they are willing to accept feelings of guilt proferred them by intellectual minorities for "despoiling the earth" and the like. Nor are they and most of the politicians who represent them prepared to endorse environmental reforms to the point of endangering the shibboleth of "full employment." And on the evidence of present restiveness, some indeterminate point of cost in higher prices and taxes might well arouse determined opposition.

At the moment the majority do favor "ecology," but primarily as consumers of a better life. Thus water-pollution abatement is much more popular than that of air. Public bodies handle the first and the price is hidden, while the latter not only entails a threat to many jobs but requires self-discipline and personal sacrifice, in the case of automobile exhaust. And how much the majority will insist upon sacrificing ecological concerns to the famous "energy crisis" of 1974 is not yet clear.

Of all the social problems we shall examine in some detail, at the present time poverty has the most equivocal status. Far beyond any other social problem, poverty embodies the sentiment of humanitarianism, which is shown in the next chapter to be the historic vehicle of concern about all social problems (19). Poverty embodies that sentiment, but the present majority find antipoverty programs already in operation and others being promoted not at all to their liking.

Actually the will to help others has not slackened at all; indeed in recent years the *proportion* of total income from wages and salaries which is assigned to voluntary contributions has been rising. Involuntary contributions are another matter, and political programs to alleviate poverty have suffered ideological defection. For an apparently growing number of people in the majority the "problem of poverty" does not, as many others so define it, call for augmented welfare checks, or a guaranteed annual income, or more control of the political process by people on welfare. The problem of poverty instead includes a pressing need to "get loafers and cheaters off the relief rolls" so that tax levies can be reduced.

Social-Problem Perception

"Facts" have very limited power to modify images already impressed upon the mind, a matter expanded upon in Chapter 4. In the hypothetical case of hard evidence that nine-tenths of all adult male relief recipients are physically unable to seek employment or hold a job, there are people who would still demand that all welfare programs be cut back, and their image of healthy but lazy and crooked parasites carousing at public expense would not fade. Conversely, in the hypothetical case of hard evidence that nine-tenths of the same category had lied about their financial status, there are other people who would ignore or deny it and preserve untarnished an image of innocent victims persecuted by an unjust system.

The social problem of population growth provokes much less majority-minority dispute. This belief, that there are too many people and too many more to come for present and foreseen resources to accommodate, does not capture the attention or interest of the majority. Many Americans have never heard about it. Most of those who do hear about it then ignore it, unless it is described as a problem in some far-off land.

They do not perceive the issue of population growth, when they perceive it at all, as affecting their lives in the short term. They lack that ability and willingness of political-intellectual minorities to project public concern into a future beyond the narrow circle of the familiar and the personally known. Of the five social problems cited, this one is the least controversial, but only because the majority have greater awareness and knowledge about the others.

Ancillary aspects of the problem, such as abortion and the movement against economic growth, are different matters. The majority are very much aware of abortion, and ambivalent about it. Recent public-opinion polls and state-referendum results indicate no clear attitude trend. The movement against economic growth stands no chance whatsoever. This fad pushed by a small intellectual coterie is unknown to the majority, who would otherwise, in light of their dominant and perceived interests, reject it out of hand.

Other recent attempts to define and promote a social problem have also failed. For example, a great deal of energy and money was spent during the sixties to create social problems out of leisure, physical fitness, and automation. Unless immediate corrections of attitudes and behavior were adopted, doom was prophesied. Public reaction in some quarters was a massive yawn, in many more a sheer lack of awareness that anything at all was happening. Yet all three subjects were featured in social-problems textbooks written during the sixties, especially automation. Such books written during the seventies rarely mention them.

Of the five social problems, ecology and population growth arouse much less emotion than do race relations, poverty, and crime. They engender more concern than did automation; yet to the majority they also remain matters of relative unawareness or indifference, notably so in the case of population growth. That is why they are more vulnerable than poverty, race relations, and crime to modification in the face of structural change. Prophecy is ill-advised because so infrequently fulfilled, but it does appear likely that a decade hence these two social problems will be specified in much different terms than at present, and possibly they will retain less of their present public interest than the other three hardier perennials.

The "Majority" and "Minority" Concepts

The majority are not a membership, do not comprise a solid and organized array which is self-consciously aware of unified purpose; they do not express collective opinion and take collective action on matters of common concern as does a constituency. If they did, social problems could hardly exist, for their agreements and rejections would be systematically implemented as well as enunciated. Group and bloc conflicts would subside as *vox populi* resounded loud and clear, not so much reacting to events and pressures, as at present, but directing them.

As used here, the concept refers to a numerical majority of the population who are dispersed in social space and have in common only an allegiance to tradition which *at any given moment in time* exceeds that displayed by various intellectual-political minorities. The latter espouse progressive causes, and attempt with differing measures of success to make social problems of those causes. The matter of relativity is crucial. The majority are in no absolute sense traditionalistic; although they remain more so than the intellectual-political minorities who try to move them, they are much less so than they were in the recent past *(20)*.

The majority are no more monolithic in interest than they

comprise a conscious membership. They vary in occupation, age, race, ethnic group, religion, income, education, and political affiliation. Each individual within it often finds himself in a situation of cross-purpose in which, say, his occupational interest fails to mesh with his interest as part of some other category. Nor do the majority possess power commensurate with their numbers. They more react than act when some reform measure they deem "goes too far" is presented them by the individually much more powerful and strategically placed minorities in the courts, church, academe, and communications media.

Not all persons within the majority remain silent, which is to say that many professors, judges, clergymen, journalists, TV program directors, and writers are part of the majority, of that broad spectrum within the population which is relatively traditionalistic in outlook. Still, these spokesmen for majority attitudes represent a much smaller proportion of their own occupations than do those people who work in much less vocal trades, such as farming, service jobs, and factory and office employment.

The apparent key factor in recent years, however, has not been occupation but higher education. When large numbers are examined, a striking correlation between attendance at or graduation from institutions of higher learning and an innovative, antitraditional, liberal-to-radical reformist stance is revealed *(21)*. As here defined in relativistic terms, the size of the majority can hardly diminish, but very likely, at least in the short term, the intensity of their traditionalistic attitudes will continue to diminish as higher education becomes more accessible and utilized *(22)*.

As for the various political-intellectual minorities, in one way they are separate in outlook. A certain minority may be primarily concerned about a single cause (such as prison abolition or Zero Population Growth) and utilize public meetings, media presentations, and political lobbying to promote that cause. They thus compete with one another for attention, donations, support, and power.

But in another way they are not separate in outlook at all; they are united by a common rejection of cultural traditionalism. They share a dim view of the majority, especially of the majority's basic satisfaction with present institutional arrangements and patterns of consumership. They also share a distaste for business and industry, a distaste which is not entirely absent *within* business and industry. All these themes are expanded upon in subsequent chapters, especially Chapter 5.

ATTITUDES AND SOCIAL-PROBLEM CONDITIONS

The present approach stresses not conditions but attitudes, especially moral judgments. It should be kept in mind that no social-problem condition exists at all apart from an attitude which directs and controls the perception of it. With reference to social problems, an unorganized majority on one side and one or more minorities which usually cooperate informally on the other either share or share in part, contest or contest in part, certain attitudes about a condition or set of conditions *which themselves* are defined with attitudes.

Illustrations for the sovereign operation of attitudes in defining social-problem conditions as well as social problems themselves can be found in the written work of social scientists. Some of them assert that the condition of modern American blacks is institutional racism, one of physical and psychic violation by the brutal operations of government, business, education, and social service agencies. Others argue that the condition of modern American blacks has been vastly and demonstrably improved, a "fact" proved by trends in housing, education, election of black officeholders by white voters, jobs, government subsidies, even favored treatment by police and the courts (23). Here as elsewhere, social "facts" are screened, sorted or distorted, by whatever images dominate the mind of a given perceiver, a subject enlarged upon in Chapter 4.

Persistent attempts by social scientists to identify social problems objectively, that is, in terms of stated conditions apart from or even in conjunction with attitudes, have not succeeded *(24)*. The danger of inducing boredom with iteration is worth risking: attitudes produce social problems, whether cited conditions are claimed to be better or worse, here as compared with there, now as compared with then. Nevertheless, as in previous decades attempts are still being made to identify social problems on the basis of one or both of two supposedly objective criteria, social disorganization and deviance.

Social Disorganization

The reality of social disorganization, apart from attitudes of disapproval, can be questioned in two ways. First, what has been called social disorganization in the sociological literature is not that at all, but disapproval of some aspect of a social institution which is structurally inseparable from that institution. War has been frequently cited as an example of social disorganization, but war, or the persisting potential for war, accompanies national sovereignty, which the majority in every nation, as well as most sociologists, endorse with settled habit, tradition, and loyalty.

Divorce has been termed a social problem, a breakdown, an indication of social disorganization, and yet divorce is found in universal company with the universal institution of the family. Nowhere approved in principle, divorce has always and everywhere been provided for stated reasons. Actually, the "social disorganization" of divorce is in a real sense a consequence of marriage and the family. In the hypothetical case of totally "free" sexual relations, divorce could not occur. In seeming paradox, however, an upsurge of hedonistic attitudes toward sexual expression in any society has always been followed by higher divorce rates, because the institutions of marriage and the family remain permanent. Interestingly enough, many people, including some who write about these subjects, laud free sexual expression while they deplore the consequent high divorce rate.

Crime is less a manifestation of social disorganization than it is an inevitable consequence of universal rules designed to protect life and property. Attitudes toward poverty in time may range from acceptance of widespread malnutrition to concern about the psychological deprivation of jobs which lack honorific status; yet some people in every society have less than others, a consequence of the division of labor, which is the foundation of social organization in all societies, past and present, and regardless of political ideology.

Pollution and similar condemned phenomena are a presently undesired consequence of desired high levels of productivity, employment, and material levels of consumption. Race riots and like disturbances have been generally disapproved results of widely approved attempts to establish racial equality. In every case cited, "social disorganization" reveals not a technical breakdown of existing social structure but an underlying attitude that idealized perfection should be realized, a wish that cake should be had and eaten.

Second, much of what is labeled social disorganization is demonstrably highly organized, but morally disapproved, as in the following quotation. The "type of social problem involved in disorganization arises not from people failing to live up to the requirements of their social statuses, as is the case with deviant behavior, but from the faulty organization of those statuses into a reasonably coherent system" (25). The key words here are "reasonably coherent" and "faulty," which are judgments of value and not of technical failure. The system of statuses within organized crime is surely coherent enough. Nazi Germany and antebellum American slavery could be accurately characterized in a similar way. We simply lack evidence that organized behavior which most of us deem nefarious is any less coherent than organized behavior which most of us approve.

The above quotation, as well as the work from which it is cited, does not deny coherence to disapproved systems. But what is "faulty" in social disorganization "refers to inadequacies or failures in a social system of interrelated statuses and roles such that the collective purposes and individual objectives of its members are less fully realized than they could be in an alternative workable system" (26). This leap into utopia has become a common practice among writers on social disorganization, as they repudiate the ideal standard of judgment applied by their sociological predecessors, that of rural America past, and seek a new one.

Note that any "alternative system" remains an ideal, a moral ideal, above all an untested ideal. Every social order remains in a constant state of failing to measure up to ideal attitudes, those applied to the present by the majority as well as those projected into the future by minority revisionists. Ideals are beacons of aspiration without which the human spirit would have to settle for less than it does. But they beckon forever beyond human reach.

At a more prosaic level, in the incessant conflict of material as well as ideal interests, any present social organization serves well the perceived interests of some, ill the perceived interests of others (27). When dissatisfied and insurgent contingents succeed in promoting "an alternative workable system," that system will leave former "have" contingents in a relative "have-not" condition. There is simply no way to break this circle with attempts to establish technical, inevitably pseudotechnical, assessments of the point at which social organization becomes social disorganization. Only attitudes, particularly those of moral judgment, can be utilized.

Deviance

Again, the concept of deviance indicates an attitude of moral judgment and not a technical description. Such is denied in one definition which is taken from the source cited above. Deviant behavior "cannot be described in the abstract but must be related to the norms that are socially defined as appropriate and morally binding for people occupying the various statuses." Deviant behavior, then, presumably is that which departs from what most of the people believe other people should do.

In one sense there is nothing wrong with this definition. Deviance always has been viewed as violation of moral standards. But it is precisely because moral standards have lost much of their erstwhile clear enunciation that the moral and nontechnical status of the concept has been revealed.

The strength of moral standards has never depended upon universal compliance. A few have always systematically violated them, and the many have always cut corners when convenient occasion arose. The strength of moral standards instead derives from shared belief and sentiment, derives not so much from what people do as from what they affirm should be done. When what should be done is in relative degree widely agreed upon, then deviance is relatively easy to ascertain in the sheer weight of expressed attitudes of moral disapproval. There is now much less such agreement than prevailed in the recent past.

What exactly constitutes deviance has become a blurred designation. Life-styles which in significant phrase are dubbed alternative rather than deviant proclaim their moral rightness and superiority. The majority, although less certainly and securely than heretofore, do attempt to maintain their traditional standards. But they receive diminishing support from institutional authority figures—clergymen, judges, professors, editors, and other leaders of thought and opinion—in what was once an unexamined assumption that their way of life is the baseline from which deviance can be measured *(28)*.

New suspicions and doubts aimed at the legitimacy of conventional norms, roles, statuses blur their sharp outline. Alternative life-styles and even idiosyncratic behavior become less vulnerable to being hedged in by majority prejudice. The baseline of moral judgment evades precise location. Surely the number of adolescent male pot-smoking runaways has become a sizable fraction of the Boy Scout enrollment. And since more than a few Boy Scouts are reported to be pot smokers, which affiliation constitutes deviance? Who, in other words, is deviating from whom as well as from what?

The Role of the Professional

A social problem, whether regarded by sociologists as a manifestation of social disorganization or deviance or something else, basically remains a matter of *public* concern. That concern is neither universal nor uniform, nor are the attitudes which create a social problem. Every social problem is embroiled in conflict of varying degree about what should be done about it, and in some cases even about whether it exists and merits public attention.

The professional's role permits only that he assess and analyze this welter of opinion, pressure, and conflict. It is not, to repeat an earlier observation, to go out into society and discover social problems by applying technical criteria of his own devising. His function instead is to observe, record, and interpret what other people are saying and doing. People other than sociologists make, define, resist, deny this or that social problem. With whatever insight and conceptual acumen he may possess, the job of the sociologist is to reveal more clearly than was previously known the what and the why of such data.

What he cannot do, in his function as social scientist, is pass moral judgment. Since social problems are created by the attitudes of *other* people, he bears no license conferred by science to declare that certain widely accepted social problems do not deserve acknowledgement or alternatively claim that he has discovered social problems which are not, or not yet, of public concern. Conditions of environmental pollution, for example, may have been almost as "bad" in 1964 as they were in 1974, but there was no warrant for any sociologist to declare them a social problem in 1964 (none actually did) because the attitudes which created that social problem had not yet emerged.

The limits of the professional's role are now more often exceeded than in the recent past. When majority opinion and public concern were relatively fixed and supported by institutional authority figures, the very data the professional dealt with circumscribed his role. Now, however, a relative deterioration of public consensus not only makes the professional's task more difficult but also offers a temptation to forsake the role of analyst for that of judge. In some cases, that temptation has apparently proved overwhelming.

In the recent social-problems literature can be found claims that the real focus of deviance, the real sources of social disorganization, are "compulsive conformity" to outmoded definitions of moral conduct, roles and statuses. The real social problems are not the so-called deviates but those who label them as such, those who "wield power." Or deviance does not exist, only oppression and persecution, perpetrated by business and political leaders who do much more harm than rapists and murderers. Or, as in the single theme of one social-problems textbook, "social pathologies" result solely from majority opinion and behavior; conformity to majority opinion and behavior is *the* social problem.

No moral judgment can be proved wrong, or proved right for that matter. Neither should any denunciation of the above moral judgments be inferred. The only pertinent question is whether what the majority do and believe can properly be defined as social problems.

With no canon of science can an entire society be indicted as a social problem, because the recognition of social problems occurs only among the people who compose it. A social problem is always defined as an unwanted phenomenon which is potentially remediable *within the ongoing context of a given society.* A social problem is a *public* issue of narrow focus which is so defined by a public.

A social problem, now as ever, exists only because of widespread and shared recognition of it. Even in those cases where a social problem is promoted by one or more minorities, the majority must be aware of the specific issue, whether they agree or disagree with, or oppose, what is being promoted. In any case, the concern and attitudes of a large public must be involved, else the matter under consideration cannot be a social problem.

The primary emphasis placed upon a study of the attitudes of others in this chapter affords a much more rigorous focus of attention than might appear at first assessment. With it, the reader is spared what Pitirim A. Sorokin called "fads and foibles of sociology." Nor is the reader subjected to arbitrary claim and propaganda disguised as scholarship.

A final word. The sociologist as *citizen* has a perfect right to assume the role of social critic, and support any political or social-reform effort he chooses. Indeed he can hardly avoid so doing, for only the rare and hapless citizen remains indifferent to whatever drift in his own society he perceives. It is only in his role as sociologist that he relinquishes any right to preach and promote. In as disinterested a posture as he can assume he analyzes what is, and strives to control the universal impulse to insist upon what should be, for no "ought" can be derived from any "is."

No science, sociology included, can tell us what should be or what we should do. That is the job of social reformers, clergymen, politicians, newspaper editors, and perhaps even the sociologist in his separated role of private citizen. Any sociologist who claims that sociology provides a blueprint for what we *should* do has abandoned his professional role, and he deserves no more attention than that ordinarily accorded any other publicist for a social cause embroiled in promotional claim and counterclaim. Scientific judgment is restricted to assessing the technical appropriateness of means adopted to achieve *given* ends.

These and all the other issues mentioned in this chapter are treated at much greater length in the chapters which follow. Now that the basic point of view of this book has been stated, the student's task of reading should become easier.

REFERENCES

1   Herbert Blumer has pointed out that "sociologists discover social problems only after they are recognized as social problems by and in a society" (p. 299 of "Social Problems as Collective Behavior," *Social Problems,* **18**:298–306, 1971). Professor Blumer correctly locates the

initial designation of social problems *in* a society, but possibly *by* a society is too inclusive an assumed scope. No social problem is ever recognized in the same way by a total population, and every social problem involves a conflict of attitudes among various segments of a total population.

2 According to one enumerator, the values which laymen share with scientists in the modern world are: (a) rationality—an approach to *"all* the phenomena of human existence in the attempt to reduce them to ever more consistent, orderly, and generalized forms of understanding"; (b) utilitarianism—"the predominant interest modern man has in the affairs of this world," as opposed to the supernatural realm; (c) universalism—a refashioning of the Christian ideal of the brotherhood of man in God into a sanctification of the opportunity to find that calling which fits a man's aptitudes; (d) individualism—"the moral preference for the dictates of individual conscience rather than for those of organized authority"; and (e) a faith in combined progress and meliorism which, in added provision, fosters a belief that social problems can as well as should be solved. See Bernard Barber, *Science and the Social Order,* Free Press, Chicago, 1952, pp. 62–65.

The above are sentiments, moral judgments, nonscientific dogmas of faith. Although historically associated with the rise of modern science, they have nothing at all to do with evidential proof or the method of inquiry. A widespread and erroneous view has nevertheless arisen of science as "an all-sufficient, exclusive form of human adjustment" (p. 224). Professor Barber further points out that within or outside of any conceivable moral context, "science" cannot prove any code of behavior right or wrong, nor can it pass judgment upon the meaning of life, justice, and so on. It would then follow that scientific method cannot specify what should be designated a social problem, what should be rejected as a social problem, and what in either case should be done about it.

3 Attitudes *selectively define* social conditions as well as social problems themselves. Effective opinion about both conditions and problems results from the balance of power—ideological, political, and economic—within a society at any given moment in time. That balance of power fosters the spread and intensity of attitudes in one or another direction.

The formation of effective opinion, the spread and intensification of attitudes which selectively define conditions and designate a social problem, requires a belief that remedial action is possible. In ancient Greece and Rome the few influential voices which denounced slavery went largely unheeded. A rudimentary technology made slavery an economic necessity, at least in the settled opinion of those, a probable majority, who wished to maintain a level of living which the emancipation of forced labor would have sacrificed. This particular factor—the belief that remedial action is possible—is enlarged upon in the next chapter.

4 Richard Lewinsohn, *A History of Sexual Customs,* Alexander Mayce (trans.), Harper, New York, 1958, p. 56. See also G. Simpson Marr, *Sex in Religion,* G. Allen, London, 1936, especially chap. 4.

5 By the twelfth and thirteenth centuries organized charity supplemented individual almsgiving. See Will Durant, *The Age of Faith,* Simon & Schuster, New York, 1950, especially pp. 830–831. Nevertheless, at no time in medieval Europe did the attitude arise that poverty called for any structural change.

6 Taking scalps on a sort of free enterprise basis is admittedly a somewhat different case than the threat of mutual annihilation from a nuclear exchange. The difficulty, a persisting one as we proceed, stems from applying the same term—for example, war—to forms of behavior which in total context have radically dissimilar consequences. The Crow and Comanche Indians, however, did maintain very different attitudes toward killing, toward the risk of violent death in a collective enterprise, than those which have become prevalent in the modern West. See Ralph Linton, *The Study of Man,* Appleton-Century-Crofts, New York, 1936, and Fred W. Voget, "Warfare and the Integration of Crow Indian Culture," in Ward H. Goodenough (ed.), *Explorations in Cultural Anthropology,* McGraw-Hill, New York, 1964, pp. 483–509.

7 Adolf Hitler, *Mein Kampf,* Ralph Manheim (trans.), Houghton Mifflin, Boston, 1942, p. 599, underscored in original. According to an American journalist, it was precisely because war was a social problem in France and England but not in Germany that the French and English were helpless to resist or even blunt the initial acts of German aggression in World War II. See Edmond Taylor, *The Strategy of Terror,* Houghton Mifflin, Boston, 1940.

8 Blumer, reference 1, p. 299.

9 George Gallup and Evan Hill, "The American Woman," *Saturday Evening Post,* Dec. 22 and Dec. 29, 1962, pp. 15–18 and 26–32.

10 Anthony Downs, "Up and Down with Ecology—The Issue-Attention Cycle," *The Public Interest,* **28**: 38–50, 1972, p. 39, underscored in original.

11 Only within a context of comparison can such value-loaded terms as better or worse retain a vestige of scientific applicability. Conditions

of poverty or racism or male dominance can only be objectified when better or worse is translated into more or less, based solely upon time and/or place comparisons. One: the present can be compared with the recent or distant past in this country. Two: the present in America can be compared with the situation in other urban-industrial nations. Differences of this kind can be crudely demonstrated, especially in statistical terms. At least for poverty and race relations if not male dominance, we have readily available national time-series on income, education, housing, employment opportunities, and so on.

There are pitfalls in such usage, especially the implication of complacency when graph lines are shown to march onward and upward. Such explicit comparisons, on the other hand, can give pause at the edge of more dangerous pitfalls, such as the gratuitous labeling and rhetorical totalism now so endemic that it can be found in formal sociological discourse. The following example is cited from a recent issue of the journal *Social Problems:* "More generally, in an unjust and exploitative society, no matter how 'humane' agents of social control are, their actions necessarily result in repression." So "rampant racism" pervades "our tortured society," where blacks are "oppressed" and "persecuted." In their of-course assumptions and tautological excess, moral judgments such as these cannot be refuted, for they are not couched in comparative terms. Conditions couldn't be worse, period, end of discussion.

12 Stuart Chase, *American Credos,* Harper, New York, 1962, chap.11.

13 Hadley Cantril, *The Pattern of Human Concerns,* Rutgers, New Brunswick, N.J., 1965. In particular, see pp. 35 and 162. There are deviations from the American norm. Israelis, for example, are more concerned about the social problem of war than Americans, which is understandable enough.

14 Daniel P. Moynihan, "The Soulless City," *American Heritage,* February 1969, pp. 5–8 and 78–85, p. 84.

15 Only a very few social problems are, so to speak, clearly the property of either a majority or a political-intellectual minority. The division between them appears most often when the same *name* is applied to a social problem which each side defines quite differently and wants very different things done about it. A majority of modern Americans approach the "crime problem" with very different attitudes than does, say, for example, the American Civil Liberties Union.

16 See Arnold W. Green, *Recreation, Leisure, and Politics,* McGraw-Hill, New York, 1964.

17 Such a range of popular attention and concern: first crime and, in descending order, race relations, "ecology," poverty, population

growth, will doubtless hold only for a short span of time. Owing to probable economic and political changes, and shifts of power within the society, not only could the above sequence become scrambled, but newly emerging and presently unforeseen social problems could move to the forefront of public attention. More attention was focused upon poverty in 1973 than was the case in 1963. In 1963 race relations was only starting to attract the attention and engage the concern of the majority, and "ecology" was a term encountered only in the writings of many professional biologists and a few professional sociologists.

18 The term "ecology," here used in the popular sense, is actually a misnomer. Ecology is not a crusade but a branch of natural science engaged in the study of interrelationships between biological organisms and the physical environment.

19 The relationship between humanitarianism and various social problems is not a constant one. Humanitarianism is classically expressed by the sentiment of directly helping others who live outside the circle of the personally known. The invocation of humanitarian concern for future generations expressed in ecology and population growth lacks the focus and immediacy of old-fashioned (individual and voluntary) charity. The case of crime as a social problem is quite interesting in this connection; selective humanitarianisms operate, one for victims, the other for perpetrators, and they clash head on.

20 In a famous, if somewhat inelegant and misleading phrase, the present majority has been characterized as "unpoor, unblack, and unyoung." With it, only a majority of all voters is specified. The majority concept herein employed includes most of the poor (of whom more are white than black), most blacks, and possibly more than half of the young—if the 1972 voting records of people aged eighteen to twenty-five signify ideological commitment.

The increasing "liberalism" of the majority has been for the most part restricted to personal-interest claims on the welfare state. (See Samuel Lubell, *The Hidden Crisis in American Politics,* Norton, New York, 1970, especially chap.7.) They remain relatively traditionalistic on those social issues which are commonly regarded as social problems. They endorse "law and order" and conventional morality, and deplore student disorders, pornography, and legalization of pot, although majority attitudes on pot do appear to be softening. "This is the apparent paradox of attitudes in the seventies; conservative on the Social Issue, liberal on the bread-and-butter issues." Richard M. Scammon and Ben J. Wattenberg, *The Real Majority,* Coward-McCann, New York, 1970, p. 76.

21 The relationship in recent years between higher education and a lib-

eral-to-radical orientation has been thoroughly documented. Only the explanation for that relationship remains controversial. There are some who believe that the superior worth of progressive attitudes is manifested, while others argue that college students are being indoctrinated by their instructors. This last charge cannot be proved, or disproved. But beyond dispute is the preponderant liberal-to-radical stance of college instructors in certain fields of study. See Seymour Martin Lipset, *Political Man*, Anchor Books, Doubleday, Garden City, N.Y., 1963, p. 337. Lipset also documents the consistent ideological orientation of those referred to here as political-intellectual minorities. See pp. 335–341.

22 Any further diminution of traditionalistic attitudes among the majority would probably result more from the indirect than the direct effects of higher education. It has been estimated that by 1976 less than one-third of the electorate will have attended any college for any period of time. Nevertheless the number and proportion of college graduates will increase, and thus doubtless swell the number of those who embrace, in Lionel Trilling's phrase, "the adversary culture." Models presented the public in art and literature, even in mass media such as television and especially the movies, already verge upon the nihilistic. An increasing number and proportion of college graduates should expand the market for a crusade to overwhelm traditional sensibility.

We lack certain evidence whether, one, the majority turn to amusements they dislike because nothing else is made available to them by public-communications channels controlled by minorities who foist their own dissent upon a helpless audience, or, two, whether the majority suffer from a kind of nonclinical schizophrenia, simultaneously clinging to old beliefs and shibboleths while actively enjoying themes of rejection, degeneration, and casual betrayal of trust in personal relationships, themes which surpass in morally erosive potential those famous literal portrayals of "sex and violence."

In one view, a possibly intemperate one, there is no such split. Opposition between the majority and the avant-garde has disappeared. The majority have been "dispossessed of all of [their] traditions—dispossessed, above all, of [their] faith in the idea of tradition—and now [lie] supine and demoralized, awaiting the next scheduled rape of [their] sensibilities with that mixture of dread, curiosity, and bemused resignation befitting an organism no longer in control of its habitat." Hilton Kramer, "The Age of the Avant-Garde," *Commentary,* October 1972, pp. 37–44, p. 44.

23 For an example of racial conditions viewed as sheer persecution, see Alexander Liazos, "The Poverty of the Sociology of Deviance: Nuts,

Sluts, and Preverts [*sic*]," *Social Problems,* **20**:103–120, 1972. For an example of racial conditions viewed in an opposite way, see Edward C. Banfield, *The Unheavenly City: The Nature and Future of Our Urban Crisis,* Little Brown, Boston, 1970, especially chap. 9.

24 Written in 1936, Willard Waller's statement about social problems remains a theoretical landmark [see "Social Problems and the Mores," in William J. Goode et al. (eds.), *Willard Waller on the Family, Education, and War,* University of Chicago Press, Chicago 1970, pp.133–146]. Waller was one of the first sociologists to recognize the primacy of attitudes, but he considered social-problem conditions to be objectively there, whatever attitudes of avoidance, acceptance, or disapproval might be adopted toward them. Such conditions are *identified* as social problems, he said, when attitudes of moral judgment are applied to them. Largely correct though it is, this dictum still overlooks the sovereignty of attitudes in the *perception* of social-problem conditions themselves.

The reader may opt to skip what follows, yet a fuller examination of Waller's theory reveals how ephemeral some of the conditions proved to be that he regarded as permanent things. Waller conceived the conditions of social problems to stem from the "organizational mores," upon which the social order is founded: the mores of private property and individualism, of the monogamous family, Christianity, and nationalism. Alongside them he identified the "humanitarian mores," which govern the impulse "to make the world better or to remedy the misfortunes of others." Such attitudes, or value judgments in his term, "are the formal causes of social problems."

But we do not solve social problems, Waller observed, because in the inevitable "clash" between these two sets of mores the organizational always prove stronger, in men's loyalties as well as in their acceptance of the reality of vested power. Therefore, we continue to treat the symptoms of social problems instead of trying to solve them, because any change in the organizational mores is recognized to be off limits by the very people most determined to solve social problems. The pacifist, for example, does not really want to end war, for the inevitable price would be surrender of national sovereignty. Those who seek to alleviate poverty stop short at a total revision of the economic system, and so on. Humanitarians, and especially professional social workers, are thus in Waller's phrase "aim-inhibited."

Of inestimable value, Waller's statement nevertheless requires revision. As already noted, his distinction between conditions and attitudes is shaky at best. Beyond that, in the few intervening years since

Waller wrote this piece the social cohesion inherent in the organizational mores has strikingly diminished. The beliefs and loyalties and capacity to accept things as they are, which represent the personal-social reality of organizational mores, have in considerable degree eroded. The organizational mores no longer represent those iron limits that Waller envisioned. The majority are surely more confused and possibly more apathetic than they were, and various political-intellectual minorities are much less "aim-inhibited." A great many people are thinking what to Waller was the unthinkable, about sacrificing national sovereignty, about junking the economic system to end poverty and "racism," about destroying the organizational mores themselves.

25 Robert K. Merton, "Social Problems and Sociological Theory," in Robert K. Merton and Robert Nisbet (eds.), *Social Problems,* rev. ed., Harcourt Brace Jovanovich, New York, 1971, pp. 793–845, p. 823, underscored.

26 Merton, reference 25, pp. 819–820.

27 Some interests—present and foreseen—are shared and converge, while others conflict. The point of conflict is here exaggerated in order to make it. Interests are examined more fully in a later chapter.

28 Apparently the dubious compliment is reciprocated. Much less trust is granted institutional authority figures than in the recent past. Although not the majority as here defined, "an adult cross section," according to identical Harris polls conducted in 1967 and 1972, lost considerable faith in specified leaderships within five years. While 55 percent expressed faith in the leadership of major business corporations in 1967, by 1972 only 27 percent did. Like percentage comparisons for bankers, 67 and 37; the military, 62 and 27; congressmen, 41 and 19; and executive branch of government, 41 and 23; and faith in scientists dropped from 56 to 32 percent. Cited in "Newsletter/ Social Science," *Intellectual Digest,* May 1972, p. 49.

Irving Kristol does not comment on the above figures, but explains a loss of faith in leadership as the result of burgeoning bureaucracy. Our leaders have become "nameless and faceless men," team players, "representative men, not exceptional men." Power, status, and unequal income no longer are clearly entitled when they have lost their human and personal associations. See "About Equality," *Commentary,* November 1972, pp. 41–47. Granted, but more important in the view here being developed, is the gap between what leaders in general are saying and the attitudes the majority continue to hold.

The Rise of Social-Problem Consciousness

Social-problem consciousness is a product of the Western cultural tradition, and it is a late Western development. The ancient Jews, Greeks, and Romans did not create social problems. They lacked social-problem consciousness, that general tendency to define and deplore conditions of secular misfortune which befall distant others and then determine to rectify those conditions.

The ancient Jews, Greeks, and Romans were all tribal peoples who could achieve only a limited statehood. Most modern non-Western peoples can be generally characterized in the same way. Local or tribal concerns, family concerns, almost encompass the social horizon, and there is little empathy with what or who is personally unknown. It is true that social problems have begun to appear in Asia and Africa, but only where Western influence has disrupted tribal life and native political-intellectual minorities have adopted certain Western ideas and attitudes.

In this chapter we will first explore the four ideas associated with the rise of social-problem consciousness in the modern West: equality; a new image of human nature; the belief that conditions which are deplored can be rectified; and humanitarianism, the heart of the matter, the expression of concern for distant others. The ideological consequences of and reactions to the French Revolution are then examined. These are shown to have greatly affected early sociological thought, but not life in the early American Republic, except as they were derived at second hand from British sources.

Earlier voluntary and gradualistic approaches to social problems in this country are then shown to have been largely displaced by calls to revamp entire social institutions. Changes in sociology, especially changes in the attitudes of sociologists, are related to this new expression of social-problem consciousness. What does lend continuity to social-problem consciousness is the persistence of the four ideas to which we now turn.

CONJUNCTURE OF IDEAS

Most modern social problems are addressed to improving the lot of lower-status persons. When social-problem awareness first emerged, that was the sole concern. And such consciousness awaited the latter part of the eighteenth century, when a conjuncture of four developments in the realm of ideas occurred. The first was an ancient idea which hitherto could not be effectively expressed. The others were new.

Equality

The idea that all mankind are basically equal fitfully appears in the work of ancient Greek and Roman writers and throughout the Judeo-Christian tradition. With that statement before us, a short interlude to back off becomes imperative. The ancients were no more clear or in agreement about what equality is than we are. Nevertheless, throughout Western history two notions about equality have been intermittently voiced: everyone deserves respect as a human being no matter what his status may be, and some degree of equal opportunity should be granted every adult male (1).

Concern about equality has long, if thin, roots in our cultural history. The covenant of the ancient Hebrews, for example, guaranteed all men equal justice in the sight of God. Although the Old Testament does sanction enslavement of non-Jews, it frequently enjoins equal treatment at law for "strangers." And while there is no condemnation of slavery in the New Testament, kindly treatment of the "bondsman" is demanded. More important was the revolutionary doctrine that all men are equal before God, which formed a base for all later attempts to translate equality into this-worldly terms *(2)*.

The issue of equality was frequently debated by ancient Greek intellectuals. But most of them could not foresee a future when slavery would cease to be the economic necessity they deemed it to be. And even in the absence of slavery, Plato and others thought that the division of labor itself would require unequal status: some men would always have to direct the operations of other men, and the more difficult and responsible job functions would inevitably confer special esteem.

Isocrates, a contemporary of Plato's, noted a discrepancy between two notions of equality which has become a focal point of conflict in modern society. Some men, he said, insist upon the same reward to all alike (in our terms, literal equality or equality of results), while others demand that each man shall receive his due (in our terms, equality of opportunity). This latter notion, of each man's due, has provoked continuous tension in the Western tradition, because the yearning for equal opportunity has been in greater or lesser degree frustrated by the inheritance of status. The division of labor may require that some men have a superior and others an inferior status, but anyone *born* to superior status denies an opportunity to many others to strive toward superior status.

For centuries ascendant social-political power and thought, as well as assumed economic necessity, denied the hope of each man's due, equal opportunity to compete. And it was sidetracked, and has continued to be sidetracked, by another yearning, that for the same reward to all alike, or literal equality. For a long time that yearning reverted to an imagined past. Ancient Greece and Rome celebrated the myth of the Golden Age, a day gone when there was no division of labor, when all men had been equal, equally alike. The Church Fathers incorporated that myth into the political theory of the church: "natural" society was literally egalitarian; only man's corrupt nature, signified in the fall from grace of original sin, had made differences of status and coercive government necessary.

Not for centuries did a vision of literal equality in the future begin to replace that in the past. A society without distinctions of status was projected into the future for the first time in the fourteenth century (3). This new time orientation, which provided a compelling vision to many peasant revolts and religious uprisings, was not informed by social-problem or even social-reform consciousness, but by a legend of a Day of Judgment, Final Redemption, the End and the Beginning, in short, by millenarianism. Thus the first propagandist of the "new Anabaptism" claimed to be "a prophet sent by God to announce that at Whitsuntide, 1528, Christ would return to earth and place the two-edged sword of justice in the hands of the rebaptized saints" *(4)*.

The desires of the poor to improve their lot through periodic uprisings between the eleventh and sixteenth centuries were consistently transmuted into violent phantasms of total destruction, and their abortive revolts secured few allies among those of property, power, or even intellect. Martin Luther's retaliatory attitude toward restive peasants is well known, and in one way his mission may be viewed as one of reimposing discipline upon a religious enthusiasm which, at least in worldly terms, had gotten out of hand. He called for an obedient surrender to "the order of Society created by the Law of Nature" (5).

Equality and the Eighteenth Century

Then and for some time to come the idea of literal equality was denied a foothold. Except in the work of Rousseau and a few of his disciples, the notion was anathema in eighteenth-century thought prior to the French Revolution *(6)*. Even so, the men of the Enlightenment, the French intellectuals, took a few tentative steps in that direction.

Next to "Nature," the most "sacred phrase" of the eighteenth century was the "Great Chain of Being." From lower animals up to the infinite power and wisdom of the Maker, each link existed "not merely and not primarily for the benefit of any other link, but for its own sake, or more precisely, for the sake of the completeness of the series of forms . . ." (7). In social terms, the "chain" might seem to justify the principle of feudal gradation. But a new emphasis was emerging, that of concern for the welfare of those who composed the lower links of the social chain. "No creature's existence . . . was

merely instrumental to the well-being of those above it in the scale"
(8).

The eighteenth-century men of intellect stressed the need to
include the common people, to seek their compliance and participation in the new knowledge. More than that, the intellectuals appealed to the common people to reject outmoded tradition by the
exercise of private judgment *(9)*. For the first time in history, intellectuals sought potential allies against tyranny and privilege at the
lower links of the social "chain."

They went much farther in a frequent use of the words "freedom" and "equality," even though they were never clear about
exactly what they were sponsoring. To grossly oversimplify the work
of many men who differed in many particulars, they saw equality
not as the abolition of status differences but instead as a *spirit* of
brotherly comradeship, a spirit which they mistakenly assumed prevailed among Chinese sages and North American aborigines. They
remained "generally on the side of authority—virtuous, enlightened
authority, it goes without saying" (10). Without realizing where they
were going, which is man's common fate, eighteenth-century men of
intellect were nevertheless preparing the way for rhetorical totalism
in the French Revolution and demands for equality of a scope which
would have horrified them.

Human Nature

In this same period the old idea and ideal of equality found emerging ideological allies. The ancient idea that human nature is basically evil was shifted enough toward the opposite pole to have important consequences. The dominant intellectual mood of the late
eighteenth century was one of optimism, a conviction "of the intrinsic goodness of man and of man's ability to win happiness" (11).
Original sin was discredited. Not the will of God, but the nature of
man should inform the devising of ethics. Man himself is perfectible.
Rousseau had gone much farther and said that man is born good
and made evil only by evil social institutions.

To be sure, even Rousseau entertained lingering doubts about
the beneficence of man's nature. Most of his contemporaries were
much more ambivalent. They were close in time, not wholly removed in thought, from such late seventeenth- and early eighteenth-

century writers as Swift, Pope, and Goldsmith, who had depicted man as inferior in moral character to other animals. Earlier, Thomas Hobbes had declared "vanity" to be the key to an understanding of human nature, and those who immediately followed him judged man to be primarily motivated by a lust for applause and approbation, for esteem and admiration (12). Some of the Founding Fathers of this country retained as much of Hobbes's jaundiced view as they accepted the fashionable one of their own time. Thomas Jefferson, for example, said that in "questions of power let no more be said of confidence in man, but bind him down from mischief by the chains of the Constitution."

Nevertheless, in the eighteenth century the predominant opinion became one of man's *potential for perfectibility*. Without that opinion, a social-problem consciousness probably could not have developed. And although faith in man's goodness has waned in recent decades, enough of it has been retained to provide a continuity of hope that social problems *can* be solved.

Conditions Can Be Modified

"The conviction that the character and lot of man are indefinitely modifiable for good, was the indispensable antecedent to any general and energetic endeavour to modify the conditions that surround him" (13). The attack upon religion, upon what was left of medieval Catholicism and remaining attention fixed upon the next world, was deemed an essential prelude to the dawn of a new age in which reason would govern and abolish all impediments to secular happiness. Human reason can control man's world, and therefore man can make of his world what he will.

A majority of intellectuals believed with a passionate faith that man can purge his mind of ancient errors and superstitions and prejudices, and realize his innate excellence *(14)*. Holbach, for example, said that slavery and "religious terrors" were the result of sheer error, of lack of knowledge, and further, that reason teaches us to pursue our own happiness, without hurting others. Reason, it was believed, tells us what we should do and how we should live.

This belief, that reason by itself contains ethical direction, remained an unexamined article of faith among French intellectuals as the century drew to its close. What they could not find was a way to persuade nonintellectuals to reason exactly as they did. Too many others rejected the proposals for building a better world which the French intellectuals offered them. So they developed more interest in Rousseau's proposal to use the power of government to guide men's minds along the path of reason (15). Only then could one be certain that conditions would be modified in the way desired.

For the most part, though, the faith that reason itself would produce improved conditions stood firm. That faith was a conceptual error, but paradoxically it strengthened emotional denunciation of defined evils in the world (16). The new spirit of humanitarianism owed much to the mistaken assumption that reason will cure all ills.

Humanitarianism

The primary sentiment of the ideological syndrome we have been discussing is humanitarianism. A concern for the welfare of unknown others emerged, a compassion for distant others, in Harold Laski's term a "religion of service to one's fellowman." And by virtual common agreement among modern scholars, the late eighteenth century was the time of its beginning *(17)*.

For centuries pity had been expressed and charity dispensed. But eighteenth-century humanitarianism was something new. Suffering came to be seen in a new light, "not as part of the order of nature and human nature, above all, not as ordained by God, but as unnatural, as the product of accumulated human errors happily remediable now that we know what the errors are." Ad hoc attempts to alleviate it were soon organized to supplement the old pattern of Christian charities "in pressure groups aiming at legislative measure to cure or prevent given suffering . . ." (18). Suffering could then lay claim not only to the attention of the more privileged but to that of the social order itself *(19)*.

Although the term *humanitarisme* was not coined until the 1830s in France, the vogue it represented started there. In common with many other social ideas or sentiments, however, that of rendering service to others in distress was used to rationalize a great deal of the ancient behavior it was supposed to supplant. The French Revolution enshrined *humanité*—and sent its enemies to the guillotine. Robespierre on humanitarian principle denounced capital punishment and later on humanitarian principle made lavish use of it.

Rationalizations for reaction were equally ambiguous. "Following the Reign of Terror the Thermidorians massacred several hundred Jacobins, notably in southern France, 'in the name of humanity and justice'" (20). Nevertheless, the Revolution *was* associated with criminal law reform, with action to abolish slavery in the colonies, and with the extension of protective rights to Jews and Protestants. And the "influence of the Humanitarian Movement also outlived the eighteenth century. Most of the reforms enacted remained as permanent enactments . . ." *(21)*.

Despite the faith of Enlightenment intellectuals in progress through education, it should be noted that the participation of the common people in the development of humanitarianism and its three associated ideas was minimal. As ideas, apart from inchoate resentment, they left the peasants virtually unaffected and were recognized only by a few of the common people who lived in cities, whose released passions during the Revolution utilized only simple slogans of opposition. The great debate had been going on over the heads of the lower classes. The intellectuals as always took center stage; they found allies not among the masses but among those nobles who embraced the new idealism for itself and among many provincial politicians who used it, promoted it, for highly practical reasons of foreseen personal advantage which came to fruition in the Revolution (22).

Humanitarianism: France and England

The new ideas had been most enthusiastically hailed in France, but they were tempered in the more stable social order of England. It was in England, not France, that the secure foundations of modern humanitarianism were built. In England was firmly established that social-problem consciousness, a desire and will to *improve* the present for the future, which has persisted with only minor shifts and lapses to the present time.

Many of the French intellectuals had pushed beyond criticism of certain arrangements they wanted corrected to denunciation of a society they regarded as hopeless. Such an outlook breeds slogans, fanaticism, and disembodied abstractions. Respectful of French intellectuals though they remained, British intellectuals of that time were for the most part uninterested in such abstractions as the rights of man. They had already secured many rights as British citizens which were denied the French. British intellectuals simply lacked the revolutionary spirit *(23)*.

Humanitarianism in England was thus unaccompanied by an adversary spirit, a conviction that first the world must be overcome. Voluntary associations addressed themselves to specific causes of temperance, protection of animals and children (that was the sequence), an end to slavery, and so on. The English outlook of gradual improvement upon what now exists stood in marked contrast to the almost characteristically French desire to overturn established institutions and create new ones.

Most important of all, it was in England that the stodgy "middle-class" ethos emerged, that fusion of humanitarianism with utilitarian principles which social-problem consciousness has retained to this day—a statement to which essential qualifications are appended below. Utilitarian values in Crane Brinton's phrase were "conventional late Christian," lacking heroism and leaving no room for rebellion. On humanitarian grounds the poor, for instance, should be helped, but not to the point that the pleasures of laziness might outvote its pains.

With explicit intent, utilitarian concern for the "greatest number" was egalitarian as well as humanitarian, though egalitarianism was adulterated with that elitism which intellectuals never in purpose avoid, only in principle renounce, be they French, English, or American, now as always. Only with *proper guidance* could each individual achieve that combination of moral and rational conduct of which every individual is capable. In Jeremy Bentham's "principle of happiness," the greatest happiness of the greatest number is the measure of right and wrong; and the business of government is to promote the happiness of everyone within a society. The pleasures of happiness, the *true* pleasures it should be noted, are not self-indulgence but earnest moral purpose. As John Stuart Mill put it: The "happiness which forms the utilitarian standard of what is right in conduct is not the agent's own happiness but that of all concerned."

Although no direct and total adoption of British utilitarianism in our time should be inferred, for many side roads have been taken and modifications effected, much of British utilitarianism remains on the American scene. Doubtless, Jeremy Bentham would have felt almost at home at a PTA meeting or county commission office. There he would hear expressed his own faith in education, in planning, in the ultimate if not immediately perceived harmony of all interests, and in the beneficent intervention of the state. Like him, his intellectual descendants would likely be little moved by Samuel Johnson's lines: "How small of all that human hearts endure,/ That part which laws or kings can cure!"

Bentham would agree with these modern Americans that changes effected should be gradual and based upon what now exists. He would surely appreciate their concern about the greatest good for the greatest number, although he might note that his own tone of moral earnestness was strangely muted, and wonder why rewards were mentioned so much more often than punishments, and why material rather than ethical standards were stressed, as in a standard of living which all should attain or otherwise be granted. But on balance he would recognize these people as basically his own kind, for they too are humanitarians, who, although they might not be so positive as he that others should not be helped beyond the point of their own good, still retain that lingering suspicion.

IDEOLOGICAL RESPONSE TO REVOLUTION

The four ideas discussed above were emblazoned on the banners of the French Revolution. That circumstance presented severe dilemmas to Western European thought which have not been resolved to this day. Erstwhile confidence that these four ideas would usher in a new *order* was shaken in some quarters, abandoned in others. The ideas themselves, of course, have remained an integral part of the Western tradition. But they were modified and compromised in the initial reaction to the Revolution.

The impact of the Revolution upon the rise of sociology is especially noteworthy. The early sociologists strove to demonstrate aspects of permanence in human nature and society which the Revolution had challenged. Reaction in the new American nation to the Revolution was quite different from that of European societies and early sociology. America, indeed, was relatively unaffected by it. Expression of the four ideas in America was mostly derived at first from British sources, and then from the indigenous American experience. These various generalizations are expanded upon in the remainder of this section.

Temporary Retreat in Europe

The nearly unanimous response in Europe to the Revolution was intellectual disillusionment and political repression. Had the "religion of humanity" spawned demons? Were the four ideas horrible masks, equality of oppression, human virtue of vice, reason of mob hysteria, humanitarianism of hatred? Reaction was swift. In Germany rigid lines of class, almost caste, which during the Enlightenment had been relaxed, suddenly hardened. Novalis, once a revolutionary and the founder of German political romanticism, denounced natural rights, democracy, equality (24).

In France, with the restoration of the Bourbons in 1815 much of the Ancien Régime returned. Church and state cooperated to repress revolutionary and democratic ideas. The intellectuals lost heart. Sickened by revolutionary bloodletting and disastrous Napoleonic adventures, they spurned ideological abstraction in a search for moral authority; weary of intellectual analysis and agnosticism, they appealed to faith, to history, to anything that opposed the Enlightenment. "Madame de Staël, one of the greatest influences of the early nineteenth century, declared . . .: 'I do not know exactly what we must believe, but I believe that we must believe' " (25).

In England initial reaction to the Revolution was one of revulsion. A wave of repression started with a suspension of habeas corpus in 1794. The Terror had made a death's head of the word "democracy." The Anglican clergy in the House of Lords "fought as an almost solid phalanx against any reform of the penal laws, against Catholic emancipation, and against the Reform Bill" (26). At the same time, English Methodism stood opposed to the "deism, skepticism, and democratic thought of the eighteenth century." The doctrines of Methodism "stressed the necessity of preserving order in society, and the need for loyalty to the public authorities" (27).

Repression in England was short-lived. Defensive reaction against turmoil observed across the Channel failed to disrupt the basic stability of English institutions. Humanitarianism had already become so strong a sentiment that it soon united men otherwise politically opposed. "In the detestation of cruelty, Benthamite free-thinkers, Whig philanthropists such as Fox, Tory humanitarians such as Pitt, and Evangelicals who followed Wilberforce, were substantially one. . ." (28). Interestingly enough, according to Lord Dicey, "humane feeling" was constantly on the increase even during the initial period of repression. It was guided by "utilitarian individualism" or "Benthamism modified by experience" (29).

The slave trade was prohibited in 1806; partial abolition of the pillory was enacted in 1816. In 1820 the whipping of women was abolished and cruelty to animals penalized. The Combination Acts passed by Parliament in 1799 and 1800 had forbidden unions, but laws of 1824 and 1825 sanctioned collective bargaining. Reaction by these later dates had disintegrated.

Temporary Retreat in Sociology

The new science of sociology which emerged in the nineteenth century was an attempt to deal with the implications of the French Revolution. The Terror, and subsequent tyranny, mocked the Enlightenment, which had provided the slogans for both Robespierre and Napoleon. Perhaps the French intellectuals had erred, especially in their assumption that certain settled values and loyalties of medieval times could be taken for granted as being given in human nature. Was the principle of order in human society precisely those structural and psychological fences which the Enlightenment had sought to remove? Many intellectuals reverted to that opinion, and identified the primary values of European culture as honor, loyalty, and friendship. Some of them realized, others did not, that they were celebrating a medievalism gone, but in any event early sociology arose out of nostalgia for community with roots.

Modern man was viewed by the early sociologists as alienated, uprooted, alone, without secure station. "Estrangement is sovereign: estrangement from others, from work, from place, and even from self" (30). Society was declared to have become inaccessible, remote, "meaningless from its impersonal complexity." Thus the "essential unit-ideas of sociology" became: *community* "characterized by a high degree of personal intimacy, emotional depth, moral commitment, social cohesion, and continuity in time"; *authority,* the inner order of association, whether political, religious, or cultural, and given legitimacy by its roots in social function, tradition, or allegiance; and *status,* the individual's position in a hierarchy of prestige and influence that characterizes every community or association.

Some of the names which follow will doubtless be unknown to the student; such knowledge is not essential for understanding the argument. Professor Nisbet has traced in Comte, Durkheim, and Tocqueville, and to some extent even in Weber and Simmel, a compelling image of medieval society "with its localism, hierarchy, and religious constitution. . . ." What follows is an extension of his analysis. The fathers of sociological thought were all *obsessed*—the word is deliberately chosen—with one theme: the limits of possibility, the limits of possibility in human nature and the limits of possibility in the structure of society. How much the Terror continued to haunt their imagination cannot be divined, but surely a search for the limits of human possibility is as far removed from its slogans as thought can diverge.

Auguste Comte, who coined the term "sociology," did envision a "social regeneration of Western Europe," but only as a fusion of old Catholicism and authoritarianism with the new science. Emile Durkheim feared what the "biological individual" might do to himself and others when deprived of mutually beneficial social constraints. Max Weber warned that the social achievement of any value ineluctably sacrifices some other, and he had intimations that a continuing dedivinization of the world would form a "cage" for the human spirit in the near future. William G. Sumner used his analysis of folkways and mores to oppose various social reforms as either harmful or bound to fail. Vilfredo Pareto found in history no progress, only periodicity, and he insisted that all human plan and aspiration was doomed to repeat ancient thought and action. Georg Simmel posited the innovative content in social arrangements to be restricted by universal forms, and further argued that inequality is socially beneficial as well as inevitable. How temporary the retreat of sociology was is indicated in a later section of this chapter, even though, as Professor Nisbet has pointed out, modern sociologists continue to employ the "essential unit ideas" of community, authority, and status.

No Retreat in America

Recoil from the "excesses" of the French Revolution was minimal in America. France was far away, and the Americans were engaged in establishing the shaky sovereignty which followed their own "Revolution." Perhaps the main reason why the French Revolution had no appreciable consequence in the new country is disclosed in the reaction of Edmund Burke, the archenemy of the ideas embodied in the French Revolution, to the American Revolution. On balance he approved of it as a natural fulfillment of historic tradition, as the means chosen to protect the hallowed right of British citizenship which had been subverted by English politicians. To the end and beyond he sought reconciliation, for in his view the American insurrection never was a revolution.

American politicians and intellectuals, whose identities tended to overlap much more at that time than ever since, had been, of course, quite receptive to Enlightenment ideas. The Declaration of Independence and the American Constitution are suffused with the Enlightenment, with the thought of Montesquieu, Rousseau, Voltaire, as well as of Locke. A very few of them excepted, they held a modification of social conditions by rational means to be desirable and possible. They were humanitarian in outlook, might be somewhat uncertain about the inherent goodness of human nature, but they endorsed equality—in a limited way.

These men were transitional figures, heirs to a European fixed class system with some few privileges of their own to protect. They nevertheless wanted to effect orderly change and expand opportunity, whether with Jefferson's agrarian or Hamilton's urban-industrial policy. But equality of station, literal equality, equality of result, was never their aim, any more than was universal franchise. Equality before God and the law, yes, and beyond that possibly Jefferson's "natural aristocracy of talent," a somewhat compromised notion of equal opportunity, might to some extent replace the system of fixed classes.

Their world rapidly fell apart in the sheer openness of American experience. The unlimited western horizon of free land beckoned to increasing numbers of Europeans fleeing clerical oppression and feudal constraints in the Old World, and to eastern seaboard residents who wanted out of what residually remained of those conditions here. The opportunity was there for the taking, authority and conventional restraints there slackened, hence the frontiersman's boast that he was just as good as the next man and mebbe a dam' sight better. The openness of experience washed back to the eastern seaboard, and during Jackson's administration democracy in the modern sense emerged. In Tocqueville's phrase, many Americans now had the sense of being "born equal." He deemed equality in America to be largely an indigenous phenomenon.

There were two crosscurrents. The main one was the "acquisitive democracy" of "millions of go-getting Americans." Even the aristocrats of the late eighteenth century could not rely upon recognition of their inherited status, and had to work hard "in the capitalistic race." The work ethic, the social requirement of effort to achieve, and the ironic ideal of equal opportunity to make oneself unequal to the next man all combined to unify the "liberal tradition in America" which in essence was "atomistic social freedom" (31).

The other was social reform. Between Jackson's administration and the outbreak of the Civil War a seemingly endless number of social reform and utopian schemes appeared. As always, various minorities, and not the majority, agitated for them. Some of these reformers expressed revulsion for the majority's pursuit of the dollar. Others denounced the cautious creep of legislative reform *(32)*. Whatever their aims, the new causes they announced included communal experiments, socialistic schemes, abolition of slavery, emancipation of women, dress reform (bloomers), dietary fads, millenarian religious prophecy, even renunciation of monogamy itself via Mormonism and the Oneida Community. Solid citizens began to wonder what the world was coming to *(33)*.

It was almost as if such creeds of the French Revolution as progress, the perfectibility of man, the immediate re-formation of society with applied reason were belatedly embraced in America. But the Revolution's "religion of humanity" most certainly was not. Traditional religious commitment remained unshaken. "The God-oriented reformers believed that love of the Creator and love of His creatures were but opposite sides of the same golden coin of righteousness. There were no arbitrary distinctions to be drawn between religious reform and humanitarianism" (34). And actually, the new reform enthusiasm and ideas associated with it are more directly traceable to England than to France. The adoption of national in place of local voluntary organization derived from British examples. British abolition, missionary, and other national societies visited and corresponded with their counterparts in this country.

Explaining American Reformers

Most historians of this period have interpreted its reform agitation as being inevitable, a response to ideas whose time had come, ideas which fulfilled the meaning of American life, notably inherent in the Constitution. Grand conclusions of any kind are suspect, especially about history, of which Isaiah Berlin has said nothing is inevitable. Like any other period, this one exhibited a resounding clash of interests and a variety of "meanings" about America in general and the Constitution in particular. Defenders of slavery pointed to support in the Constitution, while some prominent Northern clergymen denounced public education, labor unions, women's rights, abolition, as being subversive of the American way of life as well as contrary to the teachings of Christ (35).

A few historians have seen a dark underside to the reformers' motives. The Northern abolitionists, for instance, have been called "a displaced class in American society," aliens in a new industrial society. For the most part rural New England in background, neither poor nor rich nor in business, these teachers, doctors, preachers, and educated maiden ladies viewed the monied aristocracy, textile manufacturers, and Southern slave owners as essentially one villain. Further, in this view the denunciation of slavery was an unconsciously disguised attack upon the whole new industrial system. A displaced social elite had found meaning for their lives in abolition. "The freeing of the slaves ended the great crusade that had brought purpose and joy to the abolitionists. For them Abraham Lincoln was not the Great Emancipator; he was the killer of the dream" (36).

Any such imputation of motives should be approached with caution. There is actually no way to determine how "genuine" the motives of anyone might be, whether he is a reformer or someone who seeks to discredit reformers. How "genuine" are the motives which launch crusades or prompt expression for the welfare of others? That vexing question is explored but not answered in Chapter 4. A hunger for some kind of self-vindication is doubtless involved, as Ralph Waldo Emerson averred during this same period. But that kind of judgment fails to separate sheep from goats. Every human being, now as then, seeks some form of self-vindication. The go-getters of the nineteenth century simply chose means different from those adopted by the reformers to achieve a similar emotional satisfaction.

It is likewise difficult to determine how much the reformers affected the future. The greatest of the crusades, abolition, made some contribution to the outbreak of the Civil War, but one that was probably not crucial. Many more people had opposed than supported abolition in the North, where the issue that did arouse mass emotion was the expansion of slave territory within the Union (37). All in all, what Horace Greeley called the "stammering century" subsided with the Civil War. The common people had never listened very intently anyway; their master vision remained the promised land soon to be or already secured within capitalism, the numerous Christian churches and their creeds, and Constitutional democracy. The Americans would make "all good dreams come true"—with established institutions (38).

THE MISSIONARY APPROACH TO SOCIAL PROBLEMS

In the late nineteenth and early twentieth centuries, social-reform effort by no means disappeared from the American scene. Its characteristic tone, however, departed from the utopian ferment of the 1830–1860 period. Basic institutions were no longer directly challenged. Desirable change was generally interpreted to be a gradual improvement upon what already was, by means of legislative enactment, voluntary works of charity, and the guiding of those who had never found the path or had strayed from it. The missionary did not wholly displace the agitator, but center stage now belonged to the missionary, whether he was the native white Protestant bringing knowledge to the immigrants and their children, the social worker, or the sociologist.

With some metaphorical exaggeration it can be said that in the latter part of the nineteenth century the two crosscurrents of go-getting private acquisition and social reform flowed into a single channel. The age was one of rapidly expanding wealth and power—and confidence. That confidence must be viewed with attitudes then ascendant, not those of the present. By modern standards conditions were wretched, even for the majority; they were much worse for the poor, the blacks, the immigrants. But attitudes, again, are no function of conditions, because conditions, in turn, can only be perceived with attitudes. Anyway, however conditions at that time may now be or were then judged, they did not temper the general mood of confidence and optimism and trust (39).

To a limited extent certain conditions *were* perceived as being deplorable. But the general mood decreed that they could be rectified by graduated legislative enactment, by voluntary charity, and, most important of all, by education of the "unfortunate"—they were not then the "underprivileged"— to teach them approved habits and attitudes. The example of the missionary, bringing light to dark places and a message of redemption, would enable the lost ones to *become* go-getters, of moral responsibility as well as acquisition.

Assimilation

By the turn of the century the American public school was busily engaged in transforming the children of the foreign born into Americans. Learning, as such, was a secondary goal. The main emphasis was placed upon "assimilation," upon instilling a drive to "middle-class" standards of rectitude, patriotism, ambition, responsibility, and applied effort. This same missionary approach was also utilized in a negative way. Justification of punishment for criminals, who increasingly appeared to have "foreign-sounding" names, became more righteous. And the nativist overtones of the Prohibition crusade were quite pronounced (40).

It was at this time that modern social-problem consciousness was completed in this country, a consciousness which for the most part persists today. As in the English case, it embodied much of the spirit and ideas of the Enlightenment—progress, optimism, faith in human nature, trust in rational effort, humanitarianism, and a confused egalitarianism. Yet modern social-problem consciousness notably differed in the kind of change foreseen and desired. It was neither utopian nor revolutionary, not even basically reformist, but instead assumed the intrinsic worth and viability of established institutions, which were to be gradually modified. The intention was not to overturn what exists, but to improve it.

That consciousness was more securely based at the turn of the century than it is now. Consensus was neither engineered nor planned; it rested upon the social-political and ideological dominance of white Protestants of Northern European stock. They had got here first, and in other as well as their own eyes were those who had founded the American way of life. They were what the others sought as well as were enjoined to emulate.

Those who in a modern pejorative term are called WASPs controlled the centers of social organization. Without needing to be named, their idealized and in part fictive models of behavior were unselfconsciously upheld in school, the press, business, and legislation. The chief of these models was the man who succeeds with disciplined effort and moral sobriety. There was, to be sure, that inevitable adulteration of hypocrisy which attends any presented model. Personal excellence, ideally assumed to be the means to occupational achievement, more often than not was identified with such achievement (41).

And yet the newer arrivals were not being deliberately conned. The theme of success in America had always celebrated the character ethic, with strong religious overtones. Native-born Americans did believe, or perhaps they only wanted to believe, that success inevitably awards the virtuous life. Less equivocal was the requirement that success must be justified by good works.

Some scholars have exaggerated the influence of social Darwinism upon the freebooting millionaires of the late nineteenth century. The only one known to endorse the doctrine that great wealth signifies the survival of the fittest was Andrew Carnegie. He gave away all of his own big pile to what were known at that time as worthy causes. He, and most of his kind, viewed themselves as Christian benefactors; for them, "true success" was not achieved until its fruits were philanthropically distributed (42). By funding worthy causes for the uplift of others, they too were missionaries.

Nor was any real effort ever made to define a separate place for the newer arrivals. Any foreigner could *become* an American, as no naturalized citizen of, say, Germany or France could ever become a German or a Frenchman. Respect for any individual who could make it was rarely withheld because of his background. The presented models were basically egalitarian. After all, there had never been a feudal society in America to destroy, and from the beginning native "aristocrats" were forced, like everyone else, to demonstrate personal competence in the marketplace and justify, like everyone else, their existence in terms of what they had accomplished.

The common man's populist envy of wealth and prestige has been a recurrent note in American history. But American would-be aristocrats have also been dissatisfied. They never have been able to command prestige and *deference* by reason of birth (43). The perennial question of the common man has been: What have *you* done? In America everyone was thus placed under some pressure to get ahead on his own. Paradoxically, all Americans were encouraged to struggle to achieve a high place in a society defined as classless. Those cautionary tales which schoolchildren of the period were taught always included several examples of immigrant boys who had made good in a big way.

Social Work

The early history of social work also developed a missionary emphasis. Voluntary charity had possibly been engaged mainly for the benefit of one's own soul or some more obscure psychological satisfaction. That ancient theme was still exemplified at the turn of the century in Christmas basket distribution and the Lady Bountiful image. But however much voluntary charity gratified the donor, the recipient was left essentially unchanged. The zeal of the missionary approach was left ungratified. Serious missionary work required that unfortunates be encouraged to *change* themselves and their circumstances. Charity organization was "the creation of middle-class Protestant Americans, denouncing rigid sectarianism in charitable affairs but inspired by an evangelical sense of mission" (44).

Charity organization was gradually taken over by professionals. But before social work could emerge as a profession, a case had to be made against both competing public assistance and interfering voluntarism. The new professionals tapped old prejudices by insisting that public relief encouraged the pauper way of life, while amateur volunteers would not stick with the drudgery of rehabilitating the poor. What was needed, they said, was "character rehabilitation and close supervision of the poor." Even when, by the twenties and thirties, caseworkers began to substitute "technical competence for moral and class superiority to justify interference in the lives of clients" (45), they continued to respect ancient biases. As Jeremy Bentham had taught, the poor should be helped but not to the point of "destroying their character."

Willingly or not, caseworkers allocated time and funds to those who were "deserving" at the expense of those who were not. Social workers were expected to encourage moral rectitude as well as eagerness to work. Some of the more innovative ones had to disguise what they were actually trying to do in many instances: extend help by their own definition of need, outside of official agency rules. In this transitional period the "case" was becoming the "client." But such notions as the "right to benefits" and pathos manipulation of the poor as victims of a corrupt society were not to be heard until the sixties. There was still missionary work to be done in setting the unfortunate upon the acknowledged right path.

American Sociology

We have seen that early sociology, which was largely European sociology, dealt with issues associated with the French Revolution. American sociology, like American society, was not directly affected by it. Early American sociology for the most part incorporated the missionary theme of bringing various outsiders within the common fold of an accepted way of life. Not until the advent of the New Deal did sociologists become less missionaries than advocates of social legislation designed to improve social institutions.

It has often been said that the New Deal fixed a benchmark in American history. From that time American citizens are said to have been treated not as individuals but as representatives of income, racial, occupational, and other categories with collective claims on the body politic by reason of their separate corporate interests. But the actual case was a much more gradual development.

The inception of the New Deal was no answer to public demand. The party voted into power in 1932 had promised to reduce public spending, and the candidate was pledged to "abolish useless

offices" and eliminate government functions which "are not defi-
nitely essential to the continuance of government." Nor is there any
evidence that President Roosevelt himself foresaw the ultimate consequences of his own legislation. In the late thirties he insisted that
most of the New Deal legislation would be abandoned once the
crisis of the Great Depression was over. And the recent shift of
attitudes among sociologists noted in the next section did not occur
until long after that legislation had become permanently established.

American sociologists, it is true, by the early thirties had in one
way abandoned the ideology of capitalistic individualism held by
their turn-of-the-century predecessors such as Giddings, Ross, Sumner, and to a lesser extent Cooley. Sociologists now stood in the
vanguard of intellectual support for the new social legislation. With
few exceptions they were liberals—in the new sense of advocating
governmental intervention, a reversal of earlier usage when "liberal"
meant opposition to it. They were only one step ahead of the American majority, who by the forties endorsed the new social legislation
so heartily that it was never again challenged in any serious way, not
even by the Republican party.

But such general support of social legislation requires scrupu-
lous interpretation. It was imbued with a hope of making "all good
dreams come true" with established American institutions. There
was no intention to overturn what now exists, but to improve upon
it. Attitudes, in short, remained more traditionalistic than otherwise.

This continuity with the past provoked the ire of C. Wright
Mills, who in a famous paper took to task the writers of social-
problems textbooks published during the late thirties and early forties. Their level of abstraction is low, he said, and they fail to deal
with total social structures. Most of them have a rural-Protestant
background; with attendant biases and moral judgments they therefore stress "organic community," locate all social problems in urban
areas, and favor an ad hoc gradualism. Their notions of disorganization and deviance are unsophisticated and nonstatistical and are
founded in middle-class small-town morality. Their emphasis upon
legislation and "fragmentary, practical problems tends to atomize
social objectives. The studies so informed are not integrated into
designs comprehensive enough to serve collective action, granted

the power and intent of realizing such action" (46). Although Mills makes no case here (as he later did) for revolutionary total change, the tacit advocation of it seems apparent. With Mills's paper it is almost possible to date the split in social-problem consciousness among sociologists.

RECENT SHIFT OF ATTITUDES AMONG INTELLECTUALS

The four basic ideas continue to guide social-problem consciousness. But a split has opened up among other aspects of that consciousness for intellectuals in general and sociologists in particular. The missionary approach has been well-nigh abandoned. Ours is hardly an age of confidence, and intellectuals do not ordinarily sing the praises of prevailing institutional arrangements or stress the desirability of bringing in those who might remain outside of them. Indeed, the light can be sought in erstwhile dark places. Such popular anthropologists as Margaret Mead and Ruth Benedict have preached that exotic peoples can tell *us* where *we* went wrong, especially in matters of aggression (too much) and sex (not enough).

In some other dimensions the split in social-problem consciousness is less equally shared. Most intellectuals retain considerable loyalty to a New Deal outlook, support centralized government and legislative reform. But there is a continuing drift of attitudes among intellectuals toward a scorn for social reform or any other form of gradualism, a drift toward denunciation rather than criticism of present social arrangements.

The drift is also toward endorsing special claims for segments of the population held in particular favor. The mood invoked is nevertheless more retributive than revolutionary, at least in a Marxian sense, for nothing is ever said about seizing power, only about the duty to promote more of it for those who are said to be powerless. Most sociologists who deal with social problems appear especially determined to push special claims for chosen categories of citizens.

In his presidential address at the convened Society for the Study of Social Problems, Melvin M. Tumin in August of 1967 asserted that students of social problems have allied themselves with the poor, the black, and the young—against their opposite numbers.

He inveighed against the indulgence of "personal hang-ups" and a search "for new experience under the guise of the dictates of social science." Partisan pleading of this kind, he said, the championing of "black power against white power, youth power against adult power, sexual freedom against sexual constraint, deviance against conformity," makes irrelevant any claim to special and professional expertise *(47)*.

The drift noted by Professor Tumin is evident enough, although we do not know how long it will continue. He may also have exaggerated it somewhat. The present situation is much too fluid for a content analysis of social-problems textbooks such as Mills published in 1943. A spot check will indicate a clear Tumin-pointed direction, but other such textbooks are still being written within a social-problems frame of reference, informed by an older and persisting social-problem consciousness. The drift is much less marked among textbooks than in the pages of such journals as *Social Problems* and *Trans-action* (since 1972 entitled *Society).*

Assimilation in Reverse

With this new drift the "problem of assimilation" has been turned inside out. Many sociologists and most other intellectuals now tend to regard peoples of European-Catholic ancestry with a concern opposite to that once expressed. These peoples now stand accused of embracing a literal "Americanism" which, ironically enough, is much less fashionable among WASPs than it was when their grandparents were encouraging the foreign born to "assimilate" it. And many sociologists and social psychologists, via such devices as the authoritarian-personality formulation, now label the descendants of recent immigrants a problem *(48)*!

WASPs no longer serve as a cultural model, not even to most WASPs. These newer peoples, about one quarter of the present population, now tend to regard *themselves* as the upholders of the American way of life. They are "assimilated" to the present in that Catholics "under 40 are as likely to be college graduates and to be economically successful as are comparable American Protestants," and their political attitudes and behavior on balance place them solidly within "the American liberal coalition" (49). Yet they remain "assimilated" to the recent past in the sense that otherwise they remain more traditionalistic in outlook than Protestants and Jews, when the latter are also considered *en bloc*. Opinion polls disclose Catholics to be less enthusiastic about abortion, divorce, evasion of military service, pornography, "coddling of criminals," defiance of authority, and so on, than are Protestants and Jews, again considered *en bloc*. American Catholics make up the largest crudely identifiable segment of the majority defined in the previous chapter.

The anti-Catholicism noted by Andrew Greeley (see reference 49) stems from suspicion of a Catholic traditional "Americanism" which is not forgiven despite how or for whom most Catholics might vote. But anti-Catholicism may be too strong a term. Intellectuals tend to be notably disturbed only by a small part of the Catholic population, the blue-collar contingent which lives in large cities in or contiguous to black slums. These people have resisted solutions to the "racial problem" proferred from safe and distant suburbs— such as school desegration and "open housing"—which in their view victimizes them.

Intellectuals, including some Catholic intellectuals, have generally lost interest in the other Catholics. The somewhat pejorative term "ethnics" is rarely applied to people whose names end in a vowel or are hard to spell provided they live in the suburbs and work in offices or as professionals. These people, who now constitute the Catholic majority, simply hold little interest for those who once worried about them. Puerto Ricans, Chicanos, blacks, and American Indians have replaced them.

Resentment of this fall from intellectual favor, as well as a perceived residual anti-Catholic bias, is reflected in a growing tendency among American Catholics to affirm an ethnic identity which a few years ago seemed to most of them a hindrance or a nuisance. In a way, they are victims of their own success. They can readily recall that throughout the thirties, the forties, and beyond, they were the recipients of that special concern now reserved for others. They were a prominent part of the labor movement, with which the intellectuals once identified but no longer do.

According to Professor Andrew Hacker, there are changing fashions in underdogs. Using the term "liberal" for what is essentially meant by "intellectual" above, he says that the continuity of liberal ideology, despite its changing content, "lies in identification with classes about to enter their ascendancy." Conversely, the "liberal" always becomes disenchanted once the people he has championed cease to be underdogs. Their assumed uncorrupted nature is supposed to redeem their champions, but once they cease to be underdogs they inevitably turn out to be of the same clay as the rest of humanity. The burden of expected redemption is then imposed upon those newly defined as the oppressed (50).

There is an alternative, somewhat less provocative, interpretation. Many college students today express shock that only since about the end of World War II has particular concern been expressed for the Negro, and much later for Chicanos and Indians. These people, quite literally in Ralph Ellison's term, were invisible. Sensitive and humanitarian whites did feel much subliminal remorse and guilt about that invisibility, but the weight of custom, law, mores was such that remedial effort was perforce channeled toward those who, so to speak, were only one step behind in the parade— Jews and the descendants of recent immigrants.

The flavor of the times is caught in those late-hour TV films which were made during World War II. There are no black faces, and at mail call common humanity is conferred upon only "Griswold, Feinstein, Wisniewski, Costello." It was not until 1953 that segregation in the armed forces was officially abandoned.

In any event, the people who displaced American Catholics as the focus of concern are being encouraged to separate from instead of join the rest of society, to adopt reverse assimilation as it were. This ideological shift was instigated by white political-intellectual minorities, and in all probability it remains more popular with them than with the ethnic and racial minorities addressed. According to the University of Michigan's Survey Research Center, the proportion of American Negroes who favored black separatism dropped from 6 to 3 percent between 1964 and 1968. That proportion has possibly risen since 1968. Yet it is not clear how much the rhetoric of black nationalism and black separatism actually expresses black attitudes. Various surveys indicate that a very large majority of American Negroes want in, want to become an integral part of present-day American life in every dimension. According to several black spokesmen, at the same time most blacks find in extremist rhetoric an echo of their own deep-lying resentments.

Most white intellectuals appear to persist in the assumption, one that is insecurely validated at best, that militant black voices authentically speak for all blacks. In some degree as a consequence, the goals as well as strategy of white intellectuals have become confused, with a resulting compounding of confusion among the black population. Promotion of legal enactments, pressure exerted to secure government-bureau directives, slogans themselves alternate between integration and separation. Quotas are inadmissible; yet quotas must be utilized to ensure proportionate and thus fair treatment. All facilities must be desegregated; yet other facilities must be segregated—such as the reservation at Barnard College of two dormitory floors for minority students in order to uphold "the principle of selective living for all students" *(51)*. Educational opportunity must be made equal; yet the teaching of so-called black English, the syntax and vocabulary not of educated blacks but of impoverished and uneducated ones, is being promoted in many public schools (52). If the trend toward inwardness and separatism should continue, asks America's foremost historian of assimilation, Oscar Handlin, "what will happen to the possibility of communication across group lines?" (53).

Attitudes and the "Power Structure"

The "power structure" concept is examined in a later chapter. Here the term refers simply to the present *distribution of social power,* a phrase which avoids the sloganizing value judgment which inheres in "power structure." Like other omnibus terms such as "social class" and "mass society," the term "power structure," even though qualified, may obscure more than aid analysis. But the term can hardly be avoided because it is now embedded in the educated consciousness. Without further refinement of the point, among sociologists as well as other intellectuals the drift of attitude has been away from more or less acceptance of the given distribution of social power toward more or less rejection of it.

During the forties and fifties, C. Wright Mills, Kingsley Davis, Willard Waller, and other sociologists argued in different ways that the professional as well as government-agency approach to social problems was—consciously or not—designed to perpetuate the power structure. Problems were stated and addressed so as to deal, in Waller's phrase, "with symptoms rather than causes." In the different terminology used in this present section, missionary gradualism within an assumed stable and continuous social order was still ascendant. And while sociologists at that time did not endorse the power structure, with the exception of Mills they failed to denounce it. As they saw it, they were simply describing the way things are.

The recent drift of attitudes has led many sociologists, particularly those who write about social problems, to denounce the power structure, or the way things are. How much their work has influenced the course of events would be impossible to determine. Only a few sociologists have ever served as advisors to or participants in foundation- and government-sponsored programs designed to upset the power structure. Mainly, intellectuals within the government bureaucracy itself have formed the cadres of such programs. In any event, since "the mid-1960s a new orientation to the social problems of urban poverty has evolved. It is based on community organization and community action; its advocates are professionals whose careers are tied to services for the poor or research on poverty; its resources are federal funds or foundation grants; its goals entail upsetting the power structure of the city"(54).

Negative attitudes toward the power structure have persisted among intellectuals, but the programs initiated by professionals to circumvent the power structure through "community action" have not appreciably succeeded. This judgment should be viewed with the warning posted in Chapter 1: sociology, or any other science, cannot tell us what goals we should pursue. On the other hand, the adequacy or inadequacy of means applied to achieve a given goal *can* be objectively analyzed. What failed in the Community Action programs, then, was the means adopted to achieve more control for the urban poor over the circumstances of their own lives.

The chief vehicle of the enterprise was the Office of Economic Opportunity (OEO). This federal government bureau organized programs among the "poor" to challenge public and private agencies which deal with schools, merchants, welfare, housing, and the like. Before Phillip V. Sanchez left his post as Director of OEO in 1973, he characterized the entire program as a "total failure." The product of goodwill and illusion, it failed for many reasons. "Responsible leadership" among the poor was never located. Communities could hardly organize in any serious or effective way against themselves. Public resentment became a political hot potato. And the disorganized poor as well as organized street gangs, like their intellectual spokesmen, continued to seek redress and subsidies from the power structure rather than organize to displace it. The power structure remained.

In getting the original War on Poverty under way, Sargent Shriver had listed "governmental groups, philanthropic, religious, business, and labor groups, and the poor." Governmental groups were only one among several equal participants, an illusionary listing which blinks the "unsentimental application of coercion" which is the very nature of any and all govenments (55). Established community leadership, notably political leadership, recoiled from equal participation with the "poor"; it drew closer together in a real if unacknowledged common front. At the same time, that leadership made not poverty but militancy the chief criterion in seeking authentic black spokesmen to deal with. The "War on Poverty and especially Community Action helped bring on the black separatist movement itself by making black separatism the trait most favored in recruitment and promotion into [black] leadership" (56).

Since no real basis for cooperative participation was ever established, cash was simply disbursed on the basis of greasing the squeakiest wheels *(57)*. The failure of the means adopted in the poverty war and the OEO, however, was ensured from the very beginning by a confusion of aims. Freedom of initiative was sought for people who are dependent upon the existing power structure. The "pluralistic bias of American political life" was invoked to declare community leaders equal partners in a cooperative enterprise with some who were unemployables or petty criminals, others who were inarticulate and frightened. At the same time, pluralism was treated as an obstacle to be overcome in the achievement of unity among established agencies pursuing their own bureaucratic goals (58). The OEO was designed around divided purpose: to challenge, upset—*and reinforce*—the power structure.

Social-problem consciousness, then, has become a divisive as well as a unifying outlook, and how divisive it has become is made especially apparent in Chapter 5. And yet the four basic ideas discussed in the first part of this chapter have provided a continuous focus of attention and concern, a common rallying point amidst conflicting attitudes, even when what any of the ideas really means or how it should be interpreted is disputed. In the next chapter the recent history of five social problems is discussed in terms of the most basic of the four ideas, humanitarianism.

REFERENCES

1 On the other hand, in modern as well as ancient times three manifestations of inequality (perhaps better *un*equality based upon role differentiation) have gone unquestioned. They have been traced by ethologists to our protohominid ancestry, and can be observed among modern social apes and monkeys. They are male dominance over females, subordination of children to their parents, and inequality among males which results from competition for status. Real challenges to these forms of inequality (or unequality) are quite recent developments.

   The term male dominance is an unfortunate one, for it may seem to connote browbeating or even physical abuse. As used here, it refers solely to male right of major decision making which has accompanied assumption of protection and economic responsibility for mate and children. A highly controversial treatment of the subject in today's political-social climate bases universal male dominance upon the phylogenetic effects of the hunter role. See Lionel Tiger, *Men in Groups,* Random House, New York, 1969.

   According to Tiger, the so-called matriarchal societies are only matrilineal. There, as elsewhere, the public forum remains a male forum. Institutional life is universally controlled by males; only males have the capacity to "release followership behavior" in the critical areas of economic activity, defense against outside invasion, and maintenance of internal order. Only men form those "bonds" upon which hierarchical arrangements are founded.

   Hierarchies will result from hypothetically open competition as well as from hereditary transmission of status. For a vigorous defense of the hierarchical principle, as being as necessary and inevitable in human society as in biology, see Arthur Koestler, *The Ghost in the Machine,* Macmillan, New York, 1967.

2 The origin of this New Testament idea is more Greek than Semitic. The Stoics had already characterized slavery as an unnatural condition and affirmed the equality of all men—by which they meant only that common humanity should take precedence before undeniable human dif-

ferences of worth and status. And the Sophist Alcidamas had said: "God has set all men free; nature has made no man a slave."

So the idea of slavery did not sit so easily with some Greek intellectuals as it did with Plato and Aristotle. "Because slaves are men who are defined as things, the institution has always generated tension and conflict." Nevertheless, in the ancient world "there was no assertion that slavery was an intolerable evil that should be eradicated by any civilized nation." See David Brion Davis, *The Problem of Slavery in Western Culture,* Cornell, Ithaca, N. Y., 1966, pp. 60 and 62.

3 Norman Cohn, *The Pursuit of the Millenium,* Basic Books, New York, 1957, p. 209.

4 Cohn, reference 3, p. 275. This sullying of egalitarian doctrine with the notion of an elite, a saving remnant licensed by superior knowledge and sensitivity of soul to direct the common people, remains an embarrassment to, anyway a contradiction of, egalitarianism to this day.

5 Ernst Troeltsch, *The Social Teaching of the Christian Churches,* 2 vols., Olive Wyon (trans.), Macmillan, New York, 1931, vol. 2, p. 510.

6 Narration, especially that which is chronological, imposes inevitable distortions. Perhaps most of the social ideas men have ever held remain ubiquitous in time. The human condition itself, with all its subterranean resentments and longing for vindication, makes plausible such an assumed continuity. At the same time, while men do not exchange one set of ideas for another in the passage of the centuries, dominant images of the world do change, and *some* ideas come to predominate over others, even though they never supplant them.

7 Arthur O. Lovejoy, *The Great Chain of Being,* Harvard, Cambridge, Mass., 1950 (copyright 1936), p. 186.

8 Lovejoy, reference 7, p. 207.

9 Preserved Smith, *The Enlightenment 1687–1776,* Holt, New York, 1934, especially pp. 16–26. The men of the Enlightenment had no intention to function as midwife to the French Revolution. They were not radicals. They did not, for example, insist upon the abolition of private property. What they resented was *feudal* property and the privileges attendant upon it, which were denied to them. Like many other reformers, they apparently wanted just enough equality made available to enable men like themselves to be admitted through all doors. Rousseau's demand for literal equality—in uniform subservience to the state—was unique. And while they wanted to "erase superstition" (i.e., the church), they wanted only to hobble the monarch, not to destroy monarchy. They were not the first men in history to feed a pussycat and later face a tiger.

10   Crane Brinton, *A History of Western Morals,* Harcourt, Brace, New York, 1959, p. 303.

11   Smith, reference 9, p. 21.

12   Arthur O. Lovejoy, *Reflections on Human Nature,* Johns Hopkins, Baltimore, 1961, p. 131.

13   John Viscount Morley, *Diderot and the Encyclopaedists,* 2 vols., Macmillan, London, 1921, vol. I, p. 5.

14   The *philosophes* of the late eighteenth century renounced much less of the past than they intended, and perpetuated some "errors" of their own, such as a touching faith in posterity. They not only substituted nature for God as ruler of the universe; they also substituted posterity for God as its judge. Diderot said that posterity is for the rational man what the other world is for the religious. Although men who attract favorable attention in their own time have always been concerned about being remembered as long as possible, in the late eighteenth century that concern became almost institutionalized in the concept of progress. Men of the future, it was innocently believed, would forever celebrate the nobility and contribution of the enlightened, and cherish those eighteenth-century names as perpetual reminders of what their exalted present state owed to those departed heroes.

15   Morley, reference 13, p. 172.

16   Smith, reference 9, p. 588.

17   By indirection, by stressing not values and attitudes themselves but their putative formation by structural political-economic change, one scholar appears to contest the particular time-place interpretation of the rise of humanitarianism. See David Lerner, *The Passing of Traditional Society,* Free Press, New York, 1958. He argues that any highly mobile society will heighten empathic concern for the stranger. High empathic capacity appears in any distinctively industrial, urban, literate, and participant milieu. What this thesis leaves unexplained is the evident gap between urban-industrial change and humanitarian expression in such modern nations as India, China, and Russia, which lie outside of or at best are tangential to the Western tradition.

18   Brinton, reference 10, p. 309.

19   The institutionalization of compassion "is what we mean by humanitarianism," something inseparable from the modern sentiment of equality. "For, as Tocqueville shrewdly noted, it was only when the spreading sentiment of equality made all men feel related in some degree and, more importantly, made of the same fundamental clay that it was really possible for the sufferings of some to enter the consciousness and the conscience of others." The extension of humanitarianism "to include literally all human beings in society" was quite slow, however, and only achieved in the last few decades. Robert A. Nisbet, *The Social Bond,* Knopf, New York 1970, pp. 23 and 24.

20 Shelby T. McCloy, *The Humanitarian Movement in Eighteenth-Century France,* University of Kentucky Press, Lexington, 1957, p. 3.

21 McCloy, reference 20, p. 262. On the other hand, in McCloy's opinion these same reforms "would almost certainly have come about in time without the Revolution. Some would have come earlier than others, but all were on their way. Louis XVI had already initiated a number of reforms, and enlightened monarchs throughout Europe were absorbed in the matter of reform" (p. 5).

22 For example, see Stanley Loomis, *Du Barry: A Biography,* Lippincott, Philadelphia, 1959, especially pp. 210 and 222.

23 England "had already had both its religious 'reformation' and its bourgeois revolution (though not its industrial sequel), whereas in France the forms and privileges of feudalism and of medieval religion had survived almost intact into the heart of the enlightenment, so that the new and the old confronted each other there with a sharpness of contrast which was blurred on this side of the Channel." Basil Willey, *The Eighteenth Century Background,* Beacon Press, Boston, 1961 (first published in England in 1940), p. 120.

24 W. H. Bruford, *Germany in the Eighteenth Century,* Cambridge, 1935, pp. 47–49.

25 Frederick B. Artz, *Reaction and Revolution 1814–1832,* Harper, New York, 1934, p. 49.

26 Artz, reference 25, p. 17.

27 Artz, reference 25, pp. 54 and 55.

28 A. V. Dicey, *Lectures on the Relation between Law and Public Opinion in England during the Nineteenth Century,* Macmillan, London, 1952 (first published in 1905), p. 107.

29 Dicey, reference 28, p. 125.

30 Robert A. Nisbet, *The Sociological Tradition,* Basic Books, New York, 1966, p. 265.

31 Louis Hartz, *The Liberal Tradition in America,* Harcourt, Brace, New York, 1955, p. 62.

32 As one instance, in 1843 Massachusetts "forbade the employment of children under twelve years of age for more than ten hours a day." Arthur Cecil Bining, *The Rise of American Economic Life,* Scribner, New York, 1943, p. 259.

33 Only what were considered the more radical schemes aroused much popular opposition. Labor unions, state education, various antialcohol

crusades, and the crusade against "Romanism" found more support than the others because they were proposals of change *within* existing institutions.

34 C. S. Griffin, *The Ferment of Reform, 1830–1860,* Thomas Y. Crowell, New York, 1967, p. 49.

35 A sort of free enterprise market in ideas prevented any one of them from becoming entirely successful. Different banners were carried in all directions; support was solicited for many causes in competition with one another. Leaders of one movement denounced leaders of another, notably prohibitionists and abolitionists. Meanwhile, all of them were debating over the heads of the common people, for the most part untutored folk intolerant of change demanded beyond the limits of "existing thought and present institutions." See Griffin, reference 34, especially pp. 67–71.

36 David Donald, "Toward a Reconsideration of Abolitionists," in Joseph R. Gusfield (ed.), *Protest, Reform, and Revolt,* Wiley, New York, 1970, pp. 13–23. This thesis has been termed "long on speculation and short on evidence." Donald "did not name his abolitionists, and thus no one could tell who their parents had been, or to what social class they had belonged. He could not—or would not—prove that their social displacement had led them to reform." Griffin, reference 34, p. 21.

37 Edward Channing, *A History of the United States,* vol. VI, *The War for Southern Independence,* Macmillan, New York, 1927, especially p. 119.

38 Griffin, reference 34, p. 73.

39 This generalization is based upon the popular literature of the period as well as critical assessments made by historians and literary men. But since no public-opinion polls were taken at that time, and much less concern about the "unfortunate" was voiced, one question seems legitimate enough: *Whose* age of confidence was it? We do not really know. We do know, on the other hand, that material conditions and confidence do not rise and fall together. The Survey Research Center of the University of Michigan conducted a nationwide poll in 1972 and discovered that "those at the lower range of the socioeconomic ladder indicated *more* satisfaction with American life than those higher up." Cited on p. 46 of Seymour Martin Lipset and Earl Raab, "The Election and the National Mood," *Commentary,* January 1973, pp. 43–50.

40 Joseph R. Gusfield, "Moral Passage: The Symbolic Process in Public Designation of Deviance," *Social Problems,* **15:**175–188, 1967, p. 184.

41 Robin M. Williams, Jr., "Achievement and Success as Value Orientations," in Bernard C. Rosen et al. (eds.), *Achievement in American Society,* Schenkman, Cambridge, Mass., 1969, pp. 13–17.

42 The best single treatment of the success theme in American history is Richard M. Huber, *The American Idea of Success,* McGraw-Hill, New York, 1971.

43 For the classic analysis of these themes in American history, see Hartz, reference 31.

44 Ray Lubove, *The Professional Altruist: The Emergence of Social Work as a Career 1880–1930,* Harvard, Cambridge, Mass., 1965, p. 6.

45 Lubove, reference 44, p. 122.

46 C. Wright Mills, "The Professional Ideology of Social Pathologists," *American Journal of Sociology,* **49**:165–180, 1943, p. 169.

47 Melvin M. Tumin, "In Dispraise of Loyalty," *Social Problems,* **15**:267 –279, 1968, p. 275. The orientation which arouses Professor Tumin's indignation had been manifest in nascent form at the founding of the society. According to Professor Jessie Bernard, in the early fifties a revolution occurred in a "declaration of independence of a group of rebels who, deploring the refusal of the parent organization [the American Sociological Association] to take a stand on any policy issue, established the Society for the Study of Social Problems (SSSP). Our gripes were manifold." See "Jessie Bernard's Four Revolutions," *American Journal of Sociology,* **78**:773–791, 1973, p. 774.

48 Some sociologists and psychologists have been charged guilty of distorting evidence in this general area in order to serve their own moral purposes. See Gwynn Nettler, *Explanations,* McGraw-Hill, New York, 1970, footnote, pp. 29–31. In the literature, terms applied to this "class" are often pejorative; the term "authoritarian" instead of "respectful of authority," for instance, is consistently utilized. "Repression, obedience to law and prompt acceptance of authority are [in the literature] more 'primitive' ways of dealing with reality than intellectualization, reflection on principles before obeying the law, and skepticism toward authority." Michael Lerner, "Respectable Bigotry," *The American Scholar,* Autumn 1969, pp. 606–617, p. 609. In respectable bigotry, "uneducated and inarticulate white people" are judged to be "pathological" (James Hitchcock, "The Intellectuals and the People," *Commentary* March 1973, pp. 64–69, p. 65).

49 Andrew M. Greeley, "American Catholics—Making It or Losing It?" *The Public Interest,* Summer 1972, pp. 26–37, p. 27.

50 Andrew Hacker, *The End of the American Era,* Atheneum, New York, 1970, especially pp. 149–152.

51 *Time,* Nov. 27, 1972, p. 44. In early 1974 the Barnard College reservation of two dormitory floors for minority students was rescinded.

52 J. L. Dillard, "The Validity of Black English," *Intellectual Digest,* December 1972, pp. 35–42.

53 Oscar Handlin, "The Half-Truth Way of Life," *Intellectual Digest,* March 1972, pp.73–74, p.74.

54 James S. Coleman, "Community Disorganization and Conflict," in Robert K. Merton and Robert Nisbet (eds.), *Contemporary Social Problems,* rev. ed., Harcourt Brace Jovanovich, New York, 1971, pp. 657–708, p. 679.

55 Theodore J. Lowi, *The End of Liberalism,* Norton, New York, 1969, p. 84.

56 Lowi, reference 55, p. 247.

57 For a grimly hilarious account of the bullying-blackmail tactics employed by some of those wheels to get the free cash, see the latter part of Tom Wolfe's *Radical Chic and Mau-Mauing the Flak Catchers,* Bantam, New York, 1971. At one point, street gangs were being bribed with federal grants for "job training," with ensuing fraud and community terrorization. See, e.g., Winston Moore et al., "Woodlawn: The Zone of Destruction," *The Public Interest,* Winter 1973, pp. 41–59, especially pp. 48–51.

58 Peter Maris and Martin Rein, *Dilemmas of Social Reform: Poverty and Community Action in the United States,* Atherton Press, New York, 1967. This is the most scholarly and judicious assessment of the Community Action projects available.

Humanitarianism and the Recent History of Social Problems

The four ideas associated with a recognition of social problems—equality, the essential goodness of human nature, the belief that conditions which are deplored can be rectified, and humanitarianism—continue to channel accompanying attitudes. In the last few years, however, new emphases in these ideas have emerged. Equality, yes, but the notion of equality of condition has come to challenge that of equality of opportunity quite sharply. The essential goodness of man is still widely endorsed over the opposite notion, yet a tinge of paranoia has surfaced in the confrontation of hip and square discussed in Chapter 5. The insistence that conditions must be improved, now more firmly registered than ever before, accompanies a waning faith that conditions will be modified in a desired direction

(1). And although the sheer volume of humanitarianism has probably increased, approved objects of that sentiment and ways to express it have markedly changed.

Social problems operate in two dimensions of time. The first is the rise of social-problem consciousness, which is the main theme of the previous chapter. The second, the changing character and designation of specific social problems, is the main theme of this chapter. The relationships between these changes and changes in humanitarian expression are particularly stressed. And changes in humanitarian expression are shown to have become embroiled in conflicts of interest.

HUMANITARIANISM: PAST AND PRESENT

Humanitarianism in the traditional context was in one sense cheap. Upper-status persons viewed themselves as rescuers of the downtrodden and the afflicted, as missionaries seeking to bring light to dark places, and alternatively as stern taskmasters of the recalcitrant. Later, aid and succor became more organized, and legislation was utilized to redress "social evils" deemed beyond the scope of either voluntary or group-agency effort. But that later approach remained traditional in the sense that no institutional change of any consequence was demanded. With fixed institutional boundaries assumed, no serious conflict of interest arose. The majority were left relatively undisturbed by the limited goals of reformers and other political-intellectual minorities.

That situation has changed. Humanitarianism is now frequently invoked in such a way as to require institutional modification, with resultant severe conflicts of interest. Ecology and population growth are addressed to upsetting majority practices and habits, to revising the total economy. Much older social problems, like crime, race relations, and poverty, have a long history of humanitarian pathos manipulation. Only recently has drastic change of institutional arrangements been demanded in their behalf.

In all five cases at the present time, an involuntary price is exacted from numerous nonvolunteers. In its traditional expression, humanitarianism for the most part united donor and recipient in a mutually accepted common interest. The circle of involvement has been vastly extended. A humanitarianism which demands institutional change exacerbates conflicts of interest. It is largely within this context that crime, poverty, race relations, population growth, and ecology are first discussed below. The last section of the chapter deals with how and why some social problems change more rapidly in time than do others.

CRIME

Probably the first social problem to achieve recognition was crime, and it was the first to arouse humanitarian compassion—by modern standards, to a minimal degree. By the late eighteenth century organized humanitarian pressure had improved prison conditions and through legislation had reduced the severity of sentences, especially by striking from the books most of the offenses we would regard as trivial which had carried the death penalty. But there was no question of exculpating criminal acts. The criminal was blamed for what he had done, as he still is, with a divided conscience, by the majority.

Then as now, however, no way was ever found to eradicate crime. Once urban civilization emerges, or is in prospect, apparently a near-constant proportion of any population will more or less systematically flout the laws. Our forefathers worried about the rising crime rate in Boston when, by 1680, that little theocratic village had become a bustling town and seaport. The strict Sabbath already only a memory, drink, gambling, prostitution, bastardy, and dealing with pirates flourished. The wharf taverns bred disorder and mob violence. A professional class of thieves aroused general concern, and available evidence indicates that in the first quarter of the eighteenth century "probably as many offences were committed as in communities of the same size today" (2). But the causes of criminality were as unknown then as they are now, "and the solution of this peculiarly vexing problem of city life remained as remote in the seventeenth and eighteenth centuries as today."

At the same time, a clear majority of the townsmen not only observed all the laws, but drew a clear line between themselves and burglars and pickpockets, between themselves and the disorderly element along the waterfront. They felt neither guilt nor responsibility for those others. They had failed to measure up, and they could be punished—they were punished—with a clear conscience. The law-abiding citizen failed to take alarm at the criminal element in his midst because it was outside and not within the scheme of things that mattered. It was dealt with summarily. Thus, no matter how close the comparative statistics, crime in a very real sense was *not* a social problem in the sense that it later became. While punishment "worked" no better then than now in changing criminal behavior, attitudes toward crime and punishment were more uniform.

We do not know for certain whether the crime rate has risen in recent years; if it has, we do not know how to find out how much. The case could even be that the incidence of crime is now little if any greater than it was in the early days of Boston town *(3)*. On the other hand, the present "real crime rate" might be incalculably higher. Most crimes are known to go unreported to the police, and very few of those reported are followed by arrest and further legal processing, a matter discussed in Chapter 8.

Whether the real crime rate is going up or down or stabilizing has little bearing upon our main purpose, which is the analysis of attitudes. It is not facts as such but what men believe the facts to be which determines their view of the world and their attitudes toward social problems. According to a Gallup poll taken in 1973, crime topped the list of concerns expressed by all respondents in communities of whatever size. And the weight of opinion was that crime had increased over the previous year. Thus the salient "fact" is a majority *belief* that crime *is* rising at an alarming rate, and no more than those who defend and exculpate criminals do they know what to do about it. On the other hand, the majority are confused and somewhat upset by, withal skeptical about, the stance of the latter.

Diversity of Intellectual Attitudes

Since about the turn of the century, new attitudes toward crime and criminals have emerged among intellectuals. There was at first a quantum leap of humanitarian sentiment which led intellectuals to decry punishment in favor of missionizing and exhorting criminals to return to the fold. Understanding rather than blame was stressed, and antecedent social causes were traced to explain why criminal behavior persisted. Then as now, poverty was the insecure yet favored explanation for criminal conduct *(4)*.

The general public was exhorted to a crusade. The following quotations are taken from two textbooks published during the thirties; no writer on the subject today would address the general public in this way: "Let everyone who loves humanity . . . answer the challenge." Again: "The elimination of crime . . . is the greatest undertaking in the universe which could engage the attention of man, or to which he could address himself."

In the forties and fifties the missionizing of criminals and exhortation of the public to act receded. Committed intellectuals were invited to cooperate with experts in helping to modify harsh public attitudes and reduce public control. Only in this way could punishment be replaced by "treatment." Society was said to be to blame for crime, and appeals were made to re-form social institutions in order to rescue the victims of society, those accused of crime. Criminals and delinquents themselves were held to be totally blameless; having done nothing to expiate, they were said to have done nothing to merit punishment, a state of affairs indicated in the title of one book, *The Juvenile in Delinquent Society.* The mood verged on that expressed by Norman Mailer in his desire to rescue delinquents from "a collective nausea which is encysted into the future" by a "search for arts which transmute violence into heroic activity."

A minority of sociologists and other intellectuals adopted a more extreme view which appeared in the late sixties. Spokesmen of it abandoned all hope of re-forming a society they damned as corrupt. They no longer blamed criminal behavior on society; they denied the very existence of "so-called" crime. They lost interest in the older charge that criminal acts are "determined by the environment" because their attention shifted away from criminal acts as defined at law.

They labeled "crimes" of war, business operations, and, in the words of one sociologist, the "covert institutional violence" inhering in "government lack of action," incalculably more destructive. In a transvaluation of values they hailed the criminal as hero, martyr, saint. As one student of social problems stated his case: "Every black crime is a political act, a blow for freedom." People who hold such attitudes (Jessica Mitford is possibly the most famous example) do not make a case against punishment and usually do not even mention it. Instead they fire away at those who want to "treat" criminals with diagnosis, counseling, and other attempts to modify their behavior.

The attitudes of intellectuals toward crime have, then, changed, but by no means uniformly. Most people who write on the subject continue to define the criminal as a systematic lawbreaker, as do the majority. Unlike the majority, however, in one way or another they tend to deny that the criminal is responsible for his actions. Still, while the majority continue to assign responsibility for crime to the criminal himself, they have become much less conscience-free about punishment than were law-abiding citizens of eighteenth-century Boston.

Capital Punishment

The recent history of capital punishment reads like a graph of trouble in the soul. Most citizens remain self-divided on the issue, more so than most prelates, journalists, academes; former U. S. Attorney General Ramsey Clark (who has publicly stated his opposition); the American Civil Liberties Union; and federal court judges and those sitting on the various state supreme courts. Yet opinion in high places is by no means unanimous. When the U. S. Supreme Court struck down the death penalty in 1972, almost immediately thereafter an assembly of national attorneys general voted 32 to 1 in its favor. The trend toward abrogation in recent years, however, has been clear. France and Spain are now the only West European countries to retain the death penalty.

Nevertheless, because most people on this issue react in personal and concrete terms more than they endorse abstract principle, the trend has by no means been a straight line. Ireland abolished the death penalty early in 1964, with one exception—the assassination of a head of state or visiting head of state. The murder of an American President of Irish descent was fresh in memory. In April of 1965 the West German Bundestag was discussing a proposal to reinstate the death penalty—abolished in 1949—following a wave of cabdriver murders.

A few years ago the death penalty was reinstated in ten states of this country which had previously abolished it. In every case the precipitant was a specific murder, or series of murders. For instance, in March of 1965 Governor Branigan of Indiana vetoed an abolitionist legislative bill—four days after a state trooper was shot to death. His office had been deluged with letters which urged that action. In March of 1973, the murder of two American diplomats by Sudanese terrorists led Secretary of State Rogers to observe that while he deplored the death penalty, he would approve of it in this instance in order to discourage any such future abominations. Within that week President Nixon called for the return of capital punishment in a national radio broadcast.

Abroad and at home, the public when asked opts for retention of the death penalty. A late 1972 opinion poll in France disclosed only 27 percent of respondents favored abolition. California voters in 1972 by a ratio of 2 to 1 favored restoration. Seventy percent of adults responding to a 1966 Gallup poll in England opposed an antihanging bill. In that same year the *Christian Herald* in this country polled 13,500 of its Protestant church-member readers: 64 percent answered yes to "Is the death penalty ever morally justifiable?", 32 percent said no, and 7 percent were undecided. Of the total number, 61 percent affirmed a belief that "the death penalty is a deterrent of crime."

Can one say, then, that a clear majority of people in England and America favor capital punishment? Perhaps yes, and possibly no. Many of those who so declare presumably react to the last concrete image in the mind of a specific murder, or execution, with that ambivalence and shifting identification which is—ideologues possibly excepted—the human condition. That woman who answered a *Centre Daily Times's* "Inquiring Photographer" question, Should we vote on the death penalty? as follows, has many companions: "Yes, I certainly think we should. It's so barbaric I think it should be abolished. But one recent crime was so bestial I don't think the perpetrator should be allowed to live—and I hate to think I'm contributing to his support in prison."

In a Gallup poll conducted in December of 1972, three in four adults eighteen and older said that the courts in their area do not deal harshly enough with criminals. Sixty-four percent of adult blacks shared this view. Many other similar investigations have turned up like findings. But other studies have shown that this retaliatory attitude often breaks down, in favor of gentle treatment, when not the "criminal" but a specific defendant is under consideration. Identification readily shifts between culprit and authority, between defendant and judge; identification with the victim is invariable when he is pictured as pitiable, and identification with the accused is almost as certain when *he* is thus depicted. The prevalence of exculpatory rhetoric ensures that more often than not all criminals will be described for the public as being essentially victims themselves.

The long moral crusade against punishment of criminals has been rationalized with an essentially correct proposition: punishment neither reforms nor rehabilitates them. By the same token, of course, there is no evidence that failure to punish criminals improves their character in any way either. But the majority hanker less for debating issues of this kind than for safe streets, even though they do not know how to get them. More important, any yearning for simple retaliation members of the majority might feel has been made virtually inadmissible by the humanitarianism they share, in much lesser measure, with those who place them at a moral disadvantage by proclaiming a pure and indiscriminate compassion.

The question whether punishment, especially capital punishment, "works" or not *(5)* has little bearing upon the present focus of attention—attitudes and conflicts of attitudes. What is germane is the assumed right or wrong of punishment. On this score the present moral universe contrasts sharply with that, say, at the turn of the century. While the relationship between overt behavior and definitions of right and wrong has always been ambiguous, at that time the definitions of right and wrong were more clearly enunciated and widely acknowledged. To the extent that right and wrong are now viewed as being "relative" matters, that "society" or some other hypostatized entity is charged with blame (6), then the right to punish is itself brought to question.

According to the French sociologist Emile Durkheim, punishment is a social reaction which expresses the intensity of those sentiments which have been offended by the commission of crime. In his outlook, whether punishment reforms criminals or deters potential criminals remains a secondary issue; the primary function of punishment is to reinforce the sense of right and wrong for the law-abiding majority (7). These and other collective sentiments diminish when offenses against them go unpunished. But Durkheim offered no support to those people who are now demanding tough laws and stern measures, because he further said that punishment can "serve to heal the wounds made upon collective sentiments" only when those sentiments are strong and unequivocal. When those sentiments become compromised by an aggressive and indiscriminate compassion, and for the most part remain unsupported by institutional figures of authority, they fail in considerable measure to perform their erstwhile unifying function.

Punishment can be inflicted with a relatively easy conscience when definitions of right and wrong are clear and more universally upheld than is now the case. Self-righteousness, unattractive and deplorable though it may very well be, is nevertheless required for making punishment of any kind legitimate, because self-righteousness inhibits the humanitarian impulse, the feeling and expression of sympathy and compassion for "them" (whoever they might be) by "us" (whoever we might be). The sense of self-righteousness in punishment has been eroded by what can be called an egalitarian drift of humanitarianism, an essentially new variation of humanitarianism which has dropped the stick and kept the carrot of Bentham's felicific calculus. The will to enforce rules of any kind has been softened, because rules of any kind are exclusionary. Hence the conflict of attitudes over punishment, severe between majority and the spokesmen for the new drift of egalitarian humanitarianism, manifested in lesser degree within the minds of those who constitute the majority.

POVERTY

Crime may have been the first social problem to be recognized, but poverty has been the chief historic vehicle of humanitarian sentiment. In America, as in the Western European nations, community responsibility by the late eighteenth century was assumed toward the absolutely destitute, the old, the infirm, and the immature who were without means of support. Another theme soon developed to supplement that one: collective aid designed to abolish poverty among the able-bodied, by changing their attitudes and habits, by helping them to become an integral part of a self-supporting population, as in the recent War on Poverty. Only in very recent times has a notion surfaced that a permanent "poverty class" will never become self-supporting.

Early America

In early America, poverty was regarded about as it had been elsewhere during previous centuries, an an inevitable fact of life which fortunately ennobled those who voluntarily aided the poor. Later, as in England, when poor relief first appeared in the towns, it was restricted to local inhabitants. Vagrants and strangers were encouraged or forced to move on, in order to save tax money and because the potential criminality of outsiders was unconfined by primary-group control.

"Americans' understanding and response to poverty underwent a revolution in the Jacksonian era. Beginning in the 1820's and increasingly thereafter, observers defined poverty as both unnatural in the New World and capable of being eradicated" (8). The filtering down of Enlightenment ideas made people of means less complacent about the misery of those who had none. And the populist egalitarianism of the Jacksonian era rendered the *idea* of poverty objectionable, especially in view of prevailing abundant resources and labor shortages.

Later economic expansion, the rise of large cities, and the constant westward migration all served to loosen identity with local place and heighten consciousness of national identity and responsibility. In gradual replacement of home relief for neighbors, almshouses were erected to house all of the needy, strangers as well. At the same time, a dual set of attitudes emerged which persists to this day: acceptance and even approval of public aid for the unfortunate, the "deserving poor," and disapproval of the "undeserving," those deemed able but unwilling to exert effort. This latter, negative, attitude was then much more pronounced than it is now, and all of the poor, deserving or not, became "objects" of charity, to be missionized, reformed.

The poorhouse cast a long shadow on American consciousness. There are citizens living today who can recall their parents expressing revulsion at a threat they once feared. In such cities as Boston and New York the almshouse was the sole system of relief. Within its walls the poor were subjected to iron discipline, hard labor, and bad food. But most of the inmates were not able-bodied loafers; instead they were very old, maimed, or very young. Whatever spirit of humanitarianism had informed the founding of the system, the almshouse soon became a sheerly custodial and punitive institution. Yet it persisted into the late nineteenth century as the chief instrument of public assistance, when a defeated contingent of the new immigrants from Southern and Eastern Europe vastly outnumbered native-born Americans in the poorhouse.

Turn of the Century

While no period of reform in this country has ever matched that of 1830–1860, around the turn of the century the muckrakers, social-gospel clergymen, social workers, and a sprinkling of sociologists sought to awake the national conscience, to create new attitudes toward dependency. They insisted that poverty resulted more from the impersonal crunch of periodic economic slumps and exploitation by employers than from deficiencies of character. Even more forcefully, they denounced the physical and psychological debilitation of slum living conditions. Not immorality, they believed, but dirt, disease, exhausting labor, and despair victimized the poor. They almost *said* that, but not quite; the new reformers deplored houses of prostitution, dance halls, and saloons in the ethnic slums almost as much as did those people whose attitudes toward the poor they were striving to change. This attitude, even prejudice, that the poor *should* exhibit moral rectitude may be somewhat less intensive today, but it residually persists, as in those publicized juxtapositions of illegitimacy and Aid to Families with Dependent Children rates.

Nevertheless, although the almshouse was not abolished until the advent of New Deal legislation, the reformers ended the almshouse monopoly, and new measures kept some of the poor at home in their own communities. Prior to the outbreak of World War I, the most respectable, the most "deserving" of the poor, widows with small legitimate children whose husbands had not deserted them, were granted pensions by most of the industrial states. Most of the poor still had to rely on private charities, but a beachhead had been established: some of the poor had a vested right to income from tax sources. On the other hand, not even the professionalization of social work during the twenties made much of a dent in the traditional attitude (which effectively constricted, if it was not always endorsed by, caseworkers) that the poor were in some measure responsible for their own plight.

The New Deal

The trauma of the Great Depression shook many things, notably the erstwhile confidence of the majority that poverty is a simple matter of "us" and "them," that "anyone who is willing to work can find a job." Notions of individual guilt weakened when millions of people who had never known poverty suddenly became poor, even though thousands of these new poor rejected aid of any kind in defense of principle and habit. At the bottom of the Depression, almost one in every three formerly employed people were out of work, people who had always been self-supporting, most of whom had vowed they would never accept that charity which local governments and private charities were soon without funds to dispense. Without planning, almost by default, the federal government instituted nationwide temporary measures of direct relief. Shortly thereafter the New Deal legislation was drafted which charted an unprecedented course in national life. Government responsibility for individual welfare was assumed, accompanied by a growing interpretation of poverty as a social rather than as a personal condition, even though, at that particular time, poverty as a social problem played a distant second fiddle to the social problem of unemployment.

In conception the New Deal legislation was much less revolutionary than later events proved it to have been. The WPA, for instance, was designed to obviate the "dole" (which President Roosevelt denounced) by providing jobs. Even when the Social Security Act was passed by Congress in 1935, the new order was only adumbrated. The three noncontributory programs—Old-Age Assistance, Aid to Dependent Children, and Aid to the Blind—merely elaborated upon earlier provisions for worthy widows. The two contributory programs—Old Age and Survivors, and Unemployment Insurance—were conceived and described as returns to individuals for what they themselves had paid into them *(9)*. And strict eligibility rules, at first, were rigorously applied.

Then the indiscriminate welfare state gradually emerged. Eligibility under Old Age and Survivors, for example, soon departed from any strict accounting of payments made. In some measure the assumption of government responsibility for individual welfare mushroomed because politicians seized an opportunity to create specific constituencies among recipients of aid from one expanding program after another. The welfare state achieved virtually unchallenged popularity, most significantly with the majority. They accepted, indeed have come to endorse enthusiastically, the principle of government responsibility for the rectification of perceived social ills. And there was largess for everyone, including businessmen, especially those with government contracts, and already well-to-do farmers. As for the poor, enthusiasm ran high among many political-intellectual minorities—especially the one which occupied key positions within the burgeoning bureaucracy addressed to poverty—that sheer expenditure of public funds by itself would not only end poverty, slum housing, criminality, but would also erase ignorance and improve motivation.

One obvious distinction was persistently overlooked, that between the working poor who are temporarily reduced to accepting public aid during slumps and the "disreputable poor," the people "who remain unemployed, or casually and irregularly unemployed, even during periods approaching full employment and prosperity," whose condition is recorded in illegitimacy, prison sentences, long-term dependency *(10)*. Aged and decrepit people and impoverished children excepted, the New Deal legislation had been designed to improve the lot of the working poor. The existence of the voluntarily unemployed was ignored with the "common man" slogan, which was applied to all of the poor. But only the working poor used the foothold offered by New Deal legislation to reach "middle-class status" during ensuing years of almost uninterrupted prosperity. For the most part, only the poor inured to dependency remained; this "class" expanded rapidly in absolute and proportionate numbers during those same years and even more rapidly after World War II.

The Present

The number and proportion of people resigned to dependency mounted for many reasons. American intellectuals made of the "poor" a sentimental and indiscriminate cause. The banyan-tree growth of many and overlapping private, state, and especially federal programs—separately administered by personnel who had a vested interest in the expansion of each one—made the total income of some of the poor not at all penurious. Some politicians discovered a large and solid constituency among that personnel and the people they served. And the majority, enjoying continuous prosperity and access to many "welfare programs" designed for their own benefit, remained complaisant.

Any pressure to accept work which the client might regard as demeaning was officially removed. One consequence can be seen in the census figures on occupations, in which domestic service has been declining more rapidly than any other job classification. In some jurisdictions standards of welfare income by design or default are set in terms of middle-income, not low-income, families. What jobs may be available are not attractive to most of the present beneficiaries of public welfare programs (11).

Not all of the poor, resigned or otherwise, have been fortunate. Chaotic eligibility rules reward some people handsomely and allot others very little in direct relief. Lucky ones qualify for many overlapping but separated "categories," in social work parlance; the unlucky qualify for one or two—or none. At least a technical crisis in welfare does exist, in the circumstance that no agency or authority is empowered to deal with each client in the round. Much of the widespread suspicion of "welfare chiseling" inheres in this circumstance.

Failures of direction and control reached a climax when authority was delegated to field administrators and public-assistance caseworkers to operate locally at their own discretion, to disburse funds and organize "group action." There were no operating standards spelled out, for example, in the Economic Opportunity Act of 1964, which included VISTA, Job Corps, work training, adult education, work experience, business-incentive grants, and so on. As one instance, the VISTA volunteers were instructed to "combat poverty" when, as, and how they found it (12). Some of the consequences of the Community Action programs, in which distribution of federal funds was left to the total discretion of people in distant localities, were explored under the "power structure" heading in the previous chapter.

The "welfare mess" became a term employed across the political spectrum, perhaps most frequently by the chief administrators of various welfare programs themselves. The stated reasons for disenchantment differed, but general disenchantment there was, and nothing else could explain the Family Assistance Plan announced by President Nixon in 1969. An "income strategy" was proposed by which the poor would simply be given money to spend as they saw fit to substitute for the prevailing "service strategy" of directly providing the poor with housing, food, medical care, counseling, and the like.

Even though in 1974 a research-experimental model of the plan was inaugurated, the plan has probably left the scene of effective politics, at least for some time. The proximate reason for the plan's difficulties has been its "Christmas tree" compromising in House debate. One new program after another of the already entrenched service strategy is pinned onto the plan, which then falls down from the weight of contradictory stipulations, and is sent to committee to be stripped down again. But the underlying reasons go much deeper.

An income floor for all citizens at public expense, the heart of the Family Assistance Plan, threatens many interests and surely flouts traditional values. Its backers have had to engage in doubletalk. Daniel Patrick Moynihan, the welfare advisor to three Presidents, has said that the administration dressed up the proposal with traditional appeals such as "cutting relief costs" and "encouraging workfare, not welfare." At the same time the administration recognized that a permanent dependency "class" had emerged as an "unanticipated consequence" of the political past, and it simply must be subsidized (13).

Strategies and Attitudes

That recognition of a permanent dependency class, of those who will not as well as cannot make it, was truly revolutionary, a radical departure from the historic pattern of optimism, of faith informed by hope that poverty can be eliminated. Old-fashioned liberals are distressed by such a prospect, the vested interests of personnel engaged in managing the lives of the poor are obviously endangered by it, and the majority, especially the working poor, are threatened by it—about which more below. Paradoxically enough, the recognition and philosophic acceptance of a permanent dependency "class" is least distasteful to sophisticated conservatives at one end of the political spectrum and liberal intellectuals at the other, which gives point to an old observation that on some counts people at the political extremes are closer to one another than they are to those at the middle *(14)*.

In any event, many critics interpreted President Nixon's 1974 fiscal budget as a signal that *both* income and service strategies were to be abandoned. It called for disbanding the OEO along with government subsidies for organizing neighborhood action programs. No new low-income housing was provided, or neighborhood facilities or community health centers. Urban renewal and the Model Cities programs were to be phased out.

Despite these envisioned cuts, HEW was scheduled to spend $93.8 billion, an increase of more than $10 billion over the previous year and $12.7 billion more than the Defense Department. (It should be noted that only a part of HEW's budget was earmarked for the poor, even though more money than ever before was so allotted.) Continuing programs of all kinds, such as Social Security and Medicare, had built-in expansions. The number of food-stamp recipients, which increased from 3.2 million in mid-1969 to 12.1 million in late 1972, was scheduled for further increase. Head Start was allotted more funds, and a new program, a $1 billion provision for federal scholarships in higher education, was instituted.

So it is unlikely that the service strategy faces immediate danger. At this writing Congress has already reinstated several programs which had been cut from the 1974 budget, and the vast bureaucracy engaged with them will surely continue to fight to protect their own interests by resisting publicized threats to "hold down taxes and slow the rate of inflation." There is no crystal ball to inform where we go from here. But when such a major shift in political philosophy and structure as the New Deal occurs, and that shift to governmental assumption of responsibility for individual welfare gathers momentum for decades, it is not likely to be turned off like a water tap.

The majority do not want it turned off. They may grumble about taxes and welfare and inflation and "too much government spending," but they are at cross-purposes in their demands for new programs and their loyalty to old ones which directly benefit them. Millions of military veterans since the end of World War II have benefited from educational and insurance programs designed for them. Government insurance and medical programs are now viewed as indispensable in planning family budgets and even individual careers. The majority have come to endorse the principle of collective political insurance against local and personal difficulties—a principle which is by no means narrowly selfish.

There is no evidence of any revolt by the majority against the use of tax money to relieve "poverty in the midst of plenty." Their humanitarian concern for the poor is greater than ever before, a concern now somewhat less adulterated with the traditional prejudice that those who fail to shape up and get cracking should suffer a little. On the other hand, they want only the "real poor" to get any of their tax money. They believe—and evidence on this subject is beside the essential point—that they are being conned by welfare loafers and cheaters. An image of themselves as suckers infuriates them; visit your neighborhood tavern and listen. It may be that President Nixon's 1974 fiscal budget contained a little window dressing, designed to placate exactly that kind of resentment. The ambivalance of the majority was disclosed in a recent public-opinion poll: only 20 percent of the respondents said that the government should spend less on relief; "yet almost 70 percent insisted that some or most of those actually on relief were there for dishonest reasons" (15).

The working poor are more suspicious of and incensed by such imputed dishonesty than any other segment of the majority. Moreover, they feel psychologically threatened by reports that those who meet no generally accepted standard of striving or accomplishment are materially better off than those like themselves who do the repetitive or distasteful or dirty jobs which are essential to the preservation of social life—washing dishes, sweeping floors, collecting garbage, attending hospital wards, maintaining sewerage lines, guarding prisoners, pumping gasoline, and the like. Their sense of justice has been outraged. Their incentive to work, it may safely be assumed, can be encouraged only if some income gap, however small, is maintained between them and the nonworking poor.

RACE RELATIONS

With the Emancipation Proclamation interest in the plight of American blacks flagged. The abolitionist crusade saw its objective as being achieved. Northern emotional idealism was exhausted, and the dominant mood of Reconstruction was one of hatred for the defeated Confederacy. Ensuing determination to place blacks in a dominant political position was less than high-minded. The Republican Congress in 1867 designed Negro suffrage to reduce the power of the Democratic party in the South (16). The threat of black political supremacy in the South was then arrested with illegal intimidation by the Ku Klux Klan and some other, less organized, efforts. Reconstruction formally ended in 1877 when federal troops were withdrawn.

What were white-black relationships like in the South at that time? In the North? In the South during the days of slavery? There is a vast literature on the subject. Most of the earlier statements are self-serving, either accusatory or defensive; the later ones either are safely accusatory or have become monumentally cautious. In today's ideological climate, not many white sociologists would venture this opinion offered by a black one: Where slavery in America assumed the character of a social institution, "race consciousness tended to disappear and the slaves tended to identify themselves with the master's family and the slave order" (17).

Segregation and de facto disfranchisement were imposed upon the Southern black population in the post-Reconstruction years. But then as now, events did not march in a single direction. During this period visitors from the North were said to have been impressed by a black-white "freedom of association" which was absent in the North (18). Race relations from the white side in the North were approached with abstract principle and not with much personal concern for or interest in the concrete individual black. To some extent, this North-South comparison still holds, at least according to ex-comedian Dick Gregory: "In the South they don't care how close I get as long as I don't go too high; in the North they don't care how high I go as long as I don't get too close."

Early Legislation

Until the late 1880s, enforcement of discrimination in the South was in C. Vann Woodward's phrase "erratic and inconsistent." In some communities blacks had a freedom of movement denied to them in others. There were no Jim Crow laws to separate and restrict the races in public places and accommodations. Those laws were not enacted until *after* the Supreme Court sanctioned such action.

The federal Civil Rights Acts of 1866 had guaranteed Negroes "equal benefit of the laws." Most state and federal court rulings between 1865 and 1880 held in favor of Negro rights. The federal Civil Rights Act of 1875 admitted "all persons" to full and equal accommodation in public places and services, with penalties for noncompliance attached.

Actually, no state in the union during the 1870s required separation of the races in places of public accommodation; in the South as in the North, nonadmittance was the generally accepted if illegal option of private owners and managers. But white hostility toward the illegality of that option ran high, particularly in the North. So in 1883 the Supreme Court found the Civil Rights Act of 1875 to be unconstitutional. Only then were Jim Crow laws enacted, first in Florida in 1887 and finally in the Carolinas and Virginia in the last three years of the century.

According to Professor Westin, this 1883 ruling "destroyed the delicate balance . . . which was producing a steadily widening area of peacefully integrated public facilities in the North and South during the 1870's and 1880's." It also transformed national and state politics of race. The Supreme Court "wiped out the issue of civil rights from the Republican Party's agenda of national responsibility. At the same time, those southern political leaders who saw anti-Negro politics as the most promising avenue to power could now rally the 'poor whites' to the banner of segregation" (19).

Attitudes and Later Legislation

Historically, attitudes of racial prejudice have tended to resist change as circumstances in the outer world changed, circumstances which included innovative proposals made by political-intellectual minorities. These attitudes have nevertheless been subject to modification, especially when supportive comradeship for them has waned in the face of shifts of power, legal-political coercion, and massive and consistent propaganda efforts.

When all these factors pressed in one direction, legions of unreconstructed private personalities found it expedient to present a modified public personality. Many such came to a grudging public acceptance of perceived ascending attitudes which demanded a relatively small price, like the abstract sentiment that blacks should have equal opportunities with whites. With the further passage of time, and given no interruption of factorial drift, indeterminately and by imperceptible degrees the gap between privately held and publicly expressed attitudes tended to narrow among the foot-draggers.

The dramatic reorientation of white racial attitudes which started as late as the 1940s has thus been intensified. The factors enumerated did have a base upon which to build in the historic ideas previously discussed. Discrimination and segregation had always been contested in a subterranean way by a pervasive belief in equality and feelings of guilt about departing from its celebration, by beliefs in the possibility and desirability of modifying human nature and external conditions, above all by the humanitarian sentiment. Nevertheless, in recent decades the racial attitudes of the majority changed *after* the ideological and legal intervention of determined political-intellectual minorities. (They had changed in the *opposite* direction in the late nineteenth century when most intellectuals, including such sociologists as Sumner, Ross, Small, and Giddings, in various ways rationalized the very different race relations of their day for which the Supreme Court in 1883 had provided a framework.)

Liberal intellectuals during the forties vehemently criticized the segregated and constricted life of black Americans, but during that period they recognized, if they did not accept, the life of the blacks as the way things were. Their main efforts were directed at more acknowledged evils, the social discrimination faced by Jews and the economic hardships of blue-collar workers, especially those of Eastern and Southern European ancestry. The New Deal provided the initial breakthrough by establishing equal rates of pay for blacks and whites on the WPA. Then came President Truman's "unbunching" executive order, which ended segregation in the armed forces. In 1954 the Supreme Court ruled against segregation in the public schools. Civil rights laws ended Jim Crow; opened up previously segregated stores, restaurants, and hotels; and invalidated discriminatory access to public transportation and other facilities. The Voting Rights Act of 1965 eliminated qualification tests (including proof of ability to read and write) in the Deep South, and provided that federal examiners could register voters there. Later laws and bureau directives decreed equal pay for equal work, and even preferential hiring for blacks.

Changing legislation and changing attitudes reinforced one another. William F. Buckley, Jr., editor of the conservative journal *National Review,* provides a critical instance. For many years, mainly on the principle of unwarranted and unconstitutional intrusion, he had thundered against the Warren Court's 1954 ruling and the civil rights bills which followed, especially the Voting Rights Act of 1965, which enabled a new "occupation" of the South. He continued to prophesy dire consequences, albeit with lessening surety, until his return from a recent visit to Mississippi. He reported having found a racial integration surpassing anything he had seen in the North, with relations between black and white "for the most part altogether relaxed." Were some of the methods utilized to achieve this state of affairs desirable? "Well, not as a formal proposition; though it tells you at least this: that coercive measures can breed desired results" (20).

Coercive measures may produce desired results, but such results obtain only retrospectively. No one has ever argued that the coercive measures of Reconstruction bred any desired results for anybody. What that period lacked was long preparation for attitude change in a factorial drift which included gradual, steady, and consistent legal pressure. Application of coercion in the modern period capitalized upon as well as fostered decades of Southern white anticipation of the inevitable. By degrees "Never!" was transformed into a dawning, numbed acquiescence of "The day will come." To be sure, as elsewhere the attitude change in most white Mississippians has probably not yet penetrated the private personality at deeper levels. Still, a public restraint and civility has everywhere been indeterminately achieved and imposed.

As in many other areas, the majority have been more the passive recipients of attitude change than the instigators. Political-intellectual minorities in academe, the mass media, and elsewhere pressed for coercive political measures and, more important, reinforced them. Their special contribution has been an unremitting insistence upon what is desirable, and what is deplorable, in attitude. They have largely succeeded in making unfashionable bigotry and prejudice; in making fashionable tolerance, acceptance, and, perhaps less securely, admiration. Books, articles, lectures, editorials, TV dramas and situation comedies— of signal educational power as the only source of enlightenment to reach the majority steadily and consistently—all have created a single public image of what is proper and appropriate.

The bigot, even the person who once laughed politely at "ethnic humor," begins to feel out of place, uneasy, without erstwhile support. Suddenly Indians have become the heroes of Westerns and white men the villains. Blacks, heretofore seen only as domestic servants or humorous incompetents, have become figures of authority—physicians, detectives, business managers, who straighten out situations which whites have bungled. Alternatively, Indians and blacks are presented as unaggressive victims. Anyone in the cast who prefers older stereotypes to these newer ones is set up for defeat or ridicule, and so is his counterpart in the audience.

Favorites Change Places

So-called race prejudice is actually a multidimensional phenomenon. The Irish in this country, who had been the special target of several nativist crusades in the nineteenth century, in the early decades of the twentieth achieved, or were assigned, a favored place. Lingering native-Protestant doubts and reservations were tempered with good humor, revolving about a stereotype of booze, Saint Patrick's Day parades, patriotism, and superb fighting ability. During and after World War I the Irish were romanticized in legends, popular songs, and films.

By the late fifties and early sixties they were displaced by the Jews, who were granted an equivocal status of combined lingering reservation (a considerable advance over the general social hostility of previous decades) and popularity. Yiddish phrases speckled the conversation of educated Gentiles. Jewish humor—of a benign sort—was exploited in books and the mass media, bar mitzvah references replaced any to christening on TV, and Jewish writers complained of a Gentile misappropriation of "Jewish consciousness."

Has the day of the Indian and the black arrived? The cases are not strictly comparable. The Irish and perhaps to a lesser extent the Jews earnestly sought to assimilate. American Indians, a people who cling to ancient tribal ways, cannot with undivided will choose to live in the white man's world. Most American blacks on the other hand do want in, but are resentful of those remaining barriers which are more subtle and exasperating than the old and now withdrawn ones of Jim Crow and denial of equal political rights and education and access to job training. These remaining barriers can only be imprecisely stated, perhaps only inferred from black-expressed feelings of not being needed, of being patronized, of being treated without a full acknowledgement of individual dignity. Perhaps they are best exemplified in that constant invitation extended by militant blacks to white intellectuals who seek to make common cause with them: "Whitey, get lost."

The Indian and black situations differ in another dimension. At some distance from the reservation the American Indian is being accorded a vast respect that borders on awe. He has become a formidable living legend, a repository of many guilts and regrets of an urban civilization. Modern Boy Scouts celebrate his craftsmanship and techniques of survival in city church basements; the mystique of ecology is his unwitting contribution. Although Negroes by a long chalk receive more attention than any other segment of the population, no cult of Negritude has emerged which can compare with that of the Noble Red Man—except possibly among the affluent college young. The music, the clothes (the assumed historic clothes, with custom-made patches on the pants), the speech cadence and argot, the pot and blatant sex and "cool," not of the black "middle-class" striver but of the one who embodies "soul," have been adopted or are being toyed with by well-off white youngsters who range from declared hippies to those unwilling to compromise their careers to the point of disaster *(21)*.

The Majority

Through a mixture of voluntary acquiescence and expedient bending with all of the outside pressures described above, the attitudes of the majority have changed remarkably, if not with total consistency. A fear of Negroes when encountered in large numbers persists, as many polls and the continuing "flight to the suburbs" attest. At the same time, polls indicate that throughout the country, South as well as North, most whites endorse a policy of nondiscrimination, which includes an acceptance of racial intermarriage, a declared willingness to vote for black political candidates, and a renunciation of beliefs in white racial superiority. According to longshoreman-philosopher Eric Hoffer: "All we can hope for from others is that they wish us well." When interviewed, and in the above terms, about two-thirds of the whites do wish their black fellow citizens well.

On the other hand, only about a third of them "feel bad" about "the treatment of Negroes," a proportion that has not appreciably increased in recent years (22). Many whites do feel a sense of individual guilt, but white feelings of guilt are surely not so universal as Gunnar Myrdal averred in his *An American Dilemma (23)*. The apparent discrepancy of favorable attitudes unaccompanied by guilt is explainable in these terms: most whites now want external impediments to black advancement removed; they also believe black advancement now to be primarily a black responsibility. While most whites, further, deny that the sources of Negro hardship are inborn and unchangeable, they also believe "the sources of Negro hardship to be within Negroes themselves" (24).

They could very well be mistaken, but we are dealing with attitudes and not the possibility of faulty logic and factual error. In any event, the majority are not prepared to accept any political-intellectual minority demand for extensive institutional change on behalf of blacks. The majority commitment remains with traditional humanitarianism; beyond that, most of them will, in terms of abstract sentiment, accept integration (without busing) in school, on the job, in place of residence. But they display a varying recalcitrance when the price of personal proximity is exacted. Especially is the white of modest income who cannot afford suburban escape from the "inner city" prone to resentment. For several years "he is the one who has been asked to carry the burden of social reform, to integrate his schools and his neighborhood, has been asked by comfortable people to pay the social debts due to the poor and the black" (25).

Much less frequently than in the recent past are the majority being exhorted to renounce "racial prejudice" (26). Such an appeal grants the possibility that a voluntary positive response may be withheld. The mood of avant-garde intellectuals, including some sociologists, will not tolerate either gradualism or voluntarism. Their demand for an end to "institutional racism" invokes coercive restitution for centuries of racial injustice. While a few of them call down revenge and destruction upon a "racist society," the more typical demand is for what intellectual dissenters call "reverse discrimination," in higher education enrollment, job quotas at the top as well as at the middle of the corporate hierarchy, and an application of lowered work standards to certain racial and ethnic minorities.

The main roadblock to such efforts is that, as Amitai Etzioni has put it: "The majority of Middle America now feels that Negroes already have the same or better opportunity than white Americans in getting jobs, education, housing and other advantages." The *feeling* of injustice is beyond factual disputation, and the majority show evidence of developing a sense of injustice of their own. They resent any categorical favoritism which appears to abrogate the right of equal opportunity, a matter expanded upon in Chapter 5. As they see it, the ideas of equality and humanitarianism have suddenly failed to point in the same direction.

POPULATION GROWTH

In his famous essay on population, which appeared at the turn of the eighteenth century, Thomas Robert Malthus appealed less to humanitarianism than to moral probity: early and improvident marriages should be discouraged and self-restraint cultivated as one means to avert the danger of population growth exceeding the food supply and attendant technologies. But he was less than sanguine that changes in habits and outlook would occur, and declared all social reforms helpless to arrest that poverty and misery which overpopulation would ineluctably bring, accompanied by overcrowding, disease, war, and vice. However, attendant technologies developed far beyond his ken, and the ensuing rapid increase of numbers in Europe, or elsewhere, was not to be deplored for some time.

In more recent times, changes in numbers of people *have* been viewed with alarm, an alarm tempered by a hope that something can be done about them. Humanitarian concern has replaced Malthus's resignation, a humanitarian concern about numbers in the future. The social problem of population growth in this country, however, has swung between two poles of humanitarian concern: there will be too few people; there will be too many. In the recent past, the threat of underpopulation was widely publicized; at the present time, the threat of overpopulation is widely stressed.

Looking Both Ways

During the thirties, and into the forties, intellectuals in this country worried about too few babies being born. Writers of sociology textbooks and newspaper editors, as well as demographers, pointed to disastrously low birthrates, expressed concern that not enough children were being born to maintain a "strong national life." Much attention was paid the system of payments to encourage the formation of large families in Hitler's Germany and Mussolini's Italy. In some quarters the proposal was seriously made that the government of the United States should institute a similar scheme in order to arrest a threatened decline in American power and prestige. Proposed measures to encourage fertility were also humanitarian in purpose. While poverty is now frequently blamed upon overpopulation, during the thirties "many economists argued that the Great Depression was due to a stable population" *(27)*.

At the present time, warnings and proposed social reforms all feature the term "population explosion" or one of its variants. Birth limitation, not fertility, is imperative lest we face mass starvation beyond the seven years' grace Paul R. Ehrlich, for one, is willing to concede *(28)*. Meanwhile, the birthrate in 1973 reached a record low of 15 per 1,000 people. More significantly, the general fertility rate—births per thousand women aged fifteen to forty-four—has with minor interruptions been falling since 1957. In 1972 the general fertility rate dropped to 73.4, compared with the previous low of 75.8 in 1936. This short-term trend may (although we cannot be absolutely certain) continue long enough to arrest the much feared expansion of population, in which case our grandchildren possibly might revert to the kind of population worry expressed during the thirties.

Birthrates and fertility rates went up from the end of World War II to 1957, a period of prosperity. They have gone down from 1957 to the present, a continued period of prosperity. We really do not know why. The famous pill is often given the credit. But the low birthrates of the thirties owed nothing to it; and it appeared on the scene *after* the 1958–1972 decline in the birthrate was well under way. Contraceptive devices and practices are only a means to the end of birth control. Fairly reliable ones have been in use for centuries. What varies much more in time is the motivation to use whatever may be available.

Biologist-philosopher René Dubos may be correct in his claim that the reasons why large numbers of people in a given population at one time spontaneously increase or decrease their numbers elude explanation. In any event, American women are now having fewer children than at any time in the past, and they chose to do so in too short a time to have been effectively "proseletyzed" by "friends and associates," as Dr. Paul R. Ehrlich, who organized the Zero Population Growth (ZPG) movement, has advised. In 1972 the United States level of children per family dropped *below* the ZPG rate of 2.1 to 2.03.

Some demographers, though, expect the population to continue growing; because of the immediate post-World War II baby boom, there is a "bulge" in the population pyramid of young women, and even a small rise in fertility rates among so many potential mothers would rapidly increase total numbers. On the other hand, *if* the present level of children per family were maintained, the population should level off at around 275 million at the turn of the century. Past history, however, has made any projection of future numbers a foolhardy enterprise.

In a Gallup poll taken in 1973, 47 percent of adults interviewed said the ideal number of children per family is one or two, whereas 23 percent so responded in a 1945 poll. Opinions about the ideal number of children per family have notably changed, and they could continue to affect fertility rates. The most plausible explanation of that change is a sudden heightening of nonfamilistic, individualistic, hedonistic attitudes, accompanied by an equally sudden rise in the cost of raising children. Later marriage, later childbearing, more working wives, and declining fertility rates have all become adjustments to that rising cost. Working with government figures, Sylvia Porter estimated in 1970 that a family with an income between $7,500 and $10,000 would spend almost $26,000 to raise a child to the age of eighteen. In 1972 the Commission on Population and Growth assessed the direct costs to "average parents" of a child who completed college at $40,000 from the time of his birth. Lost work time of mothers would raise that figure considerably *(29)*.

Are we dealing with a social problem that was shot down as it left the ground? Probably not; those who proclaim a crisis of overpopulation can assess *any* number as too many. But vigorous propaganda indeed will be required to maintain the social problem of overpopulation in this country—at least in the short term. The dramatic change in fertility noted above occurred swiftly, by voluntary, individual effort, without much attention being paid the political-intellectual minority who promoted it.

Actually, most American adults have never even heard about ZPG. We also know that most adults of whatever race or educational and income level resent being propagandized about what they regard as an extremely private area of their own lives. Most of them do want to control reproduction, but for their own purposes, not those of major, planned, social change. Yet although the social problem of population growth may have little interest for the majority, the means being effectively employed to reduce numbers in this country—contraception and abortion—remain, and likely will remain, ancillary social problems. They are regarded by a large contingent of the majority, ironically enough including many who utilize them, as matters of public moral concern, as part of a deplorable trend which should be arrested in the future.

Contraception and Abortion

Contraception has become a bitterly contested issue in two very sensitive areas. The first is sex education. At one extreme stands the John Birch Society, which officially views sex education as a deliberate plot to corrupt youth and destroy America. At the other can be found reformers like Dr. Paul R. Ehrlich, who states: "We need a federal law requiring sex education in school—sex education that includes discussion of the need for regulating the birth rate and of the techniques of birth control. Such education should begin at the earliest age recommended by those with professional competence in this area—certainly before junior high school" (30).

The majority, when polled, do endorse "sex education," but what they have in mind, essentially, is birds-and-bees plus reasons why premarital sex should not be. They agree with Ann Landers. They are leery of Dr. Ehrlich's "experts," and in one public school hassle after another they have protested much less "sex education" than he favors. He says what he has in mind must emphasize "sex as an interpersonal relationship, as an important and extremely pleasurable aspect of being human, as mankind's major and most enduring recreation, as a fountainhead of humor. . ." (31).

Probably what ultimately lurks in the minds of all adults who use the same phrase, "sex education," is either the desirability of encouraging premarital sexual relationships or the desirability of discouraging them. That kind of "sex education" in action which makes the pill available to unmarried teenage girls without parental consent or knowledge particularly enrages majority opinion. While such dispensation in free clinics is invariably justified with humanitarian sentiments, it arouses desperate fears that parental control of offspring is being taken away by outsiders.

The second area is race relations. Black women have a higher birthrate than white, and they give birth to over half of the illegitimate children. In a 1967 Gallup poll, 63 percent of adult American Protestants and 56 percent of American Catholics replied affirmatively to the following question: "Do you think birth-control pills should be made freely available to all women on relief of childbearing age?" No breakdown of Negro and white response was recorded, although "persons in lower-income and lower-education groups" were stated to be "least receptive to this proposal."

Several white as well as black critics have charged that official and unofficial attempts to "help women in the slums" thinly disguise a preference for white over black babies. Some black militants denounce birth-control-clinic "pill pushing" as genocide. In any event, the Family Services and Population Research Act of 1970 was designed to spend $382 million between 1971 and 1973. Most of this money has gone to "family-planning clinics," which offer medical advice and contraceptives without charge to all comers.

There does appear to be a growing official determination, backed by majority approval, to "aid the poor" in reducing the size of their families. And there is no clear-cut division between the majority and some political-intellectual minority on this issue, in which the rhetoric of humanitarianism stammers. Any disinclination to single out black women for reproductive control is countered by the plea that the state must guarantee equal rights for impoverished blacks by supplying them with the contraceptives which more comfortably situated whites can afford to buy.

Abortion, much more than contraception, arouses partisan emotions. The conflict of ideal as well as material interest which attends the issue is not likely to pass despite the Supreme Court ruling in 1973 that abortion is legal and laws to the contrary in thirty-one states are unconstitutional. That ruling was based on every woman's "right to privacy," in Judge Harry Blackmun's statement for the majority 7 to 2 opinion *(32)*.

The *Wall Street Journal* on balance approved: individual liberty was upheld in the face of unwarranted interference by government. That stand made company of a sort with the loose coalition of social scientists, lawyers, spokeswomen of Women's Liberation, which had forced the issue into the hands of the Court. Support among the majority had grown. A Gallup poll taken a week after the ruling found 46 percent of adult respondents in favor of it while 45 percent were in opposition and 9 percent undecided, as compared with a similar poll taken in 1969 when 40 percent approved abortion and 50 percent disapproved. Since that time the trend of attitude has been less clear.

Nevertheless, while opposition to abortion could continue to diminish, it is not likely to disappear. What is liberation to some remains feticide to others; arguments about *when* is life do not rebut arguments about *what* is life. The Court's decision has touched off passionate debate. On one side, technical questions about "when life begins" are declared to have no bearing on the moral question of taking human life at any state of its potentiality; according to one opponent of abortion, the fetus is a real person whose destruction is "slaughter of the innocent unborn." On the other side, according to one proponent the fetus is "a bit of vegetating matter" devoid of human attributes.

The majority will doubtless continue to be plagued by a zero-sum game of opposed humanitarian claims, very similar to the conscience division opened up by the issue of capital punishment: if human life is sacred, does the principle require that the life of a murderer should be preserved or does it demand in expiation the life of the man who has violated the principle? In the case of abortion, should the life of a woman determined to terminate pregnancy, if need be by illegal and septic means, take precedence over the life of the child in her womb?

This debate will never be resolved. At the present time, the fetus is getting a better popular press than the reluctant pregnant woman. That situation could change if continued moral-religious indignation brought about a reverse decision of the Supreme Court, if abortion were declared unconstitutional, a deprivation of life in violation of the due process of law clause in the Fourteenth Amendment. The advocates of abortion might then find more popular support than ever before.

There will always be a substantial number of women who want the service, which meets not only their perceived interest but that of many husbands, and parents of pregnant unmarried girls as well. They can always, as they do now, counter the humanitarian appeals of antiabortionists with humanitarian sentiments of their own: the health and very life of women who would otherwise abort in dangerous surroundings outside the law must be preserved, and all those unwanted children should be saved from a blighted life. And they are, of course, helping to solve the social problem of population growth.

Science and Value Judgment

The above discussion should have made the obvious point that technical means utilized in contraception and abortion operate within an inescapable moral context. There is no one who, on the basis of that "professional competence" Professor Ehrlich invokes, can determine on scientific grounds whether people should, or should not, utilize those means. Even the larger setting of which they are a part, population growth, can be debated only on the grounds of value judgment, not science.

What canon of science informs how many people there should be, in this country or any other? Demographers sometimes employ the term "optimum population," which conceals a value judgment: a higher per capita income for fewer people is more desirable than a possible deterioration in the "quality of life" for more people. But only an ethical choice guides a decision to trade off people for material welfare. "Should 10% less people be traded for 5% more income per person? Or should the trade-off be 10% less people for 1%, or for 20%, more income per person (33)?" Whatever the specification, it will not convince those who believe human life is more important than material welfare, no matter whether they are told "science says" they are wrong. On the other hand, of course, an ethical argument for reducing the number of people can be answered only with a different ethical argument.

There is the further circumstance that the "optimum population," even in "scientific" terms, can be stated only in the short term. Science can offer no answer to the question whether either population decrease or population increase in the future might be deemed advisable to accommodate unforeseeable changes in production, social organization, and knowledge (34). Demographers in the recent past have constantly changed their statements about what the optimum population might be, and they are likely to continue so doing.

ECOLOGY

As a social problem, ecology can be said to date from the publication of Rachel Carson's *Silent Spring* in 1962. Shortly after the end of World War II, plastics and new pesticides appeared and mercury use was expanded. Environmental deterioration occurred at that time, as it did in the forties when preparation for war expanded agricultural and industrial production, as it did in the latter half of the nineteenth century when railroads supplanted horse-drawn vehicles in overland transportation. But in these earlier periods, environmental deterioration received little publicity. The few voices of conservation went unheeded.

There was no *unprecedented* worsening of environmental conditions during the later period. What did happen following publication of *Silent Spring* was an upsurge of concern expressed in more books, and in articles, editorials, political speeches. Later, organized pressure groups were formed and legislation was enacted. And from some quarters issued prophecies of imminent doom unless pollution levels were immediately lowered and economic growth curtailed to preserve natural resources.

Such warnings provoked some naysaying. As so often happens

in the course of a crusade, a delayed reaction set in, and the crusaders were accused by skeptics of unwarranted hysteria, or at least of exaggeration *(35)*. However that might be, unlike population growth the social problem of ecology has continued to gain acknowledgment among the majority. And like ecological crusaders, the majority place their primary trust in government to provide a solution.

Government at Cross-Purposes

There is a strong humanitarian component in ecology. It traces back to the earlier conservation movement, with its theme of preserving a heritage for future generations *(36)*. This ideal above all others is stressed in the ecological literature, invariably accompanied by demands for institutional change, especially that of expanding governmental control over the environment *(37)*.

What such enthusiasm for ordering and forbidding techniques overlooks is the record of governments. Like the majority, governments have lagged far behind environmental reformers in adoption of the long view. Nevertheless, prevailing faith holds *the* government to be above the struggle, to be protector and guarantor of the greatest good, the common good. That notion could be true in a metaphysical sense, or might even apply to government viewed as an institution. At any given moment in time, however, *the* government is manned by people who operate, who are forced to operate, in terms of short-range interest.

That consideration sways heads of federal agencies no less than it does politicians who are elected, because top appointees come and go with the coming and going of elected officials. Both are primarily motivated to maintain, gain, or regain power; and a calculation of how this and that voting bloc will go in the next election as surely determines what will happen to an environmental-protection bill as one for a new post office or a proposed change in foreign policy. That is one reason why, from time to time, an announcement that Congress (alternatively some federal agency) has decreed a stiff pollution-control measure is followed by a later announcement that the standards have been relaxed. Among other considerations, a new balance of voting blocs may have been reckoned for the next election.

Where power is maximally concentrated in central government, as in Russia, the results of the next election are known in advance. But Russian politicians exhibit less interest in ecology than do ours. Short-term considerations of economic power, and of military power which depends to some extent upon economic power, operate more arbitrarily in Russia than in the United States. And in Russia, political-intellectual minorities are either crushed or kept on short reins. The environmental-protection laws which Russia does possess are not enforced, and the few voices of conservation are ignored (38). Why? "The diversion of government funds to control environmental disruption is generally resisted by state and enterprise officials, since this usually means that there will be that much less money available for expanding production" (39).

People at Cross-Purposes

Polls in this country indicate—and if polls were allowed in the Soviet Union they doubtless would there also—that an overwhelming majority endorse ecology. Who, after all, takes a stand *against* improvement of his environment? The goal of ecology is not in dispute, as is clearly the case in crime, to a lesser extent in poverty, and in at least the ancillary issues attendant upon race relations and population growth. Controversy instead centers upon who will pay what price for which means to achieve that accepted goal.

A widespread ignorance of the connection between ecology and increases in consumer-goods prices, and of tax costs in the offing, is apparent. Personal ease, convenience, aesthetic enjoyment, and an even higher standard of living are foreseen by most—along with the apparent belief that various prices and costs can be shoved off onto someone else. Thus bond issues for pollution abatement have proved unpopular with voters, while the belief persists that "big corporations" will (or can) absorb the costs of such control.

The very high costs of pollution abatement cannot be shifted, and a conflict of interests cannot be avoided. The swimmer who wants a harbor converted into a "crystal-clear swimming pool" at the expense of "workers, consumers, and businessmen who use the harbor for commerce and industry" is one with the oil-company stockholder who wants a maximum output from offshore oil platforms. Both are "trying to get others to subsidize their particular thing" (40).

So far, ecology has fared second best when some high and personal price has suddenly loomed. The threat of rationing during the "fuel crisis" of 1972–1973 eased air-pollution standards in many cities and some entire states (41). Under political pressure the power plants of Southern California had converted from oil to a 75 percent use of natural gas, one of the cleanest fuels. Those same power plants were allowed considerable reconversion to oil when natural-gas supplies ran short (42). Such episodes are less significant, however, than the much greater public concern shown about increasing present energy supplies than using less energy in order to reduce air and water pollution as well as conserve supplies of fossil fuels. Conservation did get a major assist from the "energy crisis" of 1974, but concerted effort to enforce and comply with energy-saving measures played second fiddle to the search for new sources of fossil fuels.

"Short-term necessity," in Sir Charles Galton Darwin's gloomy pronouncement, "will always prevail against long-term prudence." Unless human behavior in the past tells us nothing about what men will probably do now, an acute water shortage will not long be tolerated if nearby is some wilderness lake, "forever protected" by legislation. Immediate interest takes precedence over the foreseen interests of future generations, and surely over that of preserving the landscape for them. Humanitarian rationalizations for the welfare of the living have always been more presuasive than humanitarian rationalizations for the welfare of the yet unborn.

Consider the automobile, the main culprit of air pollution. Its abolition is not seriously advocated, only a smaller model with less (or different) fuel consumption. The infrastructure of service stations, roadside restaurants, motels, engineers and mechanics, highway network, oil industry, and automotive industry, even suburbia itself, holds the entire population in thrall to a collective economic interest. Perhaps a technological breakthrough in either engine design or emission control will get us off the ecological hook, but neither development at this time is certain; nor would either be likely to end conflicts of interest, within people no more than between them. Opinion polls show that a majority of voters favor outlawing the internal combustion engine by 1975 in order to force the automobile manufacturers to design a pollution-free one. Let

George do it, of course, but the enthusiasm of those same voters might slacken were they offered an expensive car that was low in power and required incessant repair.

Not abandonment but pollution abatement of the conventional engine was ordered by the Federal Clean Air Amendments of 1970. Standards set for 1975 cars require that various emissions of 1970 model vehicles be reduced by 90 percent. If these standards are met (the automotive industry insists they cannot be), it is highly unlikely that Detroit's assembly lines will be shut down by the Environmental Protection Agency. If they were met, a new army of inspectors would be required to ensure that garages, mechanics, and car owners, especially poor car owners, were not cooperating to make engine improvements of a nonecological type. Another price—that of more control and surveillance—would have to be paid.

The case is stated conditionally because there is no evidence that the federal government, however much under pressure from political-intellectual minorities, is prepared to encroach very far upon the general public's short-term interest. Full employment remains, will likely remain, the most sacred of political cows, indicated by periodic relaxations of pollution standards for car manufacturers (as well as other major producers of pollutants, such as copper-mining companies) when they have pled the necessity to save jobs. The U. S. Court of Appeals in 1973 ordered the Environmental Protection Agency to reconsider its refusal to delay by one year the application of its 1975 auto-pollution controls. Later in that year, a General Motors vice-president warned that unless that delay were granted, a complete stoppage of the entire GM production could occur. When severe economic slump became the paramount fear expressed in the public forum in late 1974, pressure mounted from various quarters for more and deeper compromises of environmental protectionism.

There is a real question about how many people are actually prepared to make personal sacrifices, even those who have made of ecology a moral crusade. "Will young people continue to treasure a program for conserving the environment when they find that it pinches their equally treasured right to do exactly as they please?" (43). In this view, only a totalitarian government could enforce the lowered standard of living, the deliberate reduction of production, that would be necessary to make "Save the environment" an over-riding consideration. But no conceivable majority would accede to a life of subsistence, and no totalitarian government, on the record, is likely to plan a subsistence economy. Immediately perceived economic interest, of citizens and their governments, is likely to continue to take precedence.

Technology and Economic Growth

Despite the above demurrers, a massive if slow shift of attitudes toward many of the goals represented by the ecological crusade appears to be taking place and very well could continue. The prospects are examined in the final chapter. Very definite exceptions are the goals of curbing technology and economic growth. Intellectual, if not political, minorities have assailed technology and economic growth as being incompatible with the environmental ethic and even destructive of civilization.

From the time of the Enlightenment Western man has had a romance with technology; in and through technology he envisioned an ever-brightening future of progress. A majority of citizens on balance still hold to that faith, but disenchanted modern critics, of whom Barbara Ward, Jacques Ellul, René Dubos, Hannah Arendt, Herbert Marcuse, Lewis Mumford, and Joseph Wood Krutch are a few, clearly outnumber other intellectuals who advocate more and better technology, such as Jane Jacobs and Peter Drucker. The opponents of technology identify technology (and some of them, science as well) as a bulldozer devoid of controlling intelligence that blindly smashes flat all humanistic purpose. "In an era of absolute technology," speaks a typical voice, "freedom and identity must take on new meanings or become meaningless. Other men can change your society, your economy and your physical environment" (44).

But hatred of technology and economic growth is not likely to enlist a sizable following. The evidence of distorted ecological balances of air and water and soil pollution and other accompaniments of technology and economic growth, has surely raised widespread disquiet. Yet popular faith in technology and economic growth has been little shaken because of the life, on balance the good life, which they are viewed as having conferred. The modest general willingness to trade off some consumer emphasis for some environmental improvement may very well intensify, but that could come about only gradually and in response to unabated propaganda zeal on the part of ecological enthusiasts.

Frontal attacks upon technology and economic growth are less likely to succeed in guiding attitudes of the majority toward appreciation of the goal others have set for them. No voluntary lowering of living standards, anyway, is acceptable to the majority. Indeed, on technical-ecological grounds themselves, attacks upon technology and economic growth have been brought to question. Leonard A. Sagan has reminded single-minded enthusiasts that "operation of tertiary water treatment systems and stack scrubbers, mass transportation systems, require more energy and technology, not less."

More to the point, whatever shift in attitudes toward ecology has occurred has not been accompanied by a companion shift in attitudes toward nongrowth. The majority do not see the two issues as twinned, any more than they view population growth and ecology together. Even among "a sample of college students—where the trend in changing ideology might be expected to be strong—a majority were concerned with environmental problems; but the concept of [population] growth was viewed by them as highly necessary and generally good" (45).

THE VARYING CONSTANCY OF SOCIAL PROBLEMS

To repeat an observation made at the beginning of this chapter, social problems operate in two dimensions of time. The first is the rise of social-problem consciousness, which is the main theme of the previous chapter. The second, the changing character and designation of specific social problems, has been the main theme of this one. Some problems change much less in time than others. Suicide and prostitution, for example, have been comparatively changeless. In part because of their constantly minimal place within the framework of social institutions, they manifest relatively unchanging behavior, meanings, attitudes, and consequences. The only notable change which occurs in either of them is statistical.

On the other hand, the very words as well as content of poverty, race relations, divorce, abortion are a different matter. Those words rapidly shift meaning in company of changes in power distribution, are subject to intellectual fads and redefinition of interest by various segments of the population, and all affect—and are affected by—changes of attitudes, in particular, moral judgments. When attitudes impinging upon the specific term which designates a particular social problem are in flux, the *description* as well as designation of that social problem becomes volatile, mercurial.

Divorce and abortion, like poverty and race relations, are descriptively inconstant in time, but they have one virtue, so to speak, which poverty and race relations lack: statistical trend lines can be imposed upon them. Divorce and abortion may now be considerably different subjective phenomena than they were ten years ago, but the number of cases then and now can be compared. Such a time-number comparison of, say, poverty, is much more difficult to make. The hypothetically average poor man today would not be poor by the official, or any other, standards of ten years ago: he would be affluent by the standards of forty years ago. And when measures of material want are abandoned for attributions of psychological-emotional deprivation, comparisons in time have no application at all *(46)*. What the *trend* of poverty might be is impossible to determine.

Trend Lines and Prediction

Basing their generalizations upon extensive opinion polling, in 1961 George Gallup and Evan Hill described "the problem of youth and politics" as one of complacency, conformity, and unquestioning acceptance of the status quo. Citing later opinion polls, in 1971 Seymour Lipset as well as other researchers described that same social problem with polar-opposed adjectives. What caused it, as perceived, to be turned upside down? Changes in such crude variables as "social forces" and "underlying conditions" during the decade were of minor scope, surely not fundamental enough to bring about that "revolution in consciousness" which is said to have occurred, at least on the campus *(47)*.

If this and other social-problem descriptions offered by students of social problems can be so ephemeral, then a consideration of shifting contexts—not so much of "facts" and conditions as attitudes and especially major changes in views of the world—are called for. Conceivable trend lines should be cautiously assessed. Some cannot be projected at all; for instance, if 1961 to 1971 had virtually zero predictive value for "the problem of youth and politics" in 1961, what about 1971 to 1981 in 1971?

Even when the specification of phenomena remains more constant in time than in the above case, trend lines never march up and off the graph paper. Some trends, such as birthrates, follow a more or less wavelike pattern when plotted over long periods of time. Others are simply arrested, such as the unlimited extension into the future of democratic government, peace, and linear progress plotted by legions of late-nineteenth-century historians and utopians.

A more homely example, which posts a warning to those people who extrapolate present numbers to standing room only in a few decades, is the sour observation made by one Dr. Kapp: If a computer a century ago had projected the then steady increase of horse-drawn vehicles, the danger of a world covered with horse manure would have been convincingly forecast. In a similar vein, a Sunday-supplement alarmist has recently warned that the continuing rise of urban crime rates and private security measures in city and suburb foretells a world resembling that of tenth-century Western Europe, where isolated enclaves preserve internal security within the midst of chaos. According to the father of sociology, Auguste Comte, the "conspicuous transient manifestations" of the present are always misleading (48).

The projection game requires a misplaced faith that not only will this or that trend continue indefinitely, but also that relationships among present trends will remain constant. They do not. Many trends can for a time move together in one apparent direction, at a later time continue, but in apparent different directions. The trend away from punishment of criminals continues unabated, and so does agitation to abolish the prison system entire; at the same time, an increasing popular demand for more punishment of any kind is making politicians come to attention. The trend toward greater opportunity for blacks, in jobs, education, housing, and the like, intensifies; but as the number of blacks who attain "middle-class" status mounts, so does the number of "underclass" blacks in the slums. A long-term drift toward hedonism and self-indulgence, agnosticism and atheism, shows no sign of slackening; yet fundamentalist sects are now growing in size and influence at the expense

of the more accommodative mainstream religious bodies, while puritanical morality and literal Christianity attract many young people
out of the counterculture to form religious communes.

We do not know, there is no way to find out, where any one
trend is actually taking us. Mainly for that reason (there are others)
"prediction" in the social sciences remains a bootless quest. Part of
the difficulty is semantic. We tend to confuse prophecy with scientific prediction. The latter is essentially timeless in orientation, merely links specific events or operations together, and states that if
events occur in specified sequence again or if certain specified operations are repeated, then there is a certain probability of a similar
or the same outcome. Prediction confirms that analysis has been
sound; it does not attempt the fruitless task of prophecy, of attempting to look "into the future as far as one can see" *(49)*.

Trends do not move in a straight line, especially not in complex
societies. The more complex a social system, the more indeterminate
it is. "The greater the number of processes going on within a given
system, the greater the possible number of mutual influences which
can occur, and hence the greater the number of outcomes" (50).
Such outcomes can only be prophesied, never predicted.

Image of the Future

Neither deplored conditions nor observed trends govern the description of social problems. Attitudes do, always influenced primarily
by one or more images of the future. Recall that social problems are
here defined in part as imagined projections into the future of present trends deemed to call for correction. Changing fashions among
intellectuals of hopes for and apprehensions about the future greatly
affect changes in social-problem attitudes, and serve to displace
concern from one social problem to another. The part played by the
more present-bound majority in this connection is quite minimal.

Among intellectuals the tradition of prophecy, or "futurology,"
until fairly recent times was for the most part optimistic, a tradition
stretching from Plato to the earlier books of H. G. Wells. Such
literary artists as Aldous Huxley and George Orwell signaled an
about-face (51). Among present-day intellectuals the future is generally foreseen as a menace, a menace which changes identity quite
often.

In 1967 Herman Kahn and Anthony J. Wiener ignored ecology

and barely mentioned overpopulation in their scenario of a future dominated by nuclear-balance politics and the danger of its imbalance. That scenario was duplicated by many other writers. It appears, it was pointed out in 1972, "that the world's long-term future has suddenly changed." The threat of nuclear war has apparently come to be discounted, as an earlier threat of enforced idleness brought about by automation apparently disappeared. "We are no longer faced by the danger of domination by an all-knowing because all-computerized bureaucracy or by a military-industrial power elite (to quote some other prophetic visions of the recent past). Instead we are told that we are living in the shadow of an overpopulated, overexploited, overproducing, and overconsuming world" (52).

Visions of satanic menace have always fascinated the imagination and provided relief from boredom. Through most of history these visions have appeared in religious guise: the Great Beast leading the forces of evil to the field of Megiddo, the Infidel holding Christ's abode in thrall, the Jew as evil incarnate, God's command that Protestants slay Catholics and vice versa, down to the nativist crusades during the 1850s when the Pope and all his minions threatened to assume total control of this country. In a secular age, however, the Devil wears a secular mask. Granted that his threats of imminent doom are now more empirically "real," they shift identity more rapidly than in the past.

The Range

Visions of the future constitute only one factor in the varying constancy of social problems. When all the factors discussed in this section are combined, it is possible to place the five social problems selected for major consideration along a range of constancy in time. That range, from most to least constant, is ecology, crime, poverty, race relations, population growth.

Of the five, ecology is the most constant simply because it has so recently arrived on the scene that divisive attitudes, clashes of interest, and awareness of personal price have only begun to arise. Crime is the oldest; yet during the last three decades the issues, controversies, arguments, and the division of attitudes accompanying it have on the whole changed very little. Poverty and race relations are quite mercurial in description; attitudes adopted toward them are in flux, even though a basic commitment to improving both has been maintained—with reservations—by the majority. Population growth is the least constant. Within recent memory it has been specified in opposite ways, in some instances by the same people. Despite its present high popularity among intellectuals, population growth has continued to be ignored by the majority, with subsidiary concerns about contraception and abortion excepted.

REFERENCES

1   There has been some falling off of that confidence in the future which was once a predominant theme in American culture. In a recent Gallup poll on optimism in ten countries, the United States ranked close to the international average on what good and bad are expected to lie in the future (cited in Milton Himmelfarb, "This Aquarian Age," *Commentary,* April 1970, pp. 38–41, p. 40). People in wealthier countries were found to be less optimistic than those living in poorer countries, and in this country blacks were found to be more optimistic than whites.

2   Carl Bridenbaugh, *Cities in the Wilderness,* Capricorn Books, Putnam, New York, 1964 (originally published by Ronald Press in 1938), p. 382.

3   Eminent criminologists like Frank E. Hartung *(Crime, Law and Society,* Wayne State University Press, Detroit, 1965) and Paul W. Tappan *(Crime, Justice and Correction,* McGraw-Hill, New York, 1960) have denied that the incidence of crime is any higher in modern times than in the past. As for the present, the FBI "uniform crime reports" are by no means uniform. Classifications have been altered from time to time, the number and kinds of reporting cities change from year to year, and so does the compliance of those sheriffs and chiefs of police who submit figures. The FBI reports do indicate a steady and rapid increase in the crime rate, but it may very well be much higher, or lower, than reported. As local record keeping becomes more standardized and cooperative, such improvements may exaggerate the "real rate." On the other hand, the weight of political pressure is such as to minimize the real rate. Even the faking of reports downward has surfaced from time to time.

    More important than police underreporting is the number of offenses never called to their attention. According to sociologist Gilbert Geis, the ratio of crimes known to the police to those committed is "possibly one out of ten, maybe one out of twenty, perhaps one out of a hundred." And juvenile delinquent statistics are totally useless. Cases of "dependency and neglect" aside, fewer of the clearly delinquent cases are heard in juvenile court than are treated as "unofficial" and then released to the parents, without any record being kept. The humanitarian impulse has benefited many criminals as well as delinquents, those whose records have been officially expunged to ensure access to jobs that would otherwise be denied them.

4   Crime and delinquency are much more prevalent in Sweden than in Turkey. Sweden is affluent; Turkey is not. Walter A. Lunden *(Statistics on Delinquents and Delinquency,* Charles C. Thomas, Springfield, Ill., 1964) has made detailed comparisons and relates that throughout the world the wealthy nations with complete welfare programs have been plagued with delinquency far in excess of that in "the less well developed nations." As for the United States, Lunden has applied indices of employment, industrial production, and business activity to the number of reported cases of delinquency in several jurisdictions, and concludes that delinquency tends to rise during years of relative prosperity.

Crime, to be sure, is more prevalent among the poor than the rich, but since most of the poor are not criminals, we cannot be dealing with any sovereign cause. Once the stage of urban civilization is reached, within given nations—and with temporal fluctuations aside—an apparently constant minority turn to crime while an equally constant majority do not. The reason is obscure; nor do we know why one *person* turns to crime while another does not. See Arnold W. Green, *Sociology,* 6th ed., McGraw-Hill, New York, 1972, pp. 391–392.

5   A few years ago the favored argument against executing those very few murderers who were apprehended and tried was the supposed failure of capital punishment to deter others. Usually, the murder rates between two states, one with capital punishment and the other without, were compared; alternatively, the murder rate in the same state was compared in time, when the provision was in effect and when at an earlier or later period it was abolished. These numerical comparisons appeared to vary almost at random. What that proves is not certain, except possibly that the death penalty failed to deter when it was uncertainly, capriciously, or not at all applied even in those jurisdictions which formally retained it. In 1966 there was one execution in this country and two in 1967; there have been none since.

6   For a refutation of the thesis that "society" causes crime, see Arnold W. Green, "The Reified Villain," *Social Research,* **35:**651–665, 1968.

7   Emile Durkheim, *The Rules of Sociological Method* (trans.), University of Chicago Press, Chicago, 1938, p. 96.

8 David J. Rothman, "Our Brothers' Keepers," *American Heritage,* December 1972, pp. 38–42 and 100–105, p. 41. This section owes much to Rothman's excellent piece, a succinct history of attempts to alleviate poverty in America.

9 At that time these contributory programs were often described in the press as essential means to force people to save money they would otherwise squander. While that judgment was accurate enough, it nevertheless signaled a coming legitimation of government direction of, as well as responsibility for, individual welfare.

10 David Matza, "Poverty and Disrepute," in Robert K. Merton and Robert Nisbet (eds.), *Contemporary Social Problems,* rev. ed., Harcourt Brace Jovanovich, New York, 1971, pp. 601–656, p. 615. As in the case of crime, a growing number of modern intellectuals do not want to see the "disreputable poor" changed except in their poverty, or tempted into a "stultifying middle-class way of life" as one critic has put it. Matza himself in the piece cited sympathizes and identifies with those he calls the disreputable poor. He invokes, in literal quotation, " 'power to the people' "—including these people.

11 *San Francisco Chronicle,* Dec. 22, 1972, p. 9.

12 The near total breakdown of control over various antipoverty programs is told in detail by Theodore J. Lowi, *The End of Liberalism,* Norton, New York, 1969, pp. 222–248.

13 "Firing Line" telecast of the Public Broadcasting Service on Jan. 28, 1973.

14 Any such "agreement" between conservatives and liberals would of course stem from different reasons. Liberal intellectuals tend to favor any proposal, including the Family Assistance Plan, which is designed to "redistribute income" and achieve a greater measure of equal treatment. Conservatives, at least sophisticated ones, regard the moribund ideology of free enterprise as beyond hope of being propped up against an apparently relentless wind. But they would like to minimize costs and political disruption. Also, as self-styled libertarians they usually try to subvert the efforts of official busybodies to tell anyone, including the poor, how they should live.

One sophisticated conservative, economist Milton Friedman, sired the Family Assistance Plan with his "negative income tax" proposal of 1962. He pointed out that most tax dollars spent on "poverty" go to the people who service such programs. The money allocated for direct welfare payments and programs of all kinds in 1961 "would have financed outright cash grants of nearly $6,000 per consumer unit [a family or unattached individual] to the 10 per cent with the lowest incomes." Their incomes could then have been raised far above the average for all consumer units in the United States. See Milton Friedman, *Capitalism and Freedom,* University of Chicago Press, Chicago, 1962, p. 194.

15 Rothman, reference 8, p. 105.

16 For a discussion of the politics behind Reconstruction, see David Donald, "Why They Impeached Andrew Johnson," *American Heritage,* December 1956, pp. 20–25 and 102–103.

17 E. Franklin Frazier, *The Negro in the United States,* Macmillan, New York, 1949, p. 530.

18 C. Vann Woodward, "The Birth of Jim Crow," *American Heritage,* April 1964, pp. 52–55 and 100–103, p. 52.

19 Alan F. Westin, "Ride-in!" *American Heritage,* August 1962, pp. 57–64, p. 64.

20 *National Review,* Jan. 5, 1973, Editorial, p. 49. At about this same time Mr. Buckley announced in favor of making marijuana use legal.

21 While aristocrats in one epoch or another have adopted the motif of *nostalgie de la boue* in Tom Wolfe's phrase, until recently the more fettered spirits at the middle rank have never declared their affinity with "primitivism." Attempted emulation of their so-called betters has been the historic pattern, in dress, deportment, recreation. Every sport, including baseball and roller-skating, was first introduced in this country by the "upper classes." See Foster Rhea Dulles, *America Learns to Play,* Appleton-Century-Crofts, New York, 1940.

22 Arnold W. Green, *Sociology,* rev. ed., McGraw-hill, New York, 1972, p. 230.

23 Myrdal's emendation, virtual repudiation, of his previous thesis has passed unnoticed. See Bernard E. Segal (ed.), *Racial and Ethnic Relations,* Crowell, New York, 1966, p. 469.

24 Howard Schuman, "Sociological Racism," *Trans-action,* December 1969, pp. 44–48, p. 46.

25 Peter Schrag, *Out of Place in America,* Random House, New York, 1970, p. 22.

26 For a sophisticated analysis of the ambiguities in the "race prejudice" concept, see Gustav Ichheiser, *Appearances and Realities,* Jossey-Bass, San Francisco, 1970, especially pp. 72–77.

27 Avery M. Guest, "Defusing the 'Population Bomb,' " in Edward Pohlman (ed.), *Population: A Clash of Prophets,* Mentor Books, New American Library, New York, 1973, pp. 67–71, p. 70. One expert who in 1932 advocated governmental intervention to arrest the alarming fall in the birthrate warned thirty years later that unless a stationary population is achieved a "Hobbesian solution" of "malfunction and strife" is bound to ensue. See selections 4 and 50 in this same book, which is essential reading for placing the great population debate in historic perspective. Every conceivable argument, from Malthus to Ehrlich, is thoroughly aired.

28   Professor Ehrlich has much company in his apparent willingness to accept a totalitarian solution: "We must have population control at home, hopefully through changes in our value system, but by compulsion if voluntary methods fail." Paul R. Ehrlich, *The Population Bomb,* rev. ed., Ballantine Books Inc., N.Y., 1971, pp. xi–xii and 130.

29   With the notable exception of census figures, those released by many government bureaus merit cautionary use. Most notorious are those figures which reflect the accomplishments of some bureau when they were gathered by a research branch of that same bureau. Other self-serving purposes of announced figures are, one, to justify requested appropriations and, two, to encourage the public to take a government-approved path. Thus government figures on the cost of raising children are not likely to be minimized during a period when the decision has been made to discourage natality. Such figures might be adjusted downward if official policy should veer toward promoting a higher birthrate. Nevertheless, while the cited figures on the cost of raising children may be generous, there can be no question that the cost of raising children—inflation discounted—has been outdistancing all other household costs.

30   Ehrlich, reference 28, p. 133.

31   Ehrlich, reference 28, p. 134.

32   The ruling will doubtless leave a trail of legal confusion for some time to come. It states in effect that a fetus is not a person under the Constitution, and thus has no right to life. But in some states abortion is declared illegal interference with an unborn child's right to inherit property. And what will happen to those state laws which make blood transfusions mandatory when the life of a religious-dissenting mother's unborn child would otherwise be endangered?

33   Julian Simon, "Science Does Not Show That There Is Overpopulation in the U. S.—or Elsewhere," in Edward Pohlman (ed.), *Population: A Clash of Prophets,* Mentor Books, New American Library, New York, 1973, pp. 48–62, p. 55.

34   Simon, reference 33, p. 61.

35   Since our concern is with attitudes and not "facts," here as elsewhere the latter receive less attention. However, because the reader has doubtless encountered more "facts" on one side than the other, a few references to rebuttal might serve in the interest of balance. The editor

of *Nature,* John Maddox *(The Doomsday Syndrome,* McGraw-Hill, New York, 1972), argues that pollution was on some counts much worse in previous centuries, and technology has always met the challenges which accompanied its own expansion, such as devising replacements for exhausted resources. Jane Jacobs *(The Economy of Cities,* Random House, New York, 1969) cites examples of both resource depletion and pollution in areas where sparse populations have failed to industrialize. She regards more people and more technology as potential advantages in efforts to clean up the environment. An economist has said that when effluent charges are made an integral part of pollution abatement strategy, as in the Ruhr Valley of West Germany and in the city of London, air and water improvements follow. (He discounts the value of regulatory legislation, which must compromise clashes of interests, and favors getting the social costs of pollution into industrial accounting systems.) See Larry E. Ruff, "The Economic Common Sense of Pollution," *The Public Interest,* Spring 1970, pp. 69–85.

36 The conservation movement, in particular the national park system, was founded upon two contradictory principles: preserve for future generations the unspoiled wilderness, and promote its enjoyment by the present generation. See Arnold W. Green, *Recreation, Leisure, and Politics,* McGraw-Hill, New York, 1964, p. 20.

37 However, the most famous proponent of clear-and-present danger, Barry Commoner, holds no such faith in the wisdom of governmental intervention. Instead he implores the general public to reform themselves. See *The Closing Circle,* Bantam Books Inc., 1972 (originally published by Knopf in 1971).

38 *Time,* Jan. 29, 1973, p. 62.

39 Marshall I. Goldman, "Another Part of the Forest," *Intellectual Digest,* December 1972, pp. 49–50, p. 49.

40 Ruff, reference 35, p. 82.

41 *U. S. News & World Report,* Feb. 19, 1973, p. 31.

42 *Eureka Times-Standard,* Jan. 21, 1973, p. 8.

43 Roger Starr, "This Is the Way the World Ends," *American Heritage,* October 1970, pp. 94–101, p.101.

44 Victor C. Ferkiss, *Technological Man: The Myth and the Reality,* George Braziller Inc., New York, 1969, pp. 21–22.

45 Population Reference Bureau Selection 41, September 1972, p. 3.

46 Attributions of psychological-emotional deprivation stem mainly from ideology, and invite rebuttal by opposed ideology, e.g.: "In Mike Harrington's America [Michael Harrington, *The Other America*], there

are 40–50 million people who are 'maimed in body and spirit'—all because they have incomes under $4000 a year. Well, that's not my America, and I don't believe it's the America of most of the 40–50 million, either." Irving Kristol, "Poverty and Pecksniff," in Burton A. Weisbrod (ed.), *The Economics of Poverty,* Prentice-Hall, Englewood Cliffs, N. J., 1965, pp. 136–142. p. 142.

47 What happened is clearer than why: a large number of college youth suddenly began to revile the goals most collegians during the fifties either endorsed or grudgingly accepted. The dissenters were the off-spring of educated-liberal, well-to-do suburban parents who had achieved those goals. Similar massive rejections of established ways have occurred many times in history, even in prehistory. Long before the dawn of history, men migrated far and wide. In many such cases, archaeologists and anthropologists have found no "good" (rational or utilitarian) reason why they left the security of an area of abundant food supply for a cold and harsh environment. The choice made by many young people during the late sixties was less drastic than that: they chose to play at being poverty-stricken and persecuted.

48 See *The Positive Philosophy of Auguste Comte,* Harriet Martineau, (trans.), Calvin Blanchard, New York, 1855, especially pp. 483–485. Ironically enough, in building his system of thought Comte totally disregarded his own warning. Like most other intellectuals, he was victim to that solipsism which views the present time as determining all important developments in the future.

49 Robert A. Nisbet, *Social Change and History,* Oxford University Press, 1969, p. 286. This book is an indispensable learning experience for any student of the social sciences.

50 Percy S. Cohen, *Modern Social Theory,* Heinemann, London, 1968, p. 224.

51 For a brief history of earlier prophecy, see Green, reference 36, pp. 38–46.

52 Rudolph Klein, "Growth and Its Enemies," *Commentary,* June 1972, pp. 37–49, pp. 38–39.

The Place of Rational Discourse

Neither science nor any other form of rational discourse determines what is or shall be a social problem. The point was made in the first chapter that sociologists do not discover social problems; they arise in the effective attitudes expressed by factions of varying size who struggle to impose their own ideas about what is wrong in the world and what should be done about it. And no more than any other interested party can the sociologist demonstrate on rational grounds that such-and-such is a more serious social problem than some other which has aroused concern and found support.

For example, how could anyone prove by logic or science that crime is a worse problem than, say, poverty? How could it be demonstrated that such scarce resources as public funds and personnel *should* be applied to crime prevention at the expense of the alleviation of poverty? Rational discourse has a secure application only in determining which technical means might be more appropriate than others provided the goal in turn is defined in narrow technical terms *(1)*. Social-problem goals, as we shall see, are not so defined.

In this chapter we will first examine rationality and its limits in determining what social problems should be addressed. Images, of the self and others, are shown to possess an incalculably greater effect upon discussion of social-problem issues. The interrelationships of images on one side, interests and power on the other, are then explored. Finally the moral, essentially "nonrational," context of social-problem discussion is stated.

WHAT IS RATIONALITY?

Much of the writing in the social-problems field assails ignorance as the chief block to an achievement of unanimous social purpose. Sheer knowledge about social problems is assumed to provide an adequate basis for ameliorative action. This "rational approach" is shared by most of those sociologists who more or less accept their social world and seek to improve it and by those sociologists who try to persuade an audience that the "system" itself is rotten and should be dismembered. Some undetermined and undefined "we" should, could, or are about to take concerted action, once we become sufficiently enlightened. But according to some dissenters neither the human mind nor the world works in quite that way.

Some Dissenters

One of them, Vilfredo Pareto, said that any plea for men to be "rational" manifests the sentiment that men should be "good" and refrain from trying to secure private advantage. He did not attack morality, or dispute its worth or essential place. He merely insisted that only moral grounds, not rational ones, support any argument that people should be concerned about others instead of themselves. And Pareto is only one writer among a minority of intellectuals who have claimed that the motivational source of humanitarianism itself is tainted with a kind of "irrationality."

According to Professor Brinton: "The favorite reproach of moderate and conservative men, that radical revolutionaries and even plain reformers do not so much pity the failure, the weak, as envy and hate the strong, the successful, is like most such stereo-

types, unfair but by no means wholly untrue" (2). Much less qualified is Professor Schoeck's assessment, that humanitarian expression stems from an envy of those whose status is superior to one's
own *(3)*. On the other hand, he does not argue that humanitarianism
is uniformly grounded in envy. There are quite apparent variations
in the "genuineness" of humanitarian expression, disclosed by the
extent of personal sacrifice.

The politician whose image on a billboard accompanies the
legend that he Cares for People may possibly be more willing to
expend other people's taxes than his own money. The college student whose vocal concern for the poor stops at denunciation of the
"system," who makes no visible effort of his own in their behalf, is
likewise vulnerable to a charge of hypocrisy. Both politician and
student could "rationally" argue that any personal effort of theirs
would count little in comparison with political reform; yet their
credentials would still look paltry alongside those of, say, young
Mennonites who go from one disaster area to another and help the
victims to rebuild their communities and their lives.

Still other dissenters have equated humanitarian concern with
self-aggrandizement. Hegel insisted that "the heart-throb for the
welfare of mankind passes into the frantic rage of self-conceit."
Henry David Thoreau said that doing good is "a foul subject," and
he located the desire to change the world in one's "own belly-ache."
Camus argued that it is simply not possibe for any human being—
apart from playing to the gallery—to be concerned about any other;
we can love only ourselves.

This is nevertheless slippery ground where, in Aldous Huxley's
dictum, an ideal "is merely the projection, on an enormously enlarged scale, of some aspect of personality." Slippery because the
reverse does not necessarily hold, that a projection of some aspect
of personality is an ideal. Further, what is to be made of the moral
concern, even anguish, expressed on almost every page of Camus
and Huxley, that man is incapable of that self-transcendence they
so obviously craved?

Camus and Huxley have been described by people who knew
them well as being almost saintly in their dealings with others. It is
an odd and possibly significant circumstance that detractors of man
in the abstract are usually better men than the human nature they

describe, often better men than those who proclaim man's basic altruism and beneficence (4). It may, then, be reasonably suspected that there is something more to positive sentiment, including humanitarianism, than any of the people cited above have allowed— even though rationality is no part of it.

David Hume anticipated all the arguments listed above, and answered them. He took the full measure of envy as man's common lot (5). He insisted that the "object" of humility as well as pride is the same—the self (6). Desire, not reason, is the wellspring of human conduct. All action stems from desire, and a desire cannot be combated or overcome with reason, only with another desire.

One desire, however, is that to express sympathy for others (7), a desire manifested in humanitarianism, a term which had not yet been coined. Sympathy Hume regarded as a "real" source of motivation, however directed toward "a view to ourselves" it might be. In a very simple way the problem of rationality was bypassed, even though Hume retained doubts about the capacity of sympathy to persist, especially in collective endeavors, as did Max Weber (8). But humanitarianism, or sympathy for distant others, however qualified and limited by the stubborn obduracy of individual psychology, and by the experienced pressure to maintain group-power relationships, is "real" enough to have become a fixed standard in modern society to which skeptics and hypocrites, as well as true believers, must pay obeisance in the public forum.

Reason and Facts

Reason, according to Hume, does not lay obligations upon us; reason is employed only to discover how we can get what we want. If men do what they "should" do, not reason but moral suasion and commitment guide their action. Further, no moral obligation can be derived from any statement of fact. And attitudes, notably those of moral judgment, are never *validated* by any statement of fact, even though statements of fact are often utilized in attempts to sway or change attitudes. According to Karl Popper: ". . . perhaps the simplest and most important point about ethics is purely logical, I mean the impossibility to derive non-tautological rules—imperatives, principles of policy, aims or however we may describe them—from statements of fact" (9).

An appeal to reason based upon facts, that is, pointing out what men ought to do on the basis of described existent conditions, as often as not fails to move the people addressed. Part of the difficulty inheres in two circumstances. First, there may be disagreement over what the facts in the case actually are. Second, when there is no such disagreement, reason will not necessarily lead to agreement on what should then be done.

As we have already seen, the facts about any social problem are themselves controversial. Some experts and nonexperts say crime is increasing; others say it is not. Some say poverty is worse and more widespread than in the past; others disagree. The claim that race relations have obviously improved in recent years is countered by the claim that racism has reached crisis proportions. Population growth and ecological imbalances are likewise matters of "fact" which depend upon which pro or con sources are cited.

Although this is not the place for epistemological discussion, a few "facts" about "facts" require spelling out, in this and the following paragraph. No fact has independent existence. A fact is not a thing or an event. A fact is a *statement* about a thing or event which is more or less empirically verifiable *within a given frame of reference.* Even within science, facts once in existence can disappear when a master frame of reference is fundamentally recast (10). Or a scientist may cling to old facts when he is faced by the prospect of their being discredited by a new frame of reference. Galileo, for example, refused to examine Kepler's evidence on the elliptical movement of planets. His retention of the Copernican system required the fact of their circular movement (11).

Although physical and biological scientists may remain so ego-attached to a challenged frame of reference that they deny the existence of uncorroborative facts, subjectivistic bias in the social sciences is much more apparent. The data examined are not out there, beyond the self and the social struggle. So close are observer and observation that Charles H. Cooley was led to remark that every sociology is in part an autobiography. Moral commitment, empathy, to a lesser degree ideology, all tend to guide the perceptions of social science practitioners—guide, not dominate. One sociologist has made a good case for the quasi-independence of perception, which ensures that conception will not totally govern what "facts" are described, a case which another sociologist independently has disputed (12).

The Path of Action

To repeat, agreement about what the facts are in any given case is not easily arrived at. And even when, by whatever means, men do reach such agreement, reason will not guarantee which path of action they then will elect to follow. No one disputes the common fate of death, at least in this life. Does it therefore follow that we must not defer or neglect any kindness that we can show to our fellow creatures? Marcus Aurelius said so, but Sydney J. Harris dismissed the sentiment as utter nonsense. Those in whom virtuous impulses predominate require no intimations of mortality to behave themselves. Blither spirits of more hedonistic bent, reminded of how brief the candle, will more than likely decide: "Why not ruin the fields, deforest the woods, litter the roads, pollute the streams, trample the flowers, and treat other people as a mere means to one's own ends?"

The warnings of ecologists could lead two men to agree that big-game species are threatened with extinction. One might then promote legislation to ban all hunting of big game while the other sought a polar-bear-head trophy before polar bears disappear. Two men might reach total accord on the seriousness of a rising crime rate, and one could cite that fact as proving the need for a get-tough policy that would end permissive encouragement of crime, while the other could insist that the same fact proves the failure of punishment to deter crime, and therefore the underlying poverty-slum conditions which cause criminality should be eliminated.

"Let us face the fact that confirmed criminals do not reform. Let us face the fact that incarceration in penal institutions is not a crime deterrent. Let us face the fact that penal institutions do not reform criminals; they serve but as finishing schools of criminality!" The writer of this passage in a letter to the *Centre Daily Times* of February 9, 1957, then continued: "Let us have done with softness in our treatment of crime and criminals." Her conclusion? Electrocution and the whipping post should be utilized on a grand scale, because the facts prove that milder forms of punishment are worthless.

The above proposal departs radically from the one usually advanced after a review of the same facts. But at a more sophisticated level of analysis, the same two roads of social policy diverge. Research has shown that the personality characteristics of criminals and noncriminals are basically alike, in the sense that these characteristics vary almost at random within the same range (13). Toward what decision does this fact point? Some have argued that since criminals and noncriminals are distinguishable, for the most part, only by a legal charge or its lack, then obviously we should not punish those who as persons exhibit superior attributes of character which make recidivism improbable. Others have countered that since criminals and noncriminals are basically alike and subject to the same temptations, we had better make the penalties more certain so that those who are still law-abiding remain that way. In other words, reasoning about the facts of crime—or about those of any social problem—can take acknowledged experts in the same opposite directions as high school students in a bull session.

Men often reach agreement about what the facts are in a given case; they can also "reason together" about what to do about them, and can oftentimes arrive at a like decision. But neither facts nor reasoning about facts will guarantee what the decision will be any more than they will ensure agreement about it. What lies behind either consensus or divergence are basic attitudes, and a varying admixture of propaganda, expediency, power, moral commitment, envy, perceived interest, sympathy and humanitarianism, revulsion, fear, loyalty, resentment, and an image of the world and the place of the self within it, all of which may sway, reinforce, or modify those attitudes. The drift of effective attitudes, not facts and reasoning about facts, determines how a social problem will be specified.

PRIMACY OF THE IMAGE

Regardless of variations in sophistication and intelligence, human minds tend to compartmentalize knowledge. Almost all modern sociologists accept the findings of Mead, Cooley, and others who demonstrated that social reality is idea, mental construct, image; many of those same sociologists also assume, like men of the Enlightenment, that social problems can be solved by exhorting other men to purge their minds of factual error. That the truth will triumph is a naïve belief expressed with equal conviction in the John Birch literature of ubiquitous Communist plot and in the assertions of those sociologists who seek to prove, like Herbert Marcuse, that right-wing ideology or even traditional values are the source of all collective difficulties.

People *can* be persuaded, although within narrower limits than is commonly assumed, to modify social views previously held. But rational discourse and the "truth" have little if any consequence for such potential change. Techniques of persuasion which alternately flatter, shame, threaten, paint portraits of right-thinking people and what they believe or know are much more effective, because they may succeed in modifying self-images and images of the other.

Self-Image

We tend to view ourselves with the stated or inferred attitudes of others toward ourselves. In its initial development, the self-image (or self-conception) is almost entirely a product of social interaction. As a person approaches maturity, however, the self-image becomes less a hostage to the reflected assessments, favorable or otherwise, of *all* others toward himself. Discrimination is exercised in choosing associates whose attitudes, values, and prejudices are compatible, so that the self-image normally develops a measure of self-protection. Moreover, investigation has revealed a consistent tendency to rate oneself higher on various positive attributes than do one's associates, whether or not they are deliberately chosen. Part of this discrepancy can be explained as a result of those "norms of deference" which govern adult social intercourse; people ordinarily conceal their harsher judgments of their fellows when they deal with them directly (14).

Another part of it is revealed by the handy catalog of excuses we all have ready to explain our own failures to fulfill the expectations of others, and even of ourselves. The final part, the most important part of that discrepancy, stems from the dynamic aspect of the self, an emergent quest for self-vindication which transcends the inferred-reflected attitudes of even selected others toward the self. While the self may remain an object to itself, as Cooley and Mead insisted, that object has fish of its own to fry.

Human beings thus relate to the world from the self, outward, and a flattering self-image is each person's most prized possession, which he seeks to protect, dramatize, aggrandize *(15)*. This proposition applies equally to a gangster, who lives in a restricted world, and to a saint, who seeks to transcend the world entire. Most people, who are neither, utilize the common currency of public issues in the world for the same purpose. Since a deep and widespread social-problem consciousness is now predominant in the public forum, they express concern about social problems, especially humanitarian concern for the welfare of distant others. All moral, normative, sympathetic action rests with celebration—not necessarily advertisement—of the self.

Every socialized human being remains self-consciously aware of himself as part of now this and now that audience which watches his own performance. We resist that knowledge when we say one person is sincere and another is a phony. Essentially what we mean is that the first appears to be less concerned about whether or not the audience claps. That may be so, and yet both are equally, inescapably, aware of the audience. And no one can be certain, least of all the sincere person himself, how much the presentation of sincerity may be part of an assumed role.

One of life's greatest pleasures, for anyone, is to be caught in the commission of an anonymous good deed. And we all secretly believe that others will finally discover what exemplary characters we really are. Neither criticism nor irony should be inferred, for none is intended. We are what we are, and without a universal primary concern about the self-image, social concern and social life itself would disintegrate.

A personal interest in social problems thus has little basis in science or rationality, and how fake or real that interest is no method of science can reveal. Such a conclusion, though, has never satisfied men in the past, and it probably never will in the future. Endless conjecture about motives is part of that incessant passing of judgment upon others which is one of the key features of social life. Exactly what the motives of others are, however, *remains* a matter of conjecture, so that the chief instruments with which social life is maintained, praise and blame, perforce operate upon deed and not inferred intention.

Only the self can be praised or blamed, and only by the self, for motives, intentions, reservations which remain covert, hidden from the world and unexpressed in it. In that sense every human being lives alone, for no one, neither mate nor psychiatrist, can really share either the conscious mind or the miasmal subconscious of another. Overt behavior, whether of word, gesture, or act, remains the only basis we have for being judged by others.

In their turn they are constantly being judged, and praised or blamed in consequence. Within social interaction, every human being simultaneously becomes judge and defendant. The ultimate source of social control, then, is verbal reward and punishment by others for deeds committed and omitted. The adult self may develop a measure of protection from the judgments of others that is denied the small child, but the adult self never achieves independence from such attitudes. Even when the deeper levels of self are not engaged, in order to preserve his reputation and those social relationships he deems essential to his private interests, each person will try to persuade others that his overt responses possess a high idealistic component. And perhaps not all but surely most people expect others to achieve higher standards of idealized rectitude than they privately set for themselves.

Ordinarily, those others do not. Very few if any overt responses are, or even can be, unalloyed with undisclosed goals, manipulative intent, and private reservation *(16)*. Every human being harbors such secrets. They are universally deplored or condemned by his associates whenever the mask slips and they are inadvertently disclosed to view.

We thus simultaneously push one another toward *both* ideal expression of conduct and "hypocrisy," and the demand side of the transaction to a considerable extent creates the supply. Recall the distinction drawn in the first chapter between private and public personality. We encourage, even require, others to act as if their private and public personalities were more integrated than they actually are. In turn, their desire for self-unity, their wish to preserve a flattering self-image, often leads them to narrow the gap in consciousness between those two aspects of personality, really as well as expediently to feel concern about whatever is going on in the public forum. Quite often there, in an age of acute social-problem consciousness, social problems are being discussed. Some degree of participation is expected, by self and others.

Images of the Other

Although expressions of social-problem concern and efforts to shore up one's self-image are not identical, we have seen that the two are inextricable. It is the self-image which promotes indication of interest in social problems. Images of the other, on the other hand, largely determine how one will *relate* to social problems, to the entire social world for that matter. Images of the other include images of personal associates and images of national, ethnic, racial, and status groups, and images of institutions, such as the "nation" or the "church," as well.

According to Charles H. Cooley, immediate social reality is one person's idea of another. The personal idea *is* the real person. In this alone "one man exists for another, and acts directly upon his mind." Willard Waller argued that even in the most intimate of all relationships, marriage, we deal not with another person but with our own image of him, or her.

If personal reality is one's image of another, that image is nevertheless somewhat modifiable by what a disinterested outsider would regard as evidence. Several studies of engaged couples, for example, show that romantic idealization of the other tends to wane in time: when short-term engaged couples are compared with long-term couples, the latter are more likely in some degree to see the intended as associates of that person describe him, or her. The image of the other, then, does not necessarily ignore "objective data," but how objective that image is or becomes remains a moot point. Distinctive traits of personality *are* "real" in the sense that a person's associates, under test conditions, will with fair consistency rate him more, or less, honest, responsible, and so on, than they rate others. Nevertheless, any one of those associates will still approach and interact with that person on the basis of his own image of what he is.

An image of the other always contains elements which are not derived from particular knowledge about that other, no matter how close the relationship may be. Persons married for many years "know" the other in many unique ways and dimensions. Such knowledge stems in part from special experience of the other, but also in part from unassailable pictures in the mind which have a history that precedes any knowledge of the other. It is a common-place observation that husband and wife can view the other with pictures of whatever relationship their own parents are thought to have had. Husband and wife also view the other with sexist stereo-types. Some of these can be positive in result even when negative in tone. Many wives become reconciled to cigar ashes on the living-room rug because "all men are sloppy."

But it is in the world outside the home and the circle of personal acquaintance, where knowledge about the other is relatively frag-mentary and superficial, that images of the other tend to become *sovereign* stereotypes. This is not to say that institutions as well as large groups have no real existence. They surely have an emergent existence, apart from whatever images of them may be in the minds of individuals. But what happens in and to institutions and large groups *is* subject to whatever images of them are held at any given time.

An army, for example, will exist for Private Jones only in terms of his image of it, an image which coheres in some ways with those images held of it by his barracks mates, in fewer ways with those held by his officers, but an image which remains, finally, idiosyn-cratic to Private Jones. At the same time, an army is a historic emergent and structural reality which persists in time. Some aspects of officer–enlisted man relationships in modern armies, for example, trace back to the Roman legions and beyond; on the other hand, those relationships are subject to continuous modification as images and attendant attitudes change. Such a change notably occurred during the divisive and unpopular conflict in Vietnam.

Images of the Other and Reality

Social reality, then, is an insecure combination of what is objectively out there and shifting images of what is assumed to be out there. Images nevertheless create the immediate appearances of reality to which men orient their behavior. In one view, the "objectivity" of the social world is something transmitted to the child within the socialization process; all institutions seem given, self-evident and unalterable. With adulthood, the social world is still experienced as something more than the human product it is, but the adult then "constructs the world *into* which he externalizes himself. In the process of externalization, he projects his own meanings into reality" (17). The writers of this quotation view objective and subjective reality as being in a "symmetrical relationship" through which "objective reality can readily be 'translated' into subjective reality, and vice versa."

There is less equivocation about the subjectivistic basis of all social phenomena in another assessment. Professor Boulding insists that "facts" do not exist for any organism, organization, or even scientist *(18)*. There are only messages, which filter through changeable value systems. Messages which cannot be fitted into prevailing images are usually ignored; those which reinforce an image already held are eagerly sought.

Scientists are not exempted. A scientist's frame of reference is a "subjective knowledge structure," as much a value to be defended as it is a means to interpret data. No orthodox psychologist, for example, would welcome evidence which might serve to substantiate the claims of ESP practitioners, any more than an advocate of ESP would welcome counterevidence. In extension of Boulding's argument, scientists no less than the untutored maintain essentially closed minds for the obvious reason that a totally "open mind" would be incapable of structuring reality for itself.

All is not random chaos, as might be assumed to be the case, for aspects of most images which are critical for the maintenance of social life are widely shared. Neither are most images immovably fixed. A person can and often does restructure his own image of the other in time, because value systems are permeable and indeterminately vulnerable to coercion, propaganda, expediency, and appeals to moral obligation. Yet once established, images of the other are usually modified, if at all, slowly and reluctantly. When images of the other change dramatically and suddenly, as in the conversion experience, they do so as a result of a crisis of self-consciousness.

Images of the other are neither delusions nor epiphenomena. These images and the attitudes they serve are the basic stuff of society. Images may be ultimately idiosyncratic, peculiar to one or another individual, but those aspects of separate images which are shared form the essential social bond. And to be shared, aspects of separate images must retain some degree of stability amidst constant change. Even "preformed stereotyped images about other people are certainly among the most important factors in the system of collective representations necessary to guarantee a minimum consensus for a group. Thus they should not be lightly dismissed as prejudices" (19).

Images of the Other and Prejudice

A great deal of confusion has resulted from the popular image—in part the result of work in social psychology—of all images as sheer manifestations of maladaptive prejudice. This moral judgment accompanies a moral exhortation: we should see other individuals as they actually, in fact, are, and not as representatives of this and that classification *(20).* Such an injunction is tantamount to asking minds to cease functioning and society to disappear. Not even husband and wife know each other entirely apart from images, classifications, stereotypes.

Initial contacts, to be sure, are especially prone to categoric interpretation. Further knowledge and association can, although not always or necessarily will, lead to filling in the image of the other with particular details. But it can reasonably be doubted that anyone has ever achieved a view of the other person as he "really is," or of a group, organization, or institution as it "really is."

Man and society exist in and through images, of self and other. These images always contain a stereotypical element, which does vary but is never eliminated. The hope that human beings can be rationally persuaded to rid their minds of such is vain. They can be persuaded to try, but not by rational means, and only to make a substitution.

Manipulation of shame and guilt are especially effective. If someone is successfully made ashamed of a certain image by someone who in his eyes has prestige, he will not rid his mind of images but will instead seek to replace his original image with another. Thus people who renounce an erstwhile prejudice (pre-judgment) adopt a new one, a counterimage with refurbished stereotypical elements (21).

At any given moment of any person's life, stereotyped images already formed of the other screen messages received from the outside world, even a message of numbers. Consider the person with an image of American business as a predatory and ruthless power structure. If he reads that between the first quarter of 1969 and the final quarter of 1970 corporate profits dropped by 21 percent and employee compensation rose by 13 percent (which, according to the Commerce Department, did occur), he can ignore that "fact." He can alternatively suspect the "big corporations" of submitting false figures, or he can picture the 13 percent rise in employment compensation as a sop offered an exploited working force to keep them contented with their chains.

Someone else, with a different image of the same other, may view the same "fact" as a victory for people's capitalism. Still another may express alarm that an industrial system "starved for capital" will soon be wrecked by inordinate demands for wage increases that are outstripping worker productivity. Since images and their subsidiary attitudes tend to cluster *(22)*, this last person may also hold an image of "hippies" as irresponsible spoiled brats. Should he read in his newspaper that a "long-haired youth" rescued a child from drowning at the cost of his own life, he might either screen out the rescuer's description or wonder why all the others are so different.

IMAGES AND SOCIAL PROBLEMS

Recognition of any social problem, the *way* it is recognized, is inseparable from images of deplored conditions and of heroes and villains. These images are projected into an imagined future when what and who are deplored will be made to stop. If these images, instead of only being shared by one or more segments of the population, were universally held, the given social problem could be addressed without conflict. Perhaps unfortunately, these images are not universally held, as is shown below.

Crime

An image about crime, or anything else for that matter, cannot fail, nor can it be refuted. Appeals to "reason" will not sway a social-problem image. One reason for this impasse is that most people remain unaware that they are partisans and not mere observers. Careful scrutiny of public statements on the social problem of crime, however, will indicate that one side is being defended, the other attacked. Politicians, judges, social reformers, as well as the so-called common man, constantly refer to the "criminal," who does not exist, except variously in this and that mind. In each mind the "criminal" conjures up a picture which reduces all criminals to a single image. At polar extremes the criminal becomes either a threatening thug or a helpless victim of society, and these images are used to blame "bleeding hearts" at one extreme, "punitive public attitudes" at the other.

Such an image can be momentarily displaced. A man who sees the criminal as a brutal assailant may or may not be able to adopt an image-of-the-moment if he reads about someone who stole money to finance expensive medical care for his wife. That thief might be excluded from his master image of the criminal. But whether he has in mind the "criminal" or "some poor guy you sure can't blame," some one picture, at any given time which he might devote to crime and criminals, will dominate his consciousness. No one, intellectual or hard hat, black or white, humanitarian or advocate of condign punishment, neither defender nor denunciator of the "criminal," is capable of simultaneously "seeing" people accused of crime as men or women, black or white, old or young, clever or stupid, vicious or pathetic, in short as a range of diverse individuals. This reason, as well as the more important one of polarized master images of the criminal, serves to perpetuate misunderstandings in any discussion of the crime problem.

Race Relations

Much the same can be said about how whites view blacks, and vice versa. We are unable to hold an image of any series of individuals entirely apart from assigning them to a collectivity. When we take an additional step and apply the concept of social problem to a series of individuals, we then see them as candidates for being "solved" in a faceless, mass way. James Baldwin says that the "racial problem" is remote from everybody. "We do not know what to do with [the Negro] in life; if he breaks our sociological and sentimental image of him we are panic-stricken and feel ourselves betrayed" (23). Baldwin says that prejudice or its lack really does not matter. In neither case is the "Negro" acknowledged, fully, to be a concrete person. The reverse, of course, also holds. Blacks tend to view "Whitey" or the "man" as a category, a stereotyped image with very few overtones of sentimentality.

Images play a complex role in the history of social problems. There is first the matter of who shall be blamed, and who shall be vindicated, through identification with those vindicated. Once a public image of hero (or heroic victim) and villain has been created by extensive pathos manipulation, there is in the short term a near total resistance to any "evidence" which might question heroism on one side and villainy on the other. Even people whose interests and prejudices might be served by such evidence can find it somehow inappropriate. It does not *fit* the image which they, perhaps reluctantly in many cases, have come to accept. Thus military historian General S. L. A. Marshall is not likely to find many takers of his thesis that the Indian wars on the Great Plains were savagely fought on both sides, without any master plan of genocide, and especially of his finding that by deliberate conspiracy Black Fox and other Sioux fired the first shots at—the site is horrendously inappropriate—Wounded Knee (24).

Other Heroes and Villians

Although the "organization man" is more villainous victim than heroic victim, his public image has become as fixed and stereotyped as that of the American Indian, and about as impervious to revision with "facts." His public image has nevertheless been disputed (an image, to repeat, cannot be disproved) by a research study based on interviews with more than 3,000 men in civilian occupations. Individuality is claimed to be less suppressed among bureaucratic than nonbureaucratic work forces. "Bureaucratization is consistently, albeit not strongly, associated with greater intellectual flexibility, higher valuation of self-direction, more openness to new experience, and more personally responsible moral standards" *(25)*.

The public image of the "alienated worker" is equally stereotyped, in educated circles if not elsewhere. Unlike the organization man, he is a heroic victim and has become a proto–social problem. Blame for his supposed plight is placed upon a mechanical villain, industrialization. A recent HEW document entitled "Work in America" reinforces his public image by discounting the "facts" therein presented! "About 85% of American workers, when asked if they are satisfied with their jobs, answer in the affirmative. 'Work in America' tries to show that they don't mean what they say." For example, any worker who said he was satisfied with his job but would like something better was listed as being "really" alienated from his work *(26).* Part of that assumed alienation stems from the stereotype set by Charlie Chaplin in *Modern Times,* the pervasive image of the robot attached to an assembly line. But the same document, in passing, located only 2 percent of all American workers on the assembly line in the new service economy. This "fact" left the authors' image of alienated workers undisturbed by their own evidence.

By no means are all efforts to create and maintain public images of heroes and villains successful. For many years criminologists and Sunday-supplement writers have portrayed the "white-collar criminal," in business, the professions, and government, as much more dangerous than the "ordinary criminal," the burglar, mugger, and rapist. The chief "fact" employed in this enterprise is the incalculably larger sum of money mulcted from the public by fraud, deceit, evasion, and supplying of illegal services than by all the depredations of ordinary criminals. But despite this extensive campaign to revise public images, and in turn change attitudes, the majority continue to view "crime in the streets" as *the* crime problem.

They do so because direct and physical coercion is practiced in most ordinary crimes, while coercion is either absent or operates from a distant source in white-collar crime. Also, in the latter case, options of retaliation or withdrawal appear to be available. The politician known or rumored to be guilty of malfeasance may be voted out at the next election. The illegal services of bookies and gambling-house proprietors need not be utilized. The physician suspected of padding his bill will lose a patient. The store proprietor or landlord who violates legally controlled prices or rents cannot prevent a customer from going to another store or a tenant from attempting to rent another apartment. In sharp contrast, no freedom of avoidance or counteraction is permitted, no option is offered, by the burglar, mugger, and rapist. Quite simply, the ordinary citizen continues to feel threatened by the street criminal in a way which he does not picture the white-collar criminal, who remains faceless and distant to him.

Ends and Means

Beyond praise and blame, images of how adopted means will succeed or fail in social problems frequently promote conflict among
groups and organizations even when an ultimate end is not in dispute. The so-called gun lobby and those who press for legislation
barring the sale of handguns agree that the crime rate must be
reduced. On one side, an image of disarmed citizens helpless to
protect themselves from pillage and murder prevails. "When guns
are outlawed, only outlaws will have guns." On the other, "control
of firearms" is pictured as somehow controlling crime. Despite the
"fact" that some 25 million unregistered handguns have already
been sold to American civilians, an idealized image is projected into
the future of would-be predators deprived of weapons. And a tinge
of paranoia attends both of these images, revealed by assertions that
the other side either wants or is complacent about crime in the
streets.

Oftentimes certain measures are demanded or agreed to which
are not themselves especially wanted, only confused with a projected image of something else. Most of the state legislators who voted
to ratify the Eighteenth Amendment quite likely did not welcome
police interference with private habits of consumption, and they
surely did not want Al Capone, bootlegging, or poisoned hooch.
Possibly most of them did want to capitalize politically on a popular
desire to put an end to the "evils of drink."

In recent polls most American adults have said that they prefer
price controls to uncontrolled prices. Can they really mean they
prefer low prices to high prices? They presumably do not want what
enforced price controls have always brought, in old Rome and contemporary Russia and Cuba as well as in this country during World
War II: rationing, empty shelves, black markets, and diversion of
productive capacity from cheap and popular items to custom-made
expensive ones *(27)*. It may safely be assumed that what they do
want is an abundant supply of goods at low prices.

The demands of blacks and Indians for control of their own
schools can be similarly interpreted. In all probability they really
want a higher grade-level achievement for their children, an image
which expands to superior occupational status and other victories

long denied. Likewise, most proponents of busing have something more in mind than shuttling white children to predominantly black schools and black children to predominantly white schools, and that is an image of racial amity, mutual respect, conflict resolved, and democracy revitalized.

Any goal of social action includes an image of what will be, but a projected image of what will (or should) be is not necessarily an end. Such an image can be a utopian vision of perfection with no means specified to attain it, such as an expectation that a worldwide adoption of the democratic way of life is imminent; or purely symbolic and essentially magical means can be enlisted, as in international conferences on world peace where politics is ignored in favor of people-to-people contacts designed to foster international understanding (28). Failure to realize wishes of this kind rarely discourages preservation of the given image.

Where ends and means are somewhat more empirically joined than in the last above instances, failure to achieve an end can still be ignored, discounted, or denied, so that an established image can be retained. Such an image can be shared by disparate types, some of whom may have no special personal stake in it. For example, the inevitability (if not desirability) of the large central city is hardly ever questioned. And the existence of an "urban crisis" is not disputed by politicians or reformers, liberals or reactionaries. Even though all known programs of so-called urban renewal have satisfied very few people, everyone, almost everyone, agrees that something should, must, be done about the problem of the cities.

Professor Irving Kristol does not. He foresees something unprecedented, an urban civilization without large central cities. He argues that it is already beginning to emerge, without anyone's particular wish and certainly by no one's conscious design. For some time population and cultural life, manufacturing, commerce, financial services, and media-associated activity have all been drifting to suburban and small-city location. The central city has pushed them out more than they have been attracted elsewhere.

Large central cities have become virtually ungovernable, "politically weakened and economically enfeebled." There has been no "candid recognition of this trend," and all proposed remedies "seem trifling." He neither points a moral nor offers advice, but does imply that attention being paid to the "urban crisis" will wane as the big city ceases to play an important role in American life *(29)*. At the present time, an "urban civilization without great cities" is almost unthinkable. That picture can be formed in the mind only by conscious effort, an effort which obviates any possibility of its becoming a public image for some time to come.

Image Protection

An effort to preserve an image of the other in which one has a considerable personal stake is the most pervasive reason why it is difficult, perhaps impossible, to judge the success or failure of a program addressed to a social problem. Has the Head Start program, started in 1965 on stated grounds of removing institutionalized lack of educational opportunity, failed or succeeded? Some critics have charged that such preschool training has not improved the school-performance scores of later enrollees in public schools. Defendants of the program insist that not enough money has been spent upon it (30).

In either event, a majority of Americans have a stake in seeing that program continued. Abandonment of this or any other humanitarian enterprise to which many people of goodwill have committed themselves would open up a moral vacuum. And as Daniel P. Moynihan has put it, "Americans really *like* poor kids to come along." According to several polls, most Americans want Head Start to be continued. They preserve an image of young blacks making good.

A much clearer effort to protect an image, in this case of racism, is revealed by an unwillingness or inability to "see" the recent advances of blacks which have largely resulted from the success of other programs. True, these improvements have not been uniformly distributed. The black slums continue to grow; yet when all whites and all blacks are compared, recent black advances in job upgrading, income, and higher education are quite marked. While income for white families rose by 69 percent during the sixties, for example, income for black families went up by 99.6 percent. The proportion of black families earning above $10,000 rose from 3 to 13 percent in 1950–1961, from 13 to 30 percent in 1961–1971—in constant dollars, with inflation discounted.

Improvements in higher education enrollment are even more pronounced. Between 1965 and 1971, the proportion of blacks aged eighteen to twenty-four enrolled in college rose from 10 to 18 percent, of whites, from 26 to 27 percent. On the other hand, the *total* black unemployment rate has for some time fluctuated around a percentage twice that of the white. And although the proportion of blacks below the official poverty line dropped from 48 to 29 percent in the 1960–1971 period, the number of blacks on welfare went from 1.3 million to 4.8 million. This last increase does not mean that more blacks are becoming poor, but that poor blacks are now more likely to receive public aid (31).

The material situation of blacks in modern America is exceedingly complex, one of simultaneous up-and-down. Blacks, on average, can be said to have made remarkable gains; but while a black "middle class" rapidly expands, its gains do not leaven the dreary statistics of mounting numbers, crime, unemployment, welfare, illegitimacy, and drug addiction in the black slums. And yet through this almost bipolar situation, some categories of black income have come to exceed white income in the same categories. According to the Bureau of the Census, in 1970 there was "no apparent difference between the incomes of white and Negro husband-wife families outside the South where the head was under 35 years old." And in young families outside the South, where both husband and wife worked, black incomes were higher than white incomes (32). Daniel P. Moynihan foresees the possibility that the discrepancy between black and white earning power will disappear as these young families grow older.

He further says that the increase of income among educated blacks owes much to government jobs of administering and servicing the black poor. They, and white professionals as well, have gotten most of the money allocated to the War on Poverty. Moynihan may have overstressed the role of government employment, however, even though figures on that score are unavailable. It appears likely that government programs of employment for blacks have had less effect upon the total situation than the "equal opportunity" efforts of unions and private employers, who have been encouraged to that end by legislation and by agency decrees as well as by indeterminate voluntary commitment.

"Facts" and a Protected Image

These "facts," of course, do not refute an image of a racist society. But they are incompatible with that image and therefore must be ignored, discounted, or denied by those people who retain it. To that image the burgeoning of black slums may be acceptable but not the simultaneous and rapid rise of a black "middle class" in which, according to Wattenberg and Scammon, slightly more than one-half of all Negro families are now enrolled. On this "enormous progress" of the 1960–1971 period, "a blanket of silence seems to envelop the liberal community" (33).

Moynihan is more blunt. Within a large sector of American opinion, everything *must* be getting worse. A "mounting radical criticism of American society" derives from concerns "only marginally related to poverty and race." Poverty and race have been seized upon "for understandable strategic reasons." The media, he says, are "sensitized" to such a view, and thus have failed to report what has happened (34). As for the slum dwellers who *can* be fitted to a racist image, there is "little serious analysis" being devoted to "the presence of welfare income as an alternative to earnings" in the deepening "pathology" of their family life (35). "Reasoned discussion" is not taking place; there has been a "failure of enquiry."

Reasoned discussion of the black condition is not taking place because black failures and successes are ignored or denied in those circles where reasoned discussion traditionally has taken place. They are ignored or denied for the same reason, to preserve untarnished the image of a racist society. As for the failure of enquiry, Moynihan admits to a small measure of personal responsibility. Work of his in the early sixties which interpreted the slum black-family situation as the result of factors other than racism was attacked as a racist argument. Had he known that his prophecy of deepening underclass conditions would prove to be as correct as it did, he says, "I might have said nothing, realizing that the subject would become unbearable, and rational discussion close to impossible. I accept that in social science some things are better not said" *(36)*.

The place and condition of blacks in American society is only one of several issues about which candor is now inexpedient and open discussion almost impossible. A social science professor at Harvard says that in 1972 the list of subjects that could not be publicly discussed in a free and open forum included "the war in Vietnam, public policy toward urban ghettos, the relationship between intelligence and heredity, and the role of American corporations in certain overseas regimes" *(37)*. People who disputed the orthodox position on these subjects at Harvard (and elsewhere) were either prevented from speaking or subjected to harassment.

INTERESTS AND POWER

Images of self and other, and their attendant attitudes, are what social problems are all about. Images and attitudes, however, are not spun out of themselves. While they may be almost invulnerable to "rational persuasion," they are informed and to a lesser extent guided by ideas, as was shown in Chapter 2. But images and attitudes are much more affected by the rhythm of harmony and clash of interests which characterizes all societies, a rhythm which is ultimately controlled by the exercise of power or the threat of its use.

All Interests Not in Harmony

The concept of interests is not an easy one to deal with. There is a possibly universal tendency to identify one's own interests with personal desire. But personal desire can contract as well as expand. A combined system of power distribution and moral containment prevails in all societies, within which men define their own interests as well as pursue them. Thus when centralized government over a period of time assumes increasing control, as has happened in all industrialized countries regardless of ideology, most men will accede to that control. They come to define their own interests within limits which would, in a previous era, have been resisted. And also while most men attempt to make money, now as always they accept moral limits, so that Willie Sutton's classic reply to the question why he robbed banks ("Because that's where the money is") would not occur to them.

But to whatever extent men voluntarily, or involuntarily, restrict the definition of their interests, their interests are never identical. Certain interests, to be sure, are common to all citizens of a given country and even to all human beings who inhabit the planet. Universal interests, however, are not the ones of which we are generally aware. We all pay more attention to diverse and clashing interests, at least the dramatic ones with which politicians, lawyers, labor leaders, newspapermen, educators, and clergymen deal. But there are many clashes of interest which are rarely acknowledged by public spokesmen.

An increase in a public-library budget, for example, may make more books available to the public, but that may be small comfort to the taxpayer whose reading is restricted to the sports pages of his daily newspaper and the racing form. A quiet household after the evening meal may be absolutely essential to the well-being of an exhausted husband and father, while his small children may find their enforced inactivity unbearable. Laws to protect householders interfere with the occupation of burglary. A moral crusade can reduce the profits of some and render life less enjoyable for others. An era of prosperity, combined with technical expertise and easy and free access to technical training, may be in the clear interest of the majority, but it diminishes the opportunity of the modern unemployed poor to blame either ill luck or the "system." When the house in which an old couple are living out their retirement years is bulldozed by "eminent domain" so that a state highway can be run through their preempted land, that enterprise may be in the interest of contractors, politicians, oil companies, possibly motorists, but surely not in the interest of the old couple.

Every social order, constantly and by necessity, thwarts interests as these would be defined by various individuals and groups. Such frustration may be accepted without question by the weak, the uncaring, and the unknowing. But it is in some measure experienced by all. They are either reconciled to frustration by the morality they accept, or they are made to fear the threat of punishment.

Individual awareness of having interests separate from those of many other people is a state of affairs commonly viewed with suspicion. The very term is generally pejorative in context; "interests," in print, is usually qualified with the adjective "selfish." The underlying moral assumption is that all interests should be in harmony. That is why, in public discourse, attempts are always made to persuade others of what their interests *really* are, apart from what these others may perceive their own interests to be. Efforts to designate social problems, and to resolve them, invariably feature appeals to an assumed "common interest."

Interest Manipulation

At any given moment in time, however, the interests of any individual or group or segment of the population *are* what they themselves preceive them to be. An interest, like an image of the other, is ultimately private—no matter the extent to which either may be shared with others. All attempts to define for others what their interests *really* are have nothing to do with either science or rationality; they are exercises in manipulation and propaganda. This circumstance is one important reason why sociologists cannot promote this or that social problem. They are social scientists. As such, they abandon their own calling if they join the other manipulators of social-problem consciousness who face a clash of immediate interests while they proclaim a harmony of long-term or ultimate interests.

Propaganda, one-sided exaggeration of a public issue in emotional terms, does nevertheless have an inevitable place. Without propaganda, no social problem could ever become widely recognized. Propaganda, oftentimes but not always admixed with coercion, must first have persuaded a varying number of nonbelievers that a social problem exists and *it is in their interest* to do something about it. The need to secure this base of ideational support sacrifices "rational discourse" to a combination of cajolery and threat aimed at the assumed interests of those addressed.

Notable examples have been the reports of Presidential or Advisory Commissions on Race or Pornography or Civil Disorders. They invariably warn of drastic personal consequences that will befall those who fail to acknowledge a social problem as it is defined for them. Unless something much more is done about the black slums at once, riots of unprecedented scale will bring total holocaust. The National Commission on the Causes and Prevention of Violence urged that $20 billion of additional money be spent each year for "general welfare" in order to prevent "a rising tide of individual and group violence." Unless live sex shows and bottomless waitresses are permitted, censorship of one's daily newspaper looms. And "the possibility of the misuse of general obscenity statutes prohibiting distributions of books and films to adults constitutes a continuing threat to the free communication of ideas among Americans—one of the most important foundations of our liberties," according to the Commission on Obscenity and Pornography.

In a similar way, ecological crusaders warn of a literal wasteland, silent of bird song, affording only poisoned food and water, unless this or that remedial measure is taken at once. And advocates of population control draw trend lines to standing room only in a few decades, unless people stop having babies. Opponents who seek to arouse resistance to propaganda of this kind utilize counterpropaganda; they, too, employ the rhetoric of crisis. ZPG has been called a plot designed by wealthy educated whites to reduce the number of black births. Ecology has been called "the new false face of socialism." We have been warned by some people that unless welfare allotments are curtailed we will all be reduced to poverty, and by others that unless the flood of pornography is dammed at once a rising number of encouraged and incited rapists will defy law enforcement.

No blanket dismissal of these various, and opposed, conclusions should be inferred. Note only should be made of a struggle for men's minds which bears little resemblance to either scientific endeavor or a scholarly seminar. Actually, such all-or-nothing pronouncements and lurid threats to assumed majority interests by political-intellectual minorities, and by their opponents, are probably essential in order to secure attention from a public whose attention span is brief and easily distracted to other objects and concerns.

Most often, however, pronouncements of this kind do not succeed, if their purpose, beyond securing attention, is to mobilize action at a single unified point. There are conflicts of interest within persons as well as across categories of persons. One man may agree that censorship of pornography does carry the danger of fostering censorship in other areas, yet remain convinced that the threat of pornography to public morality, especially what he may regard as the victimization of unsophisticated adolescents, poses a graver danger—and he may also patronize X-rated films. Another may accede to the proposition that more government aid for blacks might serve to reduce those tensions which produce destructive riots, but remain reluctant to pay the price of a higher tax rate. The attitudes of many people toward ecology are in a similar bind about the question, Who pays what price?

One's personal interest in a given social problem may be seen as being threatened by any shifting of attention to another social problem. Many black spokesmen, for example, have expressed resentment of the ecology and population-growth crusades as schemes designed to distract attention from black interests and short-change them. An expert on environmental design has been cited in such a way as to lend support to that charge: ". . . to a large extent the poor pay the bills for environmental cleanups, in which they have less interest than the middle class beneficiaries" (38).

Material and Ideal Interests

Interests are usually, and mistakenly, equated with material interests alone. Although in social action a diversity of motivations fuse, interests can be analytically separated into material and ideal ones. Ideal interests are less visibly attached to personal advantage; they primarily serve to enhance or flatter the self-image, instead of augment or protect income, position, power, or convenience, as is the case with material interests. Generally speaking, political-intellectual minorities express ideal interests in the promotion of change, the majority in the preservation of tradition. On balance, however, political-intellectual minorities far surpass the majority in the expression of ideal interests. The historic role of political-intellectual minorities was first established in areas devoid of personal material interest, such as insistence upon humanitarian treatment of the insane and imprisoned criminals. In neither these nor most subsequent like cases was any spontaneous demand for change manifested by the majority.

According to Max Weber, "interests (both material and ideal) and not ideas directly determine the conduct of men." The key phrase is "directly determine." Weber does not mean that ideas are mere epiphenomena in the course of history. He means that at the moment of social interaction ideas function mainly to subserve interests of both kinds, or, as amended, to subserve perceived interests of both kinds as they are screened through images and their attendant attitudes.

There are many ideas which are widely shared and virtually unquestioned, such as democracy and humanitarianism, but men state and act out their own rationalizations of them. Democracy can be interpreted as demanding "social justice" for selected categories of persons, alternatively as requiring disciplined self-reliance of all citizens. In the first case, the ideal interests of reformers and the material interests of potential beneficiaries are served; in the latter, the ideal interests of traditionalists and their own obvious material interest. Humanitarianism, the stated obligation to help distant others, can be, often is, interpreted in similar variant ways. For example, humanitarianism has been said to require abolition of punishment for "so-called" criminals. Alternatively, humanitarianism has been invoked to protect potential "innocent victims of crime" by putting "mad dogs in the streets in jail and throwing away the key."

What Power Is

"The course of historical development," according to Professor Popper, "is never shaped by theoretical constructions." It is always "the resultant of the momentary constellation of contesting forces" (39). One of these contesting forces is interests, another a struggle to define the moral basis of social life, discussed below, and still another is power, the final arbiter of human affairs.

The relationship between interests and power is a close one. An interest without power to make itself effectively known can only be pious wish, and likely to prove futile. Interests become effective in the social struggle to the extent that they can be used, at least as threats, to harm others or to upset their comfortable routine and habit systems. It is power which enables someone to initiate action either "to protect his interests under new external conditions or simply to promote them more effectively under existing conditions" (40). In somewhat oversimplified terms, any social order is maintained by compliance with moral limits set by shared images and attitudes, while it is moved by power and shifts of power.

Power has been frequently, mistakenly, identified with force and with authority. Power is distinct from force, that is, physical coercion. When employed by an individual for his own purposes, force has been invariably treated as an illegitimate criminal act. The only strictly legitimate force, as Max Weber pointed out, is exercised in the collective name of the state. There have been, of course, emergent gray areas in modern America, where from time to time striking union members, rioting students, rioting blacks, and property-seizing Indians have been granted special quasi-immunities from prosecution when they have used group force.

Power is likewise distinct from authority. Authority has no reality "save in the memberships and allegiances of the members of an organization, be this the family, a political association, the church, or the university" (41). The essential relationship between instructor and student, for example, is one of authority, an authority vested in the instructor's status *only* as a consequence of his presumed superior knowledge of a particular subject which presumably the student is motivated to study. Any power accruing from that position of authority is rigidly limited, and easily destroyed by those who care to dispute it for any number of institutionally acceptable reasons.

Then what is power? Simply the extent of capability to control others so that they will do what they are wanted to do. Power is relative. The ordinary citizen has much less power than labor bosses and politicians, but citizenship itself confers power, in the form of legal and political rights which are denied to aliens. And since power is relative, its location and extent are not easily specified, especially in modern America, where power may be as diffused as that in any other industrialized society.

This last point cannot be demonstrated, mainly because an image of some monolithic power structure which imposes its arbitrary will upon a helpless citizenry is so widely held. To reiterate at some considerable risk of wearying the reader, an image cannot be disproved. On the other hand, in the next chapter the lack of uniformity in that particular image *is* demonstrated. If argument continues over who or what comprises the power structure, and those accused of having the power in turn accuse their accusers of having the power, then at least the suspicion may be raised that one notable feature about power in modern America is its diffusion.

With or without relative diffusion, however, power is never equally shared. The continuity of institutions, such as the family, state, division of labor, alone ensures that some will more control others than they will be controlled. And power *itself* can neither be destroyed nor dissipated. On the other hand, any specific power can be wrested or transferred. Massive *shifts* of power can and do occur in time.

Business Power

Consider the late-nineteenth-century capitalist freebooters, who ruled a pretty big roost. One of them, Dan'l Drew, as unpleasant a crook as ever tipped a poor box, sent thousands of men to the financial wall, and then endowed a theological seminary, possibly as fire insurance. He once remarked that the law was a spider web that caught little flies and let big bees fly through. He knew whereof he spoke. Dan'l and his Erie Railroad playmates, Jay Gould and Jim Fisk, bought judges and bribed legislators and got laws passed that provided them with plenty of nectar. These were men who, in Boss Plunkitt's words, "seen their opportunities and took 'em," who committed many offenses but were never guilty of hesitation.

Men like Schwab, Morgan, Rockefeller, and Vanderbilt by no means controlled everything, but they controlled enough so that political leaders came to them for aid and advice. They never made a trek to Washington, a journey "big businessmen" now take in order to learn what they may and may not do. For the most part, and despite the angry muckrakers of the period, their considerable power went unchallenged, on ideological as well as legal grounds. Dominant attitudes at that time included respect for capital accumulation as being in everyone's interest. More than it was attacked, capital accumulation was deemed to be an indispensable source for providing jobs.

The men who run modern corporations are a different breed. These hired managers of companies they do not own, which are owned by distant, faceless stockholders, in comparative terms have been stripped of power. Their decisions are hedged in by the power of big government and of big labor as they face a hostile ideological climate. Their prices, markets, and attempts to merge operations and territories are regulated by government agencies, their hiring and firing practices by unions. The law, in response to structural changes, a discussion of which would take us far afield, was the chief instrument which reduced their freedom to operate, and the law expanded union power (42).

These "facts," of course, are more often disputed than affirmed. The dominant public image of big business remains one of enormous, unchecked, monolithic power. Whether the considerable power which does remain there is "too much" or not is a judgment of images and their attendant attitudes. Perhaps another "fact" is less open to question: compared with their nineteenth-century counterparts, modern business managers are cautious, defensive, timid. They do not see themselves as wielding power of decisive consequence. The most frequent theme expressed in their trade journals and get-togethers is one of querulous worry about their own public image. They tell one another that the public must be informed about what they are doing in the public interest, informed how low profit margins really are and of the social need for profit to expand capital investment and create jobs. They plead a firm commitment to "social responsibility" in such areas as race relations, ecology, higher education. These public relations efforts can of course be fitted into an adverse image of manipulators hoodwinking the gullible public while they gently pull the same old power strings. But at the very least, note that Dan'l Drew never talked in any such fashion. He never had to.

The specification of social problems at one time for the most part cohered with the values endorsed by or associated with men of big business. The old "missionary approach," discussed in Chapter 2, quite obviously did so. The concern for social problems expressed by modern men of big business is quite different; it is a defensive reaction to pressure from outside, to power from outside. Those who now have ideological control of social problems assign much of the blame for social problems to the men, or villains, of big business.

Intellectual Power

"He who has the bigger stick has the better chance of imposing his definitions of reality" (43). Precisely who has the bigger stick remains open to argument. The definitions of reality about social problems, however, are now clearly in the charge of intellectuals, that majority of intellectuals who stand opposed to big business, more as it once was than it now is.

At least in the perspective of what big business once was, it is an odd circumstance that modern corporate managers tend to acquiesce in rather than reject the intellectuals' definitions of reality. Educated men whose primary role is granted less legitimacy than in the recent past, in general they identify much more with intellectuals than do the majority. Witness, for example, the activities of the Ford and Rockefeller Foundations, the broadcasts sponsored by the Xerox Corporation, and the advertising of the Gulf Oil Corporation. If power is the extent of capability to control others so that they will do what they are wanted to do, then intellectuals have become more powerful than ever they were in the past.

Even though the drift has long been in evidence, the tilt was sudden. As recently as the early fifties, the so-called McCarthy era found intellectuals in academe and the media, especially in Hollywood, assailed by a popular anti-Communist crusade which accused with little examination of affiliation or complicity, in many cases with no examination at all. On several campuses *all* professors formed in a reluctant line to sign a "loyalty oath" in order to save their jobs.

Besides a fear of Russian aggrandizement there was among the majority a widespread suspicion that intellectuals were "disloyal," either because they were Communist agents or because they failed to endorse traditional values. Many more people besides Senator McCarthy failed to distinguish between spies and skeptics. How many more we do not know, but the temper of the period was one of widespread fear, suspicion, and resentment. In that climate, concerns about race and poverty and the like were temporarily eclipsed, and so was the power of the intellectuals.

By the late sixties that power was more than restored; in the area of social problems it was preeminent. Consider the key images of America celebrated in movies of the forties and early fifties: a kaleidoscope of Mom, the flag revered and American arms triumphant, the individual winning against the odds, virtue real and virtue rewarded, blacks and browns rarely encountered but always contented and complaisant, and misguided intellectuals forced to admit that they prefer swing to Bach. The common man was no member of an importunate and ridiculous silent majority; he was proclaimed to represent, along with beer, baseball, and Brooklyn, all that was right and trustworthy about America. Then reflect upon the key movie images of America today, which incorporate, in revision of

Lionel Trilling's phrase, an adversary pop culture. Possibly trivial at first consideration, the shift really does reflect a newly emergent power to define what is right and wrong and affirm what social problems are and how they should be handled.

In part, that power is a function of the vast increase in the number of intellectuals, or perhaps quasi-intellectuals, indicated by the college enrollments of the fifties and sixties. Movie scripts, as well as book and magazine marketing strategies, were soon geared to an audience assumed to be estranged from Mom and all she represented. "In an educated society reality is increasingly defined as that which the principal media of communication—including universities—recognize" (44).

THE MORAL CONTEXT

We have seen that many factors—divergent images, intransigent attitudes, the dubious place of "facts" in the determination of policy, and shifts of power while interests clash—leave little if any room for rational discourse in social-problem discussion. There is, finally, still another factor: the invariable and unavoidable moral context of any social-problem discussion. Any attempt to designate a social problem and specify the means to solve or meliorate it also states or at least implies a moral judgment, a moral judgment which fails to convince all others.

When discussing social problems even social scientists can hardly avoid blending moral with positive statements *(45)*. We have already noted that sociologists disagree among themselves about their right to propose goals of social action. But even if they all did agree that sociology is limited to devising technical means in order to achieve goals set by others, it would still remain difficult to ensure that those means would not imply a moral judgment and become embroiled in moral disputation.

Within any social order many ends are simultaneously being pursued, some of which are incompatible or in conflict with other ends. The most efficient, immediate, and technical means which might be advised to achieve one end are those most likely to compromise another. For example, not long ago a social scientist correctly affirmed that "race prejudice" is transmitted within the family. To break this connection, he advised the removal of all children from parental homes for enrollment in integrated government boarding schools where no racial epithets would ever be heard. Any attempt to enforce such means to achieve that generally favored goal would, of course, be perceived as a threat to much more highly prized ends.

Suppose the given end is that of lowering the rate of recidivism. Since some categories of convicted persons have a high probability of recidivism and others a low one, the most direct and technically efficient means to achieve that goal would apply the recidivism-probability tables developed by sociologists in order to determine whether one person should be imprisoned and another paroled. But any such attempt to lower the rate of recidivism would violate more important ends, of which justice is preeminent; justice, although undefinable, remains one of those ultimate ends upon which the continuity of any social order rests.

If the given end of lowering the rate of recidivism were still granted top priority, then the youngest offenders should be imprisoned the longest, especially those who are black and have a narcotics history, because the statistical probability of their continuing to run afoul of the law is very high. On the other hand, whites over forty who are guilty of murder or rape should receive minimal sentences because the statistical probability that they will repeat their offenses is extremely low *(46)*. To such a modest proposal, which no one has made, the near-universal reaction would be one of revulsion. Technically appropriate for a logical conclusion, it has one drawback: Who would regard it as anything other than immoral?

REFERENCES

1 Vilfredo Pareto held that most activities in agriculture, industry, commerce, and the technical sciences are rationally pursued, in the sense that the goals are "real" and not "transcendental," and demonstrably effective means are applied to achieve them. Most activities in these areas are free of the moral and ideological disputation to which social problems are subject.

2 Crane Brinton, *A History of Western Morals,* Harcourt, Brace, New York, 1959, p. 310.

3   Helmut Schoeck, *A Theory of Social Behavior,* Harcourt, Brace & World, New York, 1969, especially pp. 205–206 and 326–327. While envy, in this view, explains the promoter of humanitarian causes, guilt and a ubiquitous fear of the evil eye (the envy of those the promoter describes as victims) explains the person manipulated by the promoter.

4   Arnold W. Green, "The Nature of Man and Personal Responsibility," *Modern Age,* Spring 1973, pp. 183–194.

5   David Hume, *A Treatise of Human Nature,* 3 vols., Oxford University Press, London, 1960 (reprinted from the original edition of 1739). Book II, *Of the Passions,* p. 377.

6   Hume, reference 5, Book III, *Of Morals,* p. 280.

7   Hume, reference 5, Book III, *Of Morals,* p. 481.

8   Max Weber, *Max Weber on Law in Economy and Society,* Edward Shils and Max Rheinstein (trans.), Max Rheinstein (ed.), Harvard, Cambridge, Mass., 1954, p. 75.

9   Cited in Alan Montefiore, *A Modern Introduction to Moral Philosophy,* Routledge, London, 1958, p. 109.

10   Thomas S. Kuhn, *The Structure of Scientific Revolutions,* University of Chicago Press, Chicago, 1962.

11   Arthur Koestler, *The Sleepwalkers,* Macmillan, New York, 1959, chap. 8.

12   Compare Gwynn Nettler, *Explanations,* McGraw-Hill, New York, 1970, especially pp. 92–95; and Gustav Ichheiser, *Appearances and Realities,* Jossey-Bass, San Francisco, 1970, especially pp. 142–146.

13   Frank E. Hartung, "Methodological Assumption in a Social-Psychological Theory of Criminality," *Journal of Criminal Law, Criminology and Police Science,* **45**:652–661, 1955.

14   Jerry D. Rose, "The Role of the Other in Self-Evaluation," *The Sociological Quarterly,* **10**: 470–479, 1969.

15   The relationship between self and self-image is actually much more complex than one of incessant self-congratulation. We are more kind to ourselves than others are, but also we can be more severe in judgment. While the self flatters itself with a self-image deemed to approach an ego ideal, the self remains aware of the gap between itself and that ideal, an awareness which is the chief basis for self-blame.

     Even though we know ourselves better than we know any other, it has been argued that if we have reason to blame ourselves, there is no reason to exempt others from blame. "The more deeply we investigate the course of our own conduct, the more blameworthy our behavior may seem to us to be, the more remorse we may be disposed to feel; and if this holds for ourselves, it is not reasonable to expect us necessarily, and in all cases, to withhold it from others." Pages 58–59 of Isaiah Berlin, *Historical Inevitability,* Oxford University Press, London, 1954.

16 There is one possible and quite rare exception: a love relationship of long duration, of sustained mutual willingness to make the inferred means of delighting the other almost an integral part of the self. In such a case identification can become so close, the welfare of each so indissolubly blended with that of the other in loyalty and respect, that the "normal" barriers cited can be said to disappear. Such a union of self and other, according to David Hume, is not possible on the grand scale: "In general, it may be affirm'd, that there is no such passion in human minds, as the love of mankind, merely as such, independent of personal qualities, of services, or of relation to ourself."

17 Peter L. Berger and Thomas Luckmann, *The Social Construction of Reality,* Anchor Books, Doubleday, Garden City, N. Y. (originally published by Doubleday in 1966), 1967, p. 104.

18 Kenneth E. Boulding, *The Image,* Ann Arbor Paperbacks, University of Michigan Press, Ann Arbor, Mich., 1961 (originally published by University of Michigan Press in 1956), pp. 11–12. Professor Boulding also rejects the idea that discovery and technical change precede or cause the formation of images. "Columbus would never have thought to set sail westward had he not had an image of the round world, and a high value in his system for spices" (p. 122). And all the horse collars in the world "did not suffice to abolish slavery until the image of a free society became dominant" (p. 121).

19 Gustav Ichheiser, *Appearances and Realities,* Jossey-Bass, San Francisco, 1970, p. 62.

20 The classifications discussed in this chapter apply only to collectivities, such as criminals, the poor, and so on, because only these are germane to social problems. Another type of classified image occurs in role attribution, which is vastly more important in social life considered in its entirety. What people "are" and their roles as teacher, priest, mother, officer, and so on, are not, cannot be, distinguished by the people who approach and deal with them in roles paired, for example, with the above roles, such as student, parishioner, son and enlisted man.

21 Eliot Aronson and Burton W. Golden, "The Effect of Relevant and Irrelevant Aspects of Communicator Credibility on Opinion Change," *Journal of Personality,* **30:**135–146, 1962.

22 Psychologists who specialize in the investigation of attitudes generally ignore the clustering phenomenon (which to a sociologist is the most significant aspect of attitudes—see the next chapter), and seek to refine techniques for measuring isolated responses. One notable exception, who combines both endeavors, is Leonard W. Ferguson, *Personality Measurement*, McGraw-Hill, New York, 1952, especially pp. 111–114; see also pp. 121–122.

23 James Baldwin, *Notes of A Native Son*, Beacon Press, Boston, 1955, p. 25.

24 S. L. A. Marshall, *Crimsoned Prairie*, Scribner, New York, 1972, p. 243.

25 Melvin L. Kohn, "Bureaucratic Man: A Portrait and an Interpretation," *American Sociological Review*, 36:461–474, 1971, p. 472. The author does, however, assert that bureaucrats generally are not given "as much occupational self-direction as their educational attainments and the needs of the work allow."

26 Irving Kristol, "Is the American Worker 'Alienated'?" *Wall Street Journal*, Jan. 18, 1973, p.12. Images aside, Professor Kristol cannot establish, as is his evident intent, that the American worker is really not alienated. In some degree everyone past and present was and remains dissatisfied with his lot, disgruntled about the conditions of his work. On the other hand, "alienation" is a kind of free-floating image looking for ideological anchorage in some other; the context of its employment can become a weapon aimed at the entire social order.

27 The old warning about a people being doomed to repeat that history they will not learn is futile. The "lessons of the past" have never had corrective value for images of desires satisfied in the future by political fiat.

28 Such "understanding" does not invoke Christ's message of peace, to love one another, which requires sacrifice of all worldly things and desires. Instead it apparently assumes that sheer knowledge about nonpolitical others *within* the world as it is will dissuade national-state decision makers from seeking political-economic advantage at the expense of other national-state decision makers.

29 Irving Kristol, "An Urban Civilization without Cities?" *Horizon*, Autumn 1972, pp. 36–41. There is an alternative possibility, really conjecture, to the transference of urban civilization from the central city to its outer environs which Kristol foresees: that we are facing one of those periodic breakdowns of civilization, the manifestations of which are initially appearing in places where numbers stand at maximum agglomeration.

30 *U. S. News & World Report*, Apr. 9, 1973, p. 42.

31 Ben J. Wattenberg and Richard M. Scammon, "Black Progress and Liberal Rhetoric," *Commentary*, April 1973, pp. 35–44, p. 39. Figures cited in this and the previous paragraph of the text are taken from this source.

32 Daniel P. Moynihan, "The Schism in Black America," *The Public Interest,* Spring 1972, pp. 3–24, pp. 9 and 10.

33 Wattenberg and Scammon, reference 34, p. 42.

34 For a documentation of Moynihan's claim, see Carl Gershman, "The 'Times' Op-Ed Page: Both Ends against the Middle," *Commentary,* April 1973, pp. 45–51.

35 Moynihan, reference 32, p. 17.

36 Moynihan, reference 32, p. 7. His being accused of racism is an example of a frequent occurrence: a person who presents data which are unpopular with a given audience is accused of advocating the situation he describes.

37 James Q. Wilson, "Liberalism versus Liberal Education," *Commentary,* June 1972, pp. 50–54, p. 51. Wilson's list was later expanded to include ecology, the condition of women, and the moral or medical character of homosexuality. These "have been demanding inclusion on the index of settled issues." Norman Podhoretz, "The New Inquisitors," *Commentary,* April 1973, pp. 7–8, p. 8. This magazine editor locates "new inquisitors" off as well as on campus, notably in book and magazine publishing.

38 Edward Pohlman (ed.), *Population: A Clash of Prophets,* Mentor Books, New American Library, New York, 1973, p. 204.

39 Karl R. Popper, *The Poverty of Historicism,* Beacon Press, Boston, 1957, p. 47.

40 Weber, reference 8, p. 385.

41 Robert A. Nisbet, "The Twilight of Authority," *The Public Interest,* Spring 1969, pp. 3–9, p. 5.

42 Roscoe Pound, "Legal Immunities of Labor Unions," in Edward H. Chamberlain et al., *Labor Union and Public Policy,* American Enterprise Association, Washington, D. C., 1958, pp. 122–173.

43 Berger and Luckmann, reference 17, p. 109.

44 James Hitchcock, "The Intellectuals and the People," *Commentary,* March 1973, pp. 64–69, p. 64.

45 Boulding (reference 18, p. 21) claims that in the human world of symbols any separation of positive and normative statements is impossible. Berger and Luckmann (reference 17, p. 109), go almost as far. There is "usually a continuity between the explanatory and exhortatory schemes, which serve as legitimizations on the lowest theoretical level, and the imposing intellectual constructions that expound the cosmos. The relationship between cognitive and normative conceptualization . . . is empirically fluid; normative conceptualizations always imply certain cognitive presuppositions."

46 Martin A. Levin, "Crime and Punishment and Social Science," *The Public Interest*, Spring 1972, pp. 96–103, p. 102. Levin argues that the "tension" among the goals served by our penal and judicial systems "cannot be resolved on utilitarian grounds." He further observes that social science cannot prescribe our values for us. "What it does seem able to do—for better or worse—is to reveal to us the practical incompatibilities between the many values we accept. This is a thankless task—but not, perhaps, entirely useless."

Social Problems: Arena for Hip and Square

The main theme of the previous chapter, that rational persuasion plays a very minor role in the history of social problems, can be stated in another way. The balance of the social forces cited—notably power, interests, and images and their attendant attitudes—ensures that what happens in the case of any social problem will really satisfy few if any people. In a democratic society, the balance of social forces invariably produces a compromise of any social-reform issue, to which opponents perforce reconcile themselves, at least temporarily.

Only a totalitarian "solution" can so focus attention, effort, and collective action as to create an overriding issue, but that solution will draft social-problem concern to the service of a minority who seize power, and it will eliminate the forum of discussion and the field of maneuver. Moreover, a seizure of total power, whether

Communist or Fascist, is immediately followed by a destruction of the ideological purists who propagated the faith. The revolution always swallows its own children. Whatever social-problem solutions they died for are sacrificed to the expansion of totalitarian power.

Life in a democracy also presents difficulties, albeit less critical ones. The maintenance of social-problem consciousness, of a forum for defining and seeking ways to improve upon existing social arrangements, apparently requires two seeming contradictions. First, a high degree of value consensus must prevail among a population. Otherwise, compromise is impossible. Second, that consensus must remain conditional. Otherwise, democracy is destroyed.

Preservation of democracy depends upon widespread yet limited commitment, and checked as well as delegated power, in order to contain, *but not overtly resolve,* the tensions of contesting wills, attitudes, and interests. Such resolution is possible only within totalitarian regimes. On the other hand, a sudden and marked *polarization* of these tensions can so strip away inner controls and release power from its shackles as to create a demand for a totalitarian solution.

How serious the polarization now occurring within American society may be, what it will produce beyond itself, no one can tell. A question of this kind can be answered only retrospectively. But in cautious assessment, a totalitarian solution does not appear imminent. Polarization of intransigent degree has so far occurred only between militant squares and hip extremists. The majority, who are essentially nonideological squares, remain faithful to tradition within change, and pay less attention to the battle raging over their heads than those on either side who seek to engage their attention might wish.

IDENTITY OF OPPONENTS

Analysis of modern social problems must consider this recent polarization of attitudes, lest several critical issues go unexamined. Which side is defining and promoting a given social problem? Whose egos and life-styles are going to be symbolically vindicated, whose undermined, in the process? Is anybody winning? If so, what?

C. P. Snow described a confrontation between two "cultures," science and technology on one side and literary humanism on the other. In at least as rigorous a sense as Snow employed, another confrontation is taking place between two cultures, hip and square. And while neither the precise numbers nor the positive identities of the adversaries can be stated, sufficient information is available to sketch in broad outlines on both counts.

Hip-Square Numbers

The numbers game has become a popular sport, especially guesses about what proportion of the adult population comprise the disaffected, the renunciators, the adversary culture, the counterculture, the elite culture—all terms subsumed under the hip designation. With polling techniques as well as guesses, assigned proportions vary from 1 to 15 percent. Although exact numbers remain elusive in a milieu of rapid change, available evidence does suggest that the hip contingent has been growing in size, and more significantly, in influence.

Out of one detailed study emerged "a portrait of two divergent streams in America . . . called the Silent Minority and the Liberal Coalition." The latter is composed of countercultural protesting activists, who oppose "law-and-order and the established agents of social control," who are estimated to make up about 12 percent of the public. The Silent Minority, who stand vehemently opposed to all that the Liberal Coalition represent, are reckoned to make up about 16 percent. "The vast majority [are] in the middle" (1).

These figures are as good as any other obtainable estimate for assigning numbers to the hip and militant-square contingents, which are constantly shifting within a narrow range of whatever imprecise description may be employed (2). Exception can be taken, however, with placing the majority at the middle. Their attitudes veer much closer to one end of the range than the other. The majority, for example, surely do not stand in the middle on the law-and-order issue. Although occasionally displaced by worries about money, concern for physical safety has remained at or near the top on every recent poll. In a 1972 Gallup poll, at the head of a long list of government-spending priorities stood "combating crime" (3).

The Square Majority

The vast majority of Americans are, and remain, cultural squares, even though they are much less embattled than their militant confreres. In Professor Devine's assessment, their fealty to the Lockean liberal tradition has remained unshaken, a claim he ingeniously supports by juxtaposing the basic propositions of John Locke and the Founding Fathers with recent opinion-poll results. It matters little that less than 20 percent of American adults can name the three branches of government; a majority of undiminishing size continue to affirm a reverence for that Constitution they have never read. They state Declaration of Independence beliefs, in liberty, equality (liberty more than equality), property, religion, and the vested right to pursue happiness via the route of equal opportunity.

Devine says that they continue to follow Locke and the liberal tradition in favoring mixed sovereignty and legislative predominance over the executive branch of government. They support the right of free speech over that of any other political value reported. And their agreement with Locke that the individual is more important than the state stands in marked contrast with responses secured in Mexico and Italy.

A sense of national identity is much stronger in this country than in other Western nations. Fewer Americans have any desire to settle elsewhere. Americans are notably proud of their political institutions, and given to expect equality of treatment before the law. "For both sense of national identity and sense of community identity the United States ranks higher than any of the other countries for which data is [sic] available" (4).

The weakest link in the chain of continuity Devine attempts to forge is his virtual dismissal of the marked shift toward welfare-state attitudes which occurred among the majority in the later train of the New Deal. He regards that change as a response to "environmental stress," something essentially apart from the continuity of the "liberal tradition." In certain vital respects, that tradition was actually broken. Locke was surely abandoned by most of the respondents to a 1972 Gallup poll, in which Nixon as well as McGovern voters generally favored retention of wage and price controls, and 74 and 90 percent, respectively, endorsed government guarantees of jobs to everybody.

On the other hand, the attitudes of the majority, on balance, do remain with tradition. And they are no more alienated from their present than their past. A 1972 Gallup poll found 74 percent of Americans to be satisfied with their housing situation, 78 percent with their standard of living, and 84 percent with the work they do. These responses are higher than those secured in similar polls taken in preceding years. The majority appear reasonably content, and yet satisfaction with personal life and optimism about their personal future accompanies a growing disquiet about the general social and political situation. Basic satisfaction with American institutions has been offset by an ebbing of confidence in the future of the country (5). Whatever "alienation" the majority may feel stems mainly from an uneasy sense that control of events has passed into the hands of dissident elements.

The majority have been defined here as that major segment of the population who remain oriented to tradition. The majority stretch across age, sex, region, race, and socioeconomic status. At the same time, traditional attitudes are more likely to be expressed among certain categories than others: older people, those with modest educational attainment, people living in the Middle West, manual workers and union members, and Republicans (6). To this list might be added whites, especially so-called ethnics, and people of moderate rather than very high or very low incomes. But all these designations in combination do not make up the majority, because most of the people who fall into opposite categories *also* belong to the majority.

The Line of Distinction

The concepts of majority and minority here utilized are quite distinct from popular usage, which places WASPs on one side, various ethnic groups and blacks and Indians on the other. The salient dividing line, for present purpose, is that of attitude. With it, most American blacks can be assigned to the majority. Although the proportion of blacks who support traditional political and cultural values is smaller than the white, *most* blacks do affirm that support (7). Moreover, blacks are more optimistic about their own future prospects than are whites, and blacks exceed whites in a positive assessment of progress made in "handling the problem of black Americans in general" (8).

Since about 1968 public-opinion polls have disclosed that the American majority perceive the counterculture as the enemy, as an alien force which regards them as being misguided, in the way, and superfluous. Unlike militant squares, most of them may be uninterested in making a career of their opposition, but it remains firmly registered, and within the most crucial segment of the population. Eighty-nine percent of young people, aged twenty-one to twenty-nine, according to a Gallup poll taken in 1969, wanted college administrators to get tougher with protesting demonstrators on campus (9).

Social Types

What really separates hip from square are markedly divergent attitudes. Only at the extremes of an attitude range are identities clearly established. Only there do two clear-cut social types and two "camps" emerge.

It is true that hip tendencies on the one hand, square tendencies on the other, are more pronounced within some broad categories of persons than others. But these categories signify a limited probability of affiliation rather than identity or social type. For example, although most intellectuals by a long chalk are of the hip persuasion, there are some square intellectuals. Age, socio-economic status, education are other factors which cohere with the distinction between hip and square, but in quite limited and totally unpredictable ways.

Even badges and uniforms are no infallible indicators. There are hip clergymen who wear black robes and heavy crosses around their necks, and there are square clergymen who wear business suits and no professional adornment whatever. There are hip businessmen who remain in the office closet, and also bearded, long-haired, sandaled young men who follow a religious-puritanical regimen which prohibits extramarital sex and drugs, even tobacco and alcohol.

At the same time, the symbolic importance of uniforms and badges should not be totally discounted. Their very intention can be the separation of sheep from goats. In the last few years many squares have adopted shorter hairlength than heretofore, and paid more attention to the neatness and precision of their dress, for the explicit purpose of making an announcement to the world. Likewise, squares have been led to suspect that in most cases extreme hair length when combined with Halloween-type costumery exceeds an announcement, and slyly attempts a putdown.

Nevertheless, externals of appearance as well as population categories afford only clues to hip and square identities. They can only be established by declarations of states of mind, by expressed attitudes. Especially do political and social attitudes tend to cluster, not invariably so in any individual case, but markedly enough when large numbers are considered so that a polarization of hip and square attitudes, discussed later in this chapter, is clearly revealed. No one attitude, of course, is significant by itself. William F. Buckley, Jr., as one instance, may favor the legalization of marijuana, but he remains a square, a militant square. Unlike most people who agree with him on that particular score, he stands for law and order, military preparedness, control of pornography, equality of opportunity rather than equal results, the sanctity of the family, and traditional religious observance.

Generation Gap

There is a greater statistical probability that any one person aged eighteen belongs in the hip camp than does any one person aged fifty. That said, the prevalent myth about a generation gap will not bear close scrutiny. Most young people, like their elders, remain committed to the American way of life. A national study sponsored in 1969 by the Columbia Broadcasting System found that 91 percent of non-college youth and 87 percent of college youth affirmed, "American democracy can respond to needs." Respective percentages on "American way of life can solve problems," 95 and 93; "Hard work will always pay off," 79 and 56; "Right to private property is sacred," 87 and 75 (10).

In the recent past, the abhorrence of most of the young for continued American participation in the Vietnamese conflict was shared by an almost equal proportion of their elders. And this opposition, young as well as old, was for the most part nonideological, a wish for American withdrawal, not a hope for American defeat. Protest demonstrations against the war were deplored by both. "Even young people under 30—and by overwhelming majorities—condemned student strikes against the war" (11). As for the presidential election of 1972, universally interpreted as a hip-square confrontation, *college students* voted 54 to 45 in favor of McGovern, a plurality whose modesty surprised most of the pundits.

The factor of higher education, much more than that of youth, is associated with hip attitudes. The main dividing line is one "between college educated and non-college educated—both for youth and their parents" (12), even though most people in any educational as well as age category support traditional values. Blue-collar attitudes, on the other hand, appear to be little affected by the education factor. When education is held constant, young blue-collar workers remain much more antagonistic toward student and black protest activities than young white-collar employees. Young adults split wider apart on these two issues than do their elders, another indication that the greatest differences in social and political outlook lie "within the youth group rather than between age cohorts" (13).

There does appear to be a "generation gap" on the issues of sex and drugs, one that is probably less new than it is perennial. The young, on balance, have always yearned for a sexual freedom, and for some time for experimentation with chemical substances, which their elders, on balance, have disapproved. During the twenties people were not being polled on the issues of sex and bootleg booze (or any other issues for that matter), but if they had been, doubtless as wide a generation gap would have opened up as is the present case with sex and drugs. In any event, there is now a marked age disparity in attitudes toward sexual promiscuity and use of marijuana (14).

Herman Kahn views hedonistic orientation as a notable generation difference, one that appears likely to persist with sizable numbers of the modern young into middle age. Those who now identify with the counterculture are likely to remain there in spirit, he says, despite their awareness that the student insurrections of the sixties failed to accomplish very much. Kahn, along with other militant squares, retains a prejudiced conviction that The Movement never amounted to more than drugs and fornication, anyway. He further prophesies that erstwhile dissident college youth will settle down, marry, and raise children, but "somewhere between traditional America and the counterculture" *(15)*. He insists they constitute a minority of youth, even college youth, and estimates that two-thirds of Americans now in college are basically "achievement-oriented" and otherwise close to "Middle America."

If, as has been frequently asserted, American young people feel estranged from either "Middle America" or their elders, the reverse does not hold. In a recent Gallup poll, respondents aged eighteen to twenty-nine achieved a "composite score" of 69 in expression of "trust and confidence" in young people; those aged thirty to forty-nine, a score of 67; and those over fifty, a score of 65 (16). These "composite scores" measure response intensity, and thus possess added verisimilitude.

Generation Gap and the Depression

There does remain, however, a generation distinction of real significance, one which could not be tested with enumerations of answers to specific questions because it results from somewhat divergent images of the world. In that sense, a gulf does lie between Americans born before about 1930 and those born later. Most people with a *personal recollection* of the Great Depression live with a haunting dread of career disaster. They feel threatened by discontinuity. They tend to be less open to, more guarded against, the future, than those whose personal experience has been virtually uninterrupted prosperity and reliance as well as dependence upon a cocoon of institutional protection—"the government" for all of them, and parents and school as well for the young.

That assumed gulf of generation consciousness must be approached with caution. In a real sense, every person who ever lived has inhabited a world of his own experience. History starts anew with his own consciousness of that private world. And regardless of book knowledge about time before, his youth, the time of "maximum socialization," is subliminally assumed to be what will likely continue to be. This failure of imagination is universal. Young people during the thirties were as bored with parental recollections about walking ten miles to a mill job at age twelve as modern youngsters are likely to be with warnings that they had better apply themselves, finish school and get a "good job," before the next economic slump leaves them high and dry.

The message in most cases does not come through loud and clear. In abstract terms they may admit the possibility of severe environmental pressure, but they have known relative freedom from inner pressure. Thus it is that while most of the young remain more traditional in attitude and "achievement orientation" than is usually recognized, on average they are also more likely than their elders to be impatient with the way the world is run, more impatient than their elders were during the time of their own youth. They are less reserved about committing themselves, less calculating, more "idealistic," on average more concerned about helping others and defining and solving social problems, in part because they are much less concerned about erecting personal defenses against potential disaster. They remain virtually certain of continued security in a continuing present.

Social Classes

Whether or not the concept of class fits American social reality is not an issue for present consideration, mainly because hip and square assignments have nothing to do with social classes, however defined, including Marxian definition. The Russian press was reported to have had extreme difficulty in explaining to its readers the absence of the "working class" in McGovern's nomination and its strange voting behavior in the subsequent election. On the other hand, there can be no argument about the reality of socioeconomic status, nor of the tendency for education, occupation, and income to cohere. But even on this particular score, there are only superficial tendencies for hip and square contingents to line up.

Majority support for traditional cultural beliefs is found at all income and educational levels. Americans with the lowest incomes and least education identify closest with the nation, even though their affirmation of "community trust" is somewhat less than those with more on both counts (17). In a later, 1973, nationwide Gallup poll, 14 percent of college graduates indicated they would settle in another country if they could, compared with high school attendants, 11 percent, and grade school, 7 percent. Although more than three-fourths of those interviewed in a 1972 survey expressed satisfaction with "life in the United States today," those at the lower reaches of the socioeconomic ladder indicated *more* satisfaction than those higher up (18).

Any one rich American is more likely to express hip attitudes than any one middle-income American, and more likely also to be "liberal" instead of "conservative." Those with annual incomes of $15,000 and more indicate higher-than-average concern about "education, the problems of black Americans, and urban problems in general" (19). Thirty-nine percent of the delegates at the 1972 Democratic Convention held postgraduate degrees, compared with four percent of the general population, and thirty-one percent had incomes of more than $25,000 a year, compared with five percent of the general population (20).

The self-made rich are less likely to be of the hip persuasion than the hereditary rich, those "portions of the upper classes," in Jeane Kirkpatrick's phrase, who are "freed from concern with economic self-interest." The hereditary rich are said to feel guilty in an era which celebrates egalitarianism. Unlike the self-made rich, they can hardly choose to remain being the economically productive "middle-class strivers" they never were, so they live modestly and try to justify their existence with social-reform politics (21). In recent decades, such hereditary rich families as Kennedy, Roosevelt, Harriman, Rockefeller, and Ford have been prominent in social-reform politics.

Social-reform politics radically departs from the historic pattern of charitable and philanthropic enterprise, which, of course, the rich have by no means abandoned. There is, on the other hand, a historic continuity of a minor theme—that of nonstriving aristocrats feeling sympathy for and affinity with nonstrivers of low status, uniting with them in disapprobation of strivers at the middle. No such common cause emerged in the Victorian era, but it has surfaced now, as it did during Regency England and, with some qualification, during the period immediately prior to the French Revolution. Such affectations as radical chic and *nostalgie de la boue* are "meant to convey the arrogant self-confidence of the aristocrat as opposed to the middle-class striver's obsession with propriety and keeping up appearances"(22).

Very few of the white rich consider themselves to be racists, but neither do most whites of any income level. A great deal of behavior often judged to be "racist" more likely expresses a negative reaction to "people who are not like us," regardless of race. On the issue of open neighborhoods for example, blacks as well as whites are reluctant to see people of lower income and education levels than themselves move in next door. Only 29 percent of blacks, and 7 percent of whites, say they would be "happy" at the prospect of welcoming blacks of that description. But race is apparently a lesser consideration than social affinity on other grounds. Whites are "less reluctant to admit higher-status blacks than lower-status whites." While 24 percent of the white population would be "unhappy" about the addition of similar-status blacks, 37 percent feel the same way about lower-status whites moving next door (23).

Considerations of "social class," then, muddle the social problem of race relations. But those considerations have little bearing upon hip and square attitudes. Either set of attitudes can be associated with great wealth, apparently depending in some slight degree upon whether it was earned or inherited. Although the "middle class" remains a square stronghold, the hip contingent in general, the hip young in particular, are drawn from the upper-middle reaches of the socioeconomic scale. On the other hand, the modern "working class," especially those of more recent European ancestry, are quite solidly square.

No "class struggle" is being engaged. The hip outlook is really not very radical, not at all in the Marxian-revolutionary sense. Within and outside hip circles the rhetoric of revolution is often heard, but in any meaningful sense the term is misapplied. The overturn of a political-economic system is not being sought, nor is the displacement of one "class" by another. The basic hip stance remains that of social critic, not world changer. Only a "revolution of consciousness," in Reich's phrase, is celebrated. The hip camp essentially defines itself in a passively dependent way, as the stylistic obverse of what it opposes on ideological grounds.

Liberal and Conservative

The terms "liberal" and "conservative," like that of "class," afford little help in identifying the two camps. When applied today these terms are usually shorn of their historic meaning, and conjure up a wide variety of self and other images. For instance, Gallup-poll respondents in recent years have increasingly characterized themselves as conservatives; in 1972, 12 percent said they were "very conservative" and 29 percent "fairly conservative." But some reasons are stated below for not accepting such figures at their stated face value.

Modern scholarship has helped little to dispel semantic confusion. Many writers have stated that in the *absence* of a conservative tradition Lockean liberalism was and remains the basic American creed *(24)*. The nonconservatism of Locke's thought is usually attributed to his repudiation of all vestiges of feudalism. Nevertheless, his position on individual freedom guided by a "reason" which accepts traditional restraints expresses a basic tenet of conservatism, as does his rejection of government intervention in society and the economy.

There is very little affinity between Lockean and modern liberalism. Indeed, modern liberalism endorses government intervention in social as well as economic activities. And since the present American majority also welcome government intervention in the economy, if not very much elsewhere, on this one count they can more accurately be described as modern liberals than as Lockean liberals or conservatives *(25)*.

The liberal-conservative continuum is thus much more difficult to isolate than the hip-square. There is, to be sure, *some* obvious affinity between liberal (at least modern liberal) and hip attitudes on one side, square and conservative attitudes on the other. But exceptions and contradictions are so striking that only a minimal symmetry can be descried.

Many hip attitudes and positions echo conservative prejudices, especially "libertarian" (see reference 25) prejudices, such as passion for liberty, distrust of centralized power, and antipathy for military adventuring around the globe. Conservatives also will go to the mat for every adult's right to do his own thing—with the proviso that he accepts responsibility and pays for it himself. Square attitudes either depart from or express little interest in these particular concerns. On the other hand, while hip attitudes have a utopian cast, squares have no interest in utopia, and conservatives reject utopia as a dangerous illusion. These contrasting attitudes toward utopia in large measure reflect differences of stance upon the issue of man's goodness. In the hip outlook, human nature is spontaneously innocent and requires no external constraints.

Squares and Conservatism

Squares, the modern American majority, are actually neither liberal nor conservative. Their increasing tendency to regard themselves as conservatives stems from a reaction to what they perceive as license run amok combined with an ignorance of what conservatism means. They do remain social and political traditionalists for the most part, while they have become political liberals on welfare-state issues. Whereas the old conservative and liberal labels were once seen "primarily in economic terms, e.g., attitude toward social-security policy, governmental economic planning, trade-union rights, progressive tax policy, and the like, they now appear to apply more to feelings and attitudes on cultural and moral issues" (26). Perhaps the majority *could* be called modern political liberals and cultural conservatives, surely a state of logical confusion and contradiction, yet one also that is nondoctrinaire.

That rhetoric of conservatism which celebrates untrammeled freedom in the open market elicits an ambivalent response from a work force of employees. Of the 78 million nonfarm people at work in this country in 1972, 72 million were on payrolls, big-business and big-government payrolls for the most part. Their hearts occupy a place removed from their perceived interests. Far removed in circumstance from the small-entrepreneur economy of Adam Smith's and Thomas Jefferson's day, most of them still retain a fondness for the rhetoric of free enterprise, which remains almost a cultural compulsive; yet at the same time they implore government to rescue them from the operation of the open market.

Whatever the merits or demerits of the welfare state, the majority are quite likely going to continue to want its apparent benefits, especially a collective umbrella over their retirement years and protection from financial wipeout with subsidized medical care. But what they also want is the assurance of orderly change, the appearance, if only the surface appearance, of continuity with tradition. What they do not want is what they would perceive as drastic change in the rules they have come to accept as governing their own lives, particularly that of reward withheld until something is accomplished, or at least effort is made in that direction. They stand opposed to open assaults upon cultural tradition, to principled demands for institutional overhaul.

Hip Attitudes and Liberalism

The hip relationship to modern liberalism is as complex and ideologically confused as the square relationship to conservatism. In the liberal outlook, government help should be extended to bring what are labeled deprived elements of the population into the mainstream of American life; there is no quarrel with such political favoritism in the hip outlook, but at the same time in that outlook American life itself is deplorable, and those same elements should be vindicated in their present style of living as their standard of living is improved. The liberal impulse is to remove attributed causes of crime, while the hip tendency is to locate the "real criminals" within the institutional structure. And the predominant liberal value of free speech, which receives greater mass support than any other in a long list examined (27), is under attack at the extreme hip end of the attitude range.

That the traitor is more hated than the enemy is an old observation, and interestingly enough within hip circles "liberal" is more often used in a pejorative sense than "conservative." The characteristic liberal desire to use government in order to make everyone approximately alike is especially liable to hip ridicule. There is even more hip than liberal insistence upon equal rewards, but rewards accompanied by stylistic laissez faire.

Accompanying a hip distrust of government power is a contradictory wish to destroy what is left of the free market, and replace it with political coercion in order to bring about utopia, to solve problems of an ideological cast immediately. Unlike conservative, square, or liberal, the hip extremist wants essentially magical solutions. "Quite characteristically, the radical [read: hip extremist] wants it both ways—he wants services that are enormously costly in manpower, and he wants social measures that will encourage fewer people to work" (28).

Fascinating anomalies at both ends of the square-hip attitude range abound. Detestation of Communism and all its works is a pronounced attitude of squares, and yet much more than in their own country are the square values of hard work, puritanical restraint, respect for vested authority, and patriotism zealously propagated in Russia, China, Cuba. On the other hand, while segments of the hip young may idolize Mao and Fidel (although with less enthusiasm than during the late sixties), again, ironically, the entire hip phenomenon could only have arisen, and been maintained, by conditions of diffused affluence under a "soft" capitalism which confers subsidized leisure on an unprecedented scale.

Identity of Opponents

It has been shown that hip and square attitudes tend to concentrate in different segments of the population. It has also been shown that such tendencies are at best slight ones, because square attitudes predominate in all areas examined. Only among intellectuals, and, advisedly, lumpen intellectuals, are hip attitudes sharply registered. Nevertheless, a *drift* in the hip direction has been occurring during the last few years, in company of mushrooming college enrollments in the liberal arts divisions.

Again, while the confrontation between hip and square is real enough, it does not involve distinctive personality types or individuals so much as a range of attitudes. At the two extremes of that range emerge "ideal types," fictive embodiments of clustered attitudes who do not actually exist. Perhaps no one living person can be located at either of the two opposite poles, discussed below, in all detailed specifications. To illustrate: Eric Hoffer and James Burnham can fairly be characterized as militant squares, Norman Mailer and Herbert Marcuse as hip extremists; yet each of them has expressed attitudes and assumed positions which deviate to some extent from those of his fellow ideologue.

POLARITY OF ATTITUDES

Among social scientists there is no unanimity of opinion that a polarization of attitudes is occurring or is in prospect. In one view, represented by Irving Kristol, in the last decade or so a blending of attitudes has occurred. Squares are finding themselves captive to "the tradition of the new," and their resistance to a "new popular culture" is on the wane. In the opposite view, represented by Herman Kahn, a counterreformation or counter-counterculture is becoming solidified and hostile, a movement which makes a showdown imminent (29).

Neither view excludes or negates the other. An oxymoronic kind of segregated blending could occur. Hip attitudes have made and continue to make inroads at the square side of the range, and the hypothetical average square is less square than he was, say, ten years ago. However, although this state of affairs could possibly continue, or even accelerate, the division between the two camps may become no less obvious—indeed, there could even occur a sharpening of hostility between them.

The degree of animosity between nations, ethnic groups, social classes has never been a function of personal dissimilarity and cultural difference. The record shows that negative affect more often than not in history has accompanied marginal differences in outlook and behavior rather than a gulf between "us" and "them," a point expanded upon in a later chapter. Thus it is conceivable that the polarization of attitude content might lessen in intensity while attitudes on both sides became more *emotionally* polarized. Whether this or any other scenario will prove out, or even whether Kristol's or Kahn's image is the more "correct," of course, is at present a matter of conjecture.

Square Attitudes

Despite the above qualifications, a basic split between the two camps is apparent in moral standards. Each is simultaneously more and less moral than the other. Square standards of morality are traditional and personal. The square is by no means always or perhaps even most of the time honest, trustworthy, and ready to shoulder responsibility in personal relationships, but he does highly prize these attributes; he views them as what should be. Conversely, he is relatively tolerant of jobbery in politics and business, in part because he sees many secondary-group principles bent in the compromises forever being arranged in his workaday world.

Terms which elicit his positive verbal responses are "duty," "family," "self-control," "discipline," "responsibility," "decency," "patriotism." His patriotism is of the "My country . . ." variety. From time to time he may profoundly distrust his leaders, but they remain *his* leaders. Despite his apparent growing cynicism about politics and politicians, he respects authority and tends to blame foreign governments and their leaders when open, and dangerous, clashes of national interest erupt. He is also concerned about propriety and with keeping up appearances when propriety falters, whether in a marriage, a family, or a government crisis. He admires the man who can get things done, and thus he deprecates cleverness and intellectuality apart from the requirements of a job function, and this essentially pragmatic orientation prompts little interest on his part in the logical and principled consistency of the means employed to get a job done.

If young, he is more prone than his father or older brother to appreciate the idea of participation in decision making on the job and proposals for a more "wholistic" approach to job assignments, but young or old he lives by the work ethic. He invariably holds an image of himself as someone who works or who has worked hard, made his own way, played by the rules of disciplined self-control and self-help (30). Those rules he wants applied to all, or most, other adults, with a minimum of exceptions.

His attitudes toward work color his attitudes toward crime, poverty, and race. Since he holds himself responsible, accountable, for what he does, he wants no lesser standard applied to criminals, although he may be willing to see it modified in the case of juvenile delinquents. He reacts to the argument that society is responsible for crime with scorn and cynicism. He tends to regard the Supreme Court and especially the lower courts as being soft on criminals, but he does not know what to do about his own displeasure.

His world is much more one of concrete experience than abstraction. He relishes the retelling of instances of chiseling guile among the nonworking poor, and rejects the portrait of them as sanctified victims. He is infuriated at the sight of strapping youths paying for their groceries with food stamps. Anyone who can work, by God, should (31)! His humanitarianism is thus restricted and provisional, certain of expression only in cases where effort—to find work, to assume responsibility, to "do the right thing"—was made. However, he is no work-or-starve zealot and is quite willing to pay taxes for the benefit of the "deserving poor," children, the sick and disabled, the old, all those who "cannot help themselves."

The white square is often accused of being a racist. Perhaps he is, in the sense of behaving in ways unacceptable to people who are more sensitive than he is about the race issue. But the drift of his own conscious intention is away from racial prejudice. Although the Nixon-McGovern vote by no means revealed a clear square-hip split, it did represent a crude one, and in this division of opinion the race issue was not prominent. According to Gallup-poll figures gathered immediately after the election: "About the same percentage of white Nixon and white McGovern voters said they would be more likely to vote for a candidate who would improve opportunities for blacks; in each case these voters constituted a majority of more than 2–1" (32).

Nevertheless, this statement does beg questions. It is unlikely that all respondents who favored "improved opportunities" held the same image. The polling technique can muddy as well as clarify public issues, especially complex ones. In recent years the white square has increasingly come to accept, with varying degrees of enthusiasm, the notion of better opportunities for blacks—but on his own terms of equal opportunity, mainly thorough removal of impediments to individual black career aspirations. His self-image, that of a person who had to struggle to get what he has, makes him resentful of bloc preferential treatment. "My kind of people," said Eric Hoffer, "does not feel that the world owes us anything, or that we owe anybody—white, black, or yellow—a damn thing" (33).

The square, the white square as apart from the black square, it should be added, has come to terms with his own residual racial prejudice. He is unwilling to accept the burden of guilt assigned him by white intellectuals, for he is much more prejudiced against them than against blacks. He holds "them"—media people, professors, college students, judges, clergymen—primarily responsible for the public disruptions of the sixties (34).

The square tends to feel frustrated ("alienated" would be a farfetched exaggeration) in a typical way. This is "his" country, and yet he and all his beliefs are on the defensive. He views himself as a neglected victim, exploited by distant powers-that-be and ridiculed by smart-aleck upstarts. He senses that most other Americans share his outlook and prejudices, but he does not know how to make them effective in the public forum. While on the one hand he may observe, with a touch of smugness, that "they" need him and not he "them," on the other hand exasperation can move him to complain that "they" are taking over the country.

Hip Attitudes

Hip standards of morality are more institutional than personal. The square's tolerance of public jobbery excites hip indignation. Severe demands are made on key people within the "establishment" to eschew profit seeking, preserve the environment, eliminate institutional racism, guarantee universal peace. The square's respect for personal rectitude is ridiculed as hypocrisy. Euphemisms are applied to what the square calls vandalism, theft, and sexual promiscuity: trashing, ripping off, and swinging.

The key hip attitude is impatience with things as they are. All social institutions are long overdue for drastic reconstruction. Humanitarian sentiment is hardly at all alloyed with the square's reservations. Purity of intention is highly prized, an attitude which promotes suspicion of instrumental ends. The characteristic hip reaction to an American Legion post which funded a child-welfare camp, would be negative *if* the announced purpose was to lower the rejectee rate at army induction centers and "keep America strong."

Appreciation of dramatic style replaces the square's appreciation of propriety: flair and principled resistance and commitment to abstractions, not mediocrity and respectability and dull routine—thus the impatience with, the rejection of, all judgments of deviant behavior. The hip approach to others is ideally one of acceptance of *their* wishes, desires, gratifications, whatever the degree of personal responsibility assumed for any choices those encouraged others might make.

This particular stance is grounded upon a distinctive notion about human nature. While the general-cultural idea of essential goodness is modified by the square in his belief of a need for inner and outer controls to keep human nature that way, the less-fettered hip spirit proclaims the inherent virtue of uninhibited self-expression. In the hip scenario, once institutional shackles are removed, redeemed human innocence will achieve some form of collective reconciliation.

The stimulus of challenge to settled routine is welcomed. There is a vastly reduced interest in any cautionary protection of the individual career. Personal means and ends are not strung out on a long chain. Immediate gratification must not be sacrificed to deferred gratification. The hip camp is, therefore, more socially innovative than the square, more tolerant of, indeed insistent upon, alternative ways of thought and life.

The legitimacy of wealth and power is continuously denied with a keen sensitivity to corruption in high places. Almost obsessed with the word "equality," the hip camp is unquestionably more egalitarian than the square. But in the sense that the principle of live and let live is compromised by an aspiration to place misguided others under tutelage, it is less so. In a somewhat contradictory way, others should be permitted to do whatever they want to do, but it is also assumed that they require proper guidance *(35)*.

There is a characteristically hip approach to time, as there is a square. The square tends to live *at* the immediate future, toward which he works and for which he sacrifices present enjoyment and expressiveness, but this envisioned future is nonutopian, a mere continuity of the present when the values he absorbed as a child will confer their promised reward. The hip approach to time is both more complicated and more diverse. The present, what is now, takes precedence, as well as hedonic self-expression in the present. Imagination, however, inhabits *either* distant past or distant future, either the bucolic and essentially solitary arcadia of Hesiod's Golden Age or an equally distant utopia when all problems will cease in perfected social organization.

Hip Work Attitudes and Social Problems

Hip attitudes toward work, like square ones, color attitudes toward crime, poverty and race. The hip contingent is little represented in production and distribution, the "private sector" of business and industry, except in the production and control of word flow—the news media, book and magazine publishing, and the entertainment industry. Hip workers are mostly located in areas protected from the competitive market, such as government bureaus, subsidized higher education, social work, the clergy, and court officialdom.

Of course, by no means are all the people who work in the areas cited of the hip persuasion. Only unsubstantiated estimates are available on that point, and data presented in the first part of this chapter suggest that possibly as many squares as non squares operate within them. But the weight of opinion, from hip as well as square sources, locates the working hip contingent *within* those areas. From them are largely drawn the intellectual minorities referred to in previous chapters. The main point, for present purposes, is that the hip contingent make their living, or are conferred subsidized leisure in the case of college students, primarily by manipulating symbols instead of material objects.

An apparent exception to hip word work is the very large number of ex-college students who live in rural communes or choose to take urban jobs "below their capacity"—driving cabs, delivering mail, and like expedients which avoid the close supervision of factory and office employment. Perhaps at some risk of being unfair, it could be said that most of them are playing at work roles. Digging in gardens is widely reported to be desultory and supplemented with food stamps, while an urban job is usually regarded as a temporary arrangement, to be drifted into and out of. Whatever they may *do*, the serious interest of these young people remains intellectual—reading, meditation, discussion.

The special location of the working hip contingent within the economy fosters a characteristic set of attitudes toward work, and hence social problems. The "private sector," business and industry, is distrusted and its failings cataloged. There is little of the square's belief in the necessity of work, either to maintain self-respect or to maintain a high standard of living. The high standard of living itself is a frequent object of hip satirical comment, often, and perhaps somewhat illogically, combined with a faith that automation, a sheer push-button economy, could without much human effort produce a cornucopia of goods and services—and thus solve many problems—if only the establishment would get out of the way and permit the abundance of cybernation *(36)*. When this image of a potentially effortless and free world obdurately prevented by "them" from being realized is combined with that of a basic human innocence waiting to be reclaimed by drastically reforming the economy and other institutions, the hip approach to social problems is formulated.

As with much else, therefore, society is responsible for crime. Beyond that, the hip position tends to become ambivalent. Crime may be deplorable, but it may also be an acceptable distinctive life-style like many others, rather than something which should be solved or prevented. Considerable doubt is expressed that so-called criminals should be "rehabilitated" into the square world, and anyway the "real criminals" are to be found in the establishment. Attempts to punish "victimless crimes" such as prostitution, homosexuality, and drug use are especially condemned. Violence in any form, whether practiced by criminal, police, or the nation's armed forces, provokes more revulsion than in the square camp.

Poverty should not be permitted. Incomes should be politically redistributed, without any work requirements. The principle of equal opportunity is a cruel hoax, and it should be replaced with the principle of equal results. Various programs of quota representation are not for the most part hip-directed, but support for them, among whites, will be found at the hip end of the square-hip attitude range.

Much more concern for the welfare of blacks and Indians is expressed in the hip camp than in the square. As with poverty and crime, however, the square world is in this regard an object of contempt to be denigrated while another object of sympathy is to be lifted up. Which object takes precedence becomes especially uncertain in the charge of "institutional racism." Here as elsewhere, the hip self-image tends to be that of observer rather than active participant in society, since not only the onus of blame but the responsibility for taking action is assigned to others.

This trend became quite marked after the domestic upheavals of the sixties abated and the results of the 1972 election were known. At that time, the ranks of hip renunciating contemplatives swelled at the expense of hip political activists. There is, of course, no warrant for the belief that a reversal could not occur.

As for other social-problem issues, while squares either ignore or remain ignorant about population growth (ancillary matters of abortion and contraception excepted), the hip camp expresses alarm. Both camps are becoming increasingly worried about ecology, but the square's reservations about employment and costs are almost exclusively his. The hip determination to protect wilderness areas is much stronger than the square.

The typically square sense of frustration is matched by a typically hip one. The hip camp is withdrawn except in imagination from many objects of expressed concern, including blacks, the poor, and the supposedly alienated "working class." There is little association with people outside the far-flung network of communication maintained with in-group jargon, key-phrased attitudes, cool style, and uniforms—although this last is unessential for mutual recognition. Further, hip attitudes are chic and fashionable with most of the people who produce and direct the word flow; square attitudes at best a matter for amused condescension. Therefore, the elaborate attention paid the hip camp by intellectuals, the media, commercial entertainment, and especially horrified militant squares reinforces a sense of unity and creates an exaggerated impression of how desired changes could readily be brought about in the world outside the network.

Those within the hip camp, in short, have every reason to take themselves seriously, to believe that they are the people who really count. Periodically, however, the discovery is made anew that the troops are not there in depth. Since the ranks are thin, hip proposals and declarations are not really treated seriously at all by an overwhelming majority who persist in ancient ways and errors (37).

The hip sense of frustration stems from the disappointment of impatient demands being ignored or rejected. At the same time, inroads are being made on the square camp. Although squares continue by a long chalk to outnumber those of the hip persuasion, in recent years there has been a drift of attitudes in the hip direction. Whatever imprecise label might fit, counterculture, elite culture, or adversary culture, and the attendant inability of whatever it might be to usher in a new social order, its power to weaken tradition should not be questioned. It "has been gradually incorporated into our conventional school curriculum and, with the spread of mass higher education, has begun to shape the popular culture of our urbanized masses" (38).

SOCIAL PROBLEMS AS POWER STRUGGLE

Any understanding of modern social problems requires a grasp of the square-hip confrontation. On presumptive evidence each side is less interested in particular social problems than in scoring points against their adversaries in a struggle to protect and enforce a way of life, an image of social reality as well, deemed to be threatened by "them." Debates over what is or is not a social problem, and what should be done in either case, are also weapons whose ultimate purpose is the achievement of self-vindication. In that kind of situation, no social problem is going to be "solved" by rational persuasion, goodwill, or declared unified purpose.

It has often been said that agreement prevails about the identity of social problems, while only what means should be applied to resolve them are matters of dispute. If that state of affairs ever prevailed, it does not at the present time. Each camp may use the same names for many social problems, but characteristically each has something very different in mind. They are not addressing themselves to the same mental constructs, and overt responses to these disparate mental constructs constitute the chief source of conflict in modern America.

Whose Establishment?

Each side views itself as being victimized by an establishment (conversely, power structure) which it blames for creating social problems. The image in each case, of course, is radically different. These images have been limned in two separate books, images lacking only the idiosyncratic detail which any given individual will add for himself.

Before turning to these books, note that the separate images are held by the hip camp and by militant squares. Most squares are essentially nonideological. The attitudes they express are matters of conviction and habit, colored very little by awareness of or concern about intellectual ferment. They share with militant squares a degree of hostility toward "them," but "they" are more likely to be seen on the street or television than read about; most squares surely could not define a power-elite abstraction, nor do they possess an articulated image of one *(39)*.

The quintessential hip conception of the establishment has changed very little since C. Wright Mills's original description. A power elite rules America, through a sort of interlocking directorate of conscious personal interest which unites the political masters, the warlords or military ascendancy, and the very rich, especially the corporate rich. The real purpose of the labor unions is "to control the working class in behalf of the power elite." This power elite is the enemy, which pulls strings, foments wars, shapes human fate to its own purpose, and has transformed the public into a helpless mass. Its power is illegitimate, never mobilized for any social purpose *(40)*.

A militant square, M. Stanton Evans, has described a very different establishment. This one also rules America, but it is composed of very different types—intellectuals and "liberals" in academe, the media, and positions of power in government. This power elite espouses moral relativism, and has for its primary goal the concentration of control in its own hands. The dominance of these people is a dangerous threat to national security as well as liberty, because they locate all danger on the right, never the left, and therefore encourage dissidence at home and Communist regimes abroad at the expense of national tradition and military preparedness (41).

Doubt was expressed in a previous chapter, here, that any individual, group, class, or cabal "rules America." But no quarrel with any image, including the two cited above, will be engaged. On the other hand, Evans may have overshot his "liberal-intellectual" target.

Intellectuals have always insisted that the world could be run better, and throughout history they have criticized the social life around them. Until very recent times, though, their main complaint has been about the glaring contrast between proclaimed lofty ideals and wretched performance, the gap between creed and deed. Other people were called to task for their failure to live by their own words. In this historic mission of moral and social gadfly, however, the desirability, the rightness, of those ideals was rarely questioned. A common world was assumed.

There has been a steady drift away from the assumption of a common world. Many intellectuals, or perhaps liberal-intellectuals, continue to endorse received ideals while they demand their "fuller implementation." But that position is being usurped by a hip insurgence of hostility toward received ideals themselves. While in many dimensions hip intellectuals merely push liberal-intellectual attitudes one step farther, toward rhetorical totalism, in this one dimension hip intellectualism is something new. Therefore, although the declared object of Evans's hostility is liberalism, it could more accurately be called the early breeding ground of hip intellectualism.

Whose Social Problems?

There is a natural division between race relations, poverty, and crime on one side, ecology and population growth on the other. In the hypothetical instance that the latter two were suddenly to become matters of top priority, if national attention, funds, energy were allotted to them on a scale comparable to what either World War received, the consequences of deep and ramified structural change would be incalculably greater than any similar approach to race relations, poverty, and crime. And yet these problems elicit much more square-hip hostility than ecology and population growth. They do so because they are *believed,* on one side to threaten, on the other to promise, more drastic change than either ecology or population growth.

Except for the ancillary issues of abortion and contraception, population growth is simply ignored by most squares. Ecology has been usually viewed, and has been usually presented, as a movement designed to confer equal benefit upon all citizens. Ideology either is absent or retains a low profile compared with crime, race relations, and poverty. These are the controversial problems that bring the hip-square confrontation into sharp focus. Unlike ecology and population growth, these problems are accompanied on one side by efforts to institute status changes throughout society, on the other to stop or slow down the drift of those changes. Emotions are heightened by a vague or sharp image of an establishment on the other side which is secretly working to thwart perceived interests and moral purpose.

Is the primary intent on either side to solve problems or blame the other side? That question cannot be definitively answered because sociology provides no techniques for plumbing the depths of motivation. Still, the denunciatory way in which each side tends to invoke humanitarianism is suggestive. The social problem of crime is especially liable to excite mutual hip-square accusations of bad faith.

Each side proceeds with a separate mental construct, informed by a polarized image, justified with an interpretation of opposition purpose which is slightly tinged with paranoia. Each side accuses the other at best of heartless indifference to the "problem," which on each side is defined with a different version of humanitarianism. On one side the "criminal" is not really a criminal but a victim himself; on the other the "criminal" must be punished and then closely supervised to protect his potential victims from harm.

The split between the two camps is not nearly so marked in the case of race relations and poverty. Common agreement that "something should be done," however, does leave a large unresolved area of disagreement. The square tends to drag foot and offer objections to each new proposal made, while hip demands are unnegotiable or at least open-ended, and they include an assignment of guilt and atonement to the square which is rejected. The hip camp wants immediate and total reconstruction, the square camp gradual improvement of existing institutions and established procedures at an orderly and slow pace.

There is a generous supply of animus on each side. The militant square's heartily reciprocated hatred of the hip extremist exceeds in negative affect any white-black or gentile-Jew prejudice of the recent past. The reason why is simple: although blacks and Jews were considered in varying degree to be socially unacceptable, their desire for inclusion was assumed. They were not perceived as the enemy, as detractors and spoilers of a way of life fighting for survival.

Scoring Points

Attempts to define social problems and their scope, the search for solutions, efforts to secure program-support are in some degree vitiated and rendered futile by acrimonious denunciations of the opposition. The stated conditions of social problems often appear to be of less concern than an opportunity to skewer the enemy. Feelings of righteous indignation, a need for symbolic vindication, can expand into a lust to punish.

Statements made by first two hip and then two square columnists illustrate the point. Herb Caen is San Francisco's most famous character witness. He continuously rebuts those "puritan critics" who dwell upon the city's VD rate, international reputation for pornography unlimited, gay bars, prostitution, and live sex entertainment. The beauty and cultural attractions of the city, he says, are embellished by the live-and-let-live tolerance of its citizens. The critics of San Francisco forever inveigh against sex, he says further, but they overlook something incalculably worse, brutal violence, as in the recent American bombing of Vietnamese citizens. "These 'good, square Americans,' as they like to think of themselves, have neat hair and messed-up priorities, shiny shoes and shadowy minds, a misguided pride that is heading toward the outer reaches of paranoia" (42).

Charles McCabe is ostensibly engaged in a one-man crusade to eliminate all police and court procedures against those who indulge in victimless crimes. Although there is nothing good about drugs, for example, for either the user or his companions, except that "for a while they make life seem better," their use should not be treated as a criminal act. "The crime is that you are thought to be enjoying yourself while some churchgoing nut spends his days sticking gaskets into automobiles in a large square building. He can't stand you, so he puts the blame on the drug which is most disapproved at the minute" (43).

Victor Lasky has made almost a career of unearthing what he calls "liberal hypocrisy." In 1971 he listed several aspirants to presidential nomination who were sponsoring integrated education while they sent their own offspring to private or suburban schools rather than public schools in the Washington area. "These would-be 'leaders' of mankind preach a liberalism for others, not for themselves. It's 'Do as I say,' not 'Do as I do.' " The poor have no such privilege of "copping out." And further, "_____ is not the only distinguished Negro opposed to sending his children to public schools. Our beloved _____, as well as Congressman _____, prefer white-oriented private schools for their progeny. And that goes for about every well-heeled civil rights activist in town, black as well as white" (44).

Guy Wright is more even-tempered, less prone to the insult direct. Still, his square prejudices are militant; his target is quite obvious. He says the "intelligentsia" err in their concept of victimless crime. There are direct victims, those stolen from to support the drug habit. More important is the indirect "coarsening effect on a society as a whole." No victims from a mere economic transaction between buyer and seller in prostitution? Every passing citizen. "The man and wife going out to dinner. The boy and girl on their first date. Is there no victimization when these people must learn to accept the sleeve-pluckings of a whore?" The "intelligentsia" image of prostitution and homosexuality is one of people discreetly doing their own thing in private. But things don't work out that way. "Grant sanctuary to homosexuals and soon drag queens take to the streets in flaunting parade" (45).

In the company of social problems homosexuality is granted relatively little attention, but this and other sexual issues more clearly than the major social problems measure the gulf of noncommunication between hip and square extremes of the attitude range. The square's feeling of moral affront from sex in the streets provokes hip hilarity. Openly advertised pornography, which offends the square, is in the hip view a joke, a right of free speech, or a revelation of square hypocrisy *(46)*. Hip references to the right of free enterprise in prostitution are put-downs of square complaints against the open traffic. Hip defense of homosexuality, however, is much more pronounced, and so is square revulsion against the practice.

Here, square humanitarianism is at lowest ebb. Homosexuals should act the penitent, acknowledge guilt and perhaps suffer a little, surely seek help to cure themselves of an unfortunate aberration. Whatever help is offered should be designed to change the homosexual's deviant habits and make him a whole member of society.

The hip prescription for helping the homosexual is acceptance of that way of life as a perfectly normal alternative life-style. He (or she) is not to be changed at all, only his (or her) present social status. To that end—or the end of scoring points on squares by implying their stupidity and cruelty—is addressed hip encouragement of gay parades, love-ins, marriages, lounges in universities, and, in 1973, a Gay Miss America Pageant. There is nothing *directly* self-serving about this hip attitude, because homosexuals constitute a very small proportion of the hip as well as the total population. There are even some homosexuals who are square in every way save one. They are doubly banished.

There is little hip interest in the stratagems employed by liberals to deflect hostility from objects selected for concern. The hip attitude is one of scorn for such ploys as labeling homosexuals, or criminals, or alcoholics, or drug addicts, as sick, that is, victimized by their own helplessness. The overriding hip impulse instead is to accuse the accusers of obtuse moral judgment, of false consciousness.

POLARIZED VIEWS OF EQUALITY

In his proposal for public-supported education in Virginia, Thomas Jefferson said: "Of the boys . . . sent in any one year, trial is to be made at the grammar schools one or two years, and the best genius of the whole selected, and continued six years, and the rest dismissed. By this means twenty of the best geniuses will be raked from the rubbish annually, and be instructed, at the public expence, so far as the grammar schools go" (47). Thus was expressed not only a belief in an aristocracy of talent, moribund about a quarter century after Jefferson's death, but also an affirmation of the principle of equal opportunity (the right to succeed or fail on personal merit instead of birth), which remains very much alive.

Although in general terms it can be said that squares tend to favor Jefferson's principle, while the demand for equality of results is a characteristically hip one, that blanket statement obscures more than it illuminates. Long before the emergence of the hip phenomenon, for instance, higher education of any sort that Jefferson would have recognized had become debased by a combination of, first, indiscriminate demand for educational credentials by economic organizations, and, second, "lower-middle-class" pressure—mainly parental—for easy access to and graduation from college.

Any human being, hip, square, or whatever, is prone to indulge contradictory wishes. One is a desire to secure by minimum effort those prizes which in others' eyes will be regarded as representing maximum effort. Surely everyone hankers for one free ride or another while he demands principled justice or equal treatment. These conflicts within the self antedated the square-hip confrontation by several millennia; in the life-cycle, they first appear in the nursery.

Divided impulse becomes strikingly apparent when a sought prize is once attained. A factory hand may insist that the best man for a higher assignment (usually himself) should get it, but he may also support union measures which bar potential competitors from membership and thus jobs—measures often aimed at blacks, an exclusionary practice only now being rectified. The same management trade journal which extols free enterprise may include a demand for stiffer protective tariffs and "fair-trade" legislation designed to eliminate new competitors. There is a stock graduate school joke, about the Ph.D. aspirant who complained about and even connived against this, that, and the other requirement, and who, upon securing his degree, immediately proclaimed that "the standards have got to be raised."

What Equality?

The square-hip range of attitudes on equality requires further preface. This protean word more often reveals or invokes a feeling-state, usually a positive feeling-state, than explicit meaning. Among a host of contemporary equality images are democratic manners; a shared opportunity to pursue different career goals; the same rewards for everyone; abolition of all status distinctions, including those of age, sex, and race, as well as those which prevail within the division of labor; like treatment at law; compensation for injustice perceived in historic circumstance; the same treatment for people who share a similar status or set of life conditions; and the sharing of power with people at the top of the heap. Only the more consequential notions about equality are discussed below.

It was shown in Chapter 2 that the idea of equality has provided the Western tradition with continuous tension, revealed by attempts to justify and simultaneous attempts to discredit any distribution of rewards based upon inequalities of status. Nevertheless, according to Mosca, inequality of association in history has provoked more hostility than have inequalities of status. "In the Middle Ages the first peasant revolts broke out not when feudalism was harshest but when the nobles had learned to associate with one another, when the courts of love—a conscious quest of good manners . . .—had begun to give them polish and alienate them from the rustic ways of the lonely castle" (48). Envy of superior status, even hereditary status, was minimal so long as peasants and lords shared the same social environment. Mosca extends this distinction to the modern setting: it is not the superior status of the intellectual, but his isolated status, his remote moralizing, which aggravates the sense of the "masses" that they are being treated as unequals, as inferiors.

But like everyone else, modern intellectuals inadvertently reveal confusion in the values they express. Together with most other Americans, they are more concerned about sharing a common social universe than ever were Europeans in the Middle Ages. Even squares, who cling to the principle of equal opportunity, become uneasy at its correlative purpose and result, that in the competition some will outstrip others, become unequal. Everyone should have the right to compete on his own merit for prizes, and yet it is a shame if anyone is left out.

There is thus a near-universal American willingness to spend more tax money on the education of dull children than on very bright children, a choice which has led Senator Jacob Javits to say that gifted children are "the most neglected minority in American education today." May the best man win, but somehow every man *should* win. That is why periodic demands for a reinstitution of standards of excellence make few waves. Nearly all modern Americans, square as well as hip, in the event that they should read Jefferson, would find his remark about sweeping out the rubbish more than vaguely repellent.

This nearly universal American attitude, perhaps better, feeling-state, that all should win is contradicted by a virtual obsession with this question: Who, in this or that field, is the best? Americans are fascinated by linear measurement of accomplishment. Historians as gravely ponder the best two or three Presidents as small boys argue baseball players, past and present. People who care little and know less about art still want to be told whether Picasso was or was not the greatest painter of the century. Intellectuals may champion equality, but they rank their own kind (49).

Ambivalence about Achievement

Most Americans, then, laud accomplishment yet retain some ambivalence about accomplishment being made difficult to achieve. At the same time, most Americans feel uneasy about social inequality, and the reduction of its scope has led to a seeming paradox. Resentment of inequality does not abate as social equality advances, as material conditions level out and abhorrence of deferential address rises. According to Tocqueville; "The hatred which men bear to privilege increases in proportion as privileges become fewer and less considerable." Envy reaches maximum expression not among extremely unequal children or adults but among nearly equal ones (50).

Since envy and resentment tend to rise as social inequality wanes, a fear of provoking egalitarian envy and resentment has promoted a widespread effort to make oneself accessible to others in casual relationships. To most Americans, being "democratic" does not refer to political behavior but to an open "common folks" manner in approaching others. Behavior of this kind is ridiculed

only by some intellectuals and repudiated only by those conservatives who hanker for a past when men of withdrawn dignity as well
as substance had not yet been rendered obsolete by Jacksonian
populism.

With few exceptions, then, Americans celebrate democratic
manners. Democratic manners require a touch of mutual familiarity
with the waitress. It is not expected or even desired that she should
fawn and simper, a new development, since "servants" were expected in Jackson's time and until recently to act like servants. She may
indeed make as much money as many of her patrons, and the chef
makes more than most of the people whose food he prepares.

Democratic manners, of course, required that leveling out of
the material base which has taken place. The welfare state, which
dispenses more largess to the well-to-do than the poor, was not the
instrument. Leveling out of the material base, and consequent diminution of social inequality to an extent unique in the modern
world, was a result of America's preeminent economic development
during the recent past. Henry Ford was the chief, albeit totally
unaware, revolutionary. He and a few other innovators forsook the
old "class market" and sought to supply and build a mass market.
Then and only then did social class in any historic sense finally
depart from America. The major shift to a classless society comes
not with Marxist dogma but when the capitalist market is attuned
to the big numbers. Privilege was a gulf when turn-of-the-century
automobile manufacturers sold only luxury, custom-made models.
Privilege becomes a series of minute gradations when General Motors offers cars for every pocketbook, cars that are almost uniformly
styled.

Equality and Status Frustration

What were once the prerogatives of the few—a well-furnished home,
long vacations, private transportation, an extensive wardrobe, access to higher education—are now the birthright of the many. The
leveling out of the material base, however, has had ironic consequences, especially that of status frustration. The poor, via the welfare state, are materially better off than ever before. A welfare
recipient lives in more comfortable circumstances than most employed citizens in some Western European countries. Yet he is prob-

ably more frustrated here than elsewhere, because only a minority are defined as poor. He cannot draw comfort from the knowledge that most other people share his plight. He may also find difficulty in convincing himself that luck or the "system" are to blame when he is constantly being urged to accept job training and similar measures of self-help, when so many others persist in regarding his low status as remediable. "Only the existence of unequal external opportunities makes it possible for the unsuccessful individual to live with himself" (51).

Those, most of the majority, who have achieved a modest success are also subject to status frustration. For them, accomplishment has become in some measure devaluated, in two ways. First, with the leveling out of the material base how does one distinguish himself except from the very poor, those whom the social workers cannot qualify for one or more relief "slots"? Everyone else apparently has a duplicate package of home, car, refrigerator, vacations, and so on. Their style of life approximates one's own; and when everybody is somebody, then nobody is anybody. Those possessions and experiences which in the recent past were symbolic of high status have been nearly equalized, and because so many people have availed themselves of an equal opportunity to get them, the fruits of equal opportunity have been somewhat spoiled (52). An unresolvable dilemma then appears in stark form: the wish for equality by any definition and the wish for recognition cannot simultaneously be gratified.

Second, the new service economy is geared to mass consumption, and, therefore, except for the very rich, there can be nothing special about the service. The "new middle class," said to comprise "six out of every ten people," are also said to feel entitled to privileges and amenities once reserved for the "old middle class." As their right, they expect protection from crime and violence. "They are upset when taxis are unavailable, when planes fall behind schedule, and when roads and recreational facilities are overcrowded. They object to the quality of service they receive from others and the lack of people prepared to wait on them in return for a reasonable payment" (53). Object? More likely mutter behind a cupped hand, because any social interchange with the waitress must celebrate democratic manners.

We have seen that one person often has a very different thing in mind from another when they endorse equality. We have also discussed reasons why many of those people whose support is sought for programs designed to improve the lot of criminals, the poor, and racial minorities harbor resentments of their own. They may feel vaguely victimized by schemes to raise the status of others when they remain dissatisfied with their own. On this count as well as many others, communication between hip and square camps is lacking.

Square Equality

Despite the above generalizations, most squares do not have much difficulty with their belief in equal opportunity. Since they lack the intellectual's ability to define abstractions as well as his interest in them, squares tend to ignore or fail to see the complexities and contradictions of their own principle. They *believe* in equal opportunity. They believe it prevails almost as much as they believe it should reign.

The sovereignty of the principle will not bear rigorous inspection. The institution of the family is the chief offender against it, for whether in Tahiti, Russia, or America, strenuous efforts are made to pass on to one's children advantages already secured. All that can be said is that in modern America greater effort than elsewhere is also exerted to reduce the scale of inherited advantage.

Even the central contradiction of equal opportunity, a principle that equal means should be provided to become unequal, to surpass one's competitors and thereby register superiority in one way or another, presents no insuperable difficulty. The principle stated that baldly, and carried to conceivable limits, would produce a few winners and a multitude of losers. But nothing of the kind has happened in this country, because the reference points of success for the majority were never very high.

The reference was impoverished compatriots in the homeland for successive waves of immigrants, and they reached success by attaining *average* American standards of education, housing, speech, dress, and comportment. For most of their children and grandchildren success has meant more education than their parents acquired, and perhaps suburban living to accompany a better job.

For most Americans of any vintage success has meant visibly moving up and out with reference to what they had and were at some previous time. With the almost uninterrupted prosperity of the last three decades, virtually everyone's scale of consumption has mounted; in a modest sense, the majority have been enabled to succeed, to take advantage, as they see it, of equal opportunity.

The square tends to ignore any passivity of his own in being carried along by this tide. His typical insistence that his own hard work has taken him to where he is overlooks the recent phenomenal growth rate of technology and economy. But he is not altogether wrong. His own effort did contribute to what he has gained.

He does work—he believes he must and should. All his friends and younger relatives work, in or outside the home. Despite airy promises of a leisure world aborning, for some time there have been more Americans working outside the home in any one year than the previous one. While population increasd by 2.4 percent in the period 1970–1973, the number of people with jobs expanded 6.8 percent.

Emotionally, psychologically, the square is not attuned to prophecies of a push-button automated cornucopia. And he believes that except in extreme circumstances everyone *should* work for what he gets; moreover, that standards of personal effort should apply to rewards. In his eyes equal opportunity also means that any special favors withheld from him should not be conferred upon others, especially those who are visible, who are close to him in circumstance.

He is relatively untroubled about those who are remote from him in circumstance, those in high authority and the rich, who operate in a different league of opportunity, equal or otherwise. He accepts the proposition that most rewards are earned, that ability and not chance determines most outcomes. Between 1939 and 1970, an increasing majority of Americans said that ability has more to do with achieving success than luck; 86 percent so affirmed in 1970 (54).

In his investigation of "upper-working-class" attitudes, Professor Lane found that most of his respondents "accepted the view that America opens up opportunity to all people, if not in equal proportions, then at least enough so that a person must assume responsibility for his own status." They regard the status of the "eminently successful" to be as deserved as their own, as appropriate to their different talents. They appreciate the responsibility that high position entails, and they want no part of either for themselves.

As for literal social and economic equality, the notion is anathema. They fear that equality of income would destroy inner tension, "deprive people of the goals of life." On the one hand, they view such equality as a threat to their established relationships with relatives, friends, and neighbors; on the other, the idea that their own hard-earned status should be conferred upon the "lower orders" as a "right and not a reward for effort seems to them desperately wrong" (55).

Hip Equality

A totally different vision of the good society than that held by Jefferson has been supported, oddly enough, with conclusions about education very similar to his. In a recent and already famous book Christopher Jencks rejects the notion that all people are "born equal," that differences of status and income must result from prejudice or discrimination on one hand, advantages conferred by parents on another. Unequal social opportunity, he says, is not to blame for unequal results. He advances the unfashionable argument that there *are* "geniuses," in the sense that genetic differences among children obviate any possibility that "cognitive equality" can be achieved with uniform educational instruction and facilities. "Exposed to identical environments, one [child] will learn more than another."

Nor will children raised in even the same home by the same parents have, as adults, equal occupational status and income. Income varies among siblings in rather striking fashion, and parental income plays no decisive part in determining what children will earn as adults. He singles out "luck" as the decisive factor, something palpably unjust, such as "chance acquaintances" steering "you to one line of work rather than another" or "whether bad weather destroys your strawberry crop . . . and a hundred other unpredictable accidents" (56).

Jencks wants this fortuitous situation rectified in order to achieve a near equality of results. Since Americans feel strongly about the money they have "earned" (his quotation marks), "egalitarians should concentrate on making the distribution of pretax wages more equal" through direct legislative control over wages, "rather than trying to use taxation as a major instrument for redistribution" (57). "Cognitive inequality" could be reduced by similar means, through an assignment of "environmental handicaps" to those who start life with genetic advantages (58).

In his attitude toward equality Professor Jencks can be assigned only a medium-hip rating, because his endorsement of imposed equal results is accompanied by some nonhip observations about innate ability. The hip extremist is not all that interested in seeing equal results imposed if his adopted constituencies simply join the rest of society. The hip extremist does not so much want to improve the status of his adopted constituencies as he wants to exalt their present condition. Nevertheless, a demand for their preferential treatment could only come from the hip *side* of the attitude range, because that treatment would require drastic changes in the institutional structure.

The wish for equal results is as old as history, the demand for them quite new. That demand was first expressed, not by hip extremists, but by disappointed intellectuals and professional people of the hip persuasion who administer and service programs for the poor. What led them to abandon their previous effort to improve conditions of equal opportunity was the realization "that schooling had little effect in raising the achievement or reducing the disparate standing of black children relative to white" (59). Like Professor Jencks, they then turned to preferential treatment in order to achieve a near equality of results—for black adults. That beachhead of principle once secured, it "spread like wildfire to other groups and categories—ethnic, sexual, or chronological—each claiming the right of preferential treatment" (60).

Such claims would have remained inchoate wishes without the intervention of effective law in the form of government-agency regulations *(61)*. The Department of Health, Education, and Welfare now calls upon universities and other institutions which receive federal monies above a certain amount or have government contracts to submit plans for, and later, statements of compliance to, employment quotas for women, blacks, Indians, and Chicanos. Its Affirmative Action programs require colleges and universities to set specific recruitment goals and timetables to ensure immediate increases in the percentages of the above categories hired for faculty and staff positions. HEW then either accepts or rejects submitted statements of compliance.

Ironically, the Equal Employment Opportunity Commission (EEOC) was established to investigate and recommend penalties for discrimination in employment against any person because of his "race, color, religion, sex, or national origin." With the passage of the Equal Opportunity Act of 1972, it was empowered to bring suit "in federal court against any employer it deems to be guilty of discrimination." EEOC now enforces a form of discrimination it is specifically charged to combat. The commission has decreed any employment practice to be discriminatory when "it results in a work force containing a smaller proportion of minorities or women than does the surrounding population," a quota system of proportional representation which is in violation of law *(62)*.

The drive for equal results has been pushed to include a category under square reprobation, convicted criminals. Ex-convicts have in many cases by new laws been successful in getting their criminal records expunged. According to the EEOC, it is illegal "to discharge or refuse to employ a minority-group person because of a conviction record unless the particular circumstance of each case indicates that employment of that particular person for a particular job is manifestly inconsistent with the safe and efficient operation of that job" (63).

Prisoners have been granted many "equal rights" hitherto denied them. In 1971 the U. S. Court of Appeals abrogated the 1952 rule of court noninterference with prison administration. Suits by prisoners against prison personnel have piled up in the courts, on such matters as uncensored mail, conjugal visits, free access to publications of any kind, and determination of menus. Some prisoner-rights attorneys and court judges have stated their intent to abolish the present prison system by "raising the cost of doing [prison] business" (64).

Education and the Two Equalities

So far, however, the main battle of the two equalities has been fought on the field of higher education. On one side the notion still holds that enrollment and graduation should bear some relationship to individual merit and effort. On the other, there is an insistence upon an absolute equality of access and equal diploma certification, contradictory and self-defeating ends, to be sure: for credibility, any badge of superior achievement must assure the beholder that some competitive standard has been met.

As have many other educational institutions, the City University of New York has abandoned individual standards of merit in favor of preferential treatment and abolition of standards in general. The policy of "open admissions" welcomes any graduate of any high school. The decision was also made to give college credit for grammar school-level "remedial work." And "City headquarters has been judging the colleges by the number of credits Open Admission students receive—and the students themselves, of course, have been learning from the grapevine about teachers who pass everybody" (65). Professor Mayer says that only very secure faculty members are in a position to resist official pressure to apply a dual set of standards, one for those who can do assigned work, another for those who cannot.

Any human being, regardless of race, creed, color, sex, or national origin, is prone to take advantage of what appears to be a change in the rules favorable to him. There is no question, here, of anyone's right to follow his own perceived interest. About the near abandonment of education standards at CUNY and elsewhere, however, two points can be made. The change was initiated not by the "disadvantaged" but by government and education bureaucrats; and some spokesmen of the "disadvantaged" argue that the change was very much against their own interest.

A black professor of economics has documented one charge with personal experience at several predominantly white colleges and universities. The authorities at these institutions actively recruit black youngsters from the slums, students whose attitudes and background guarantee their failure to appreciate or even grasp the rudiments of education at any level. Conversely, they reject the applications of qualified black youngsters.

This policy stems from a combination of outside pressure and ideological conviction. The "search for misfits" is required by HEW "guidelines," and by stipulations which accompany federal government and private foundation grants, to the effect that recruitment of black students must favor those with low-performance scores.

Cornell, for example, once denied admission to a black girl with College Board scores in the top 1 percent with the justification that "her cultural and educational background does not indicate deprivation to the extent necessary for qualification as a disadvantaged . . . student." Both of her parents were laundry workers. Nevertheless, "she has been adequately motivated by them to a point where she has achieved academic success and some degree of cultural sophistication" (66).

Recruitment and admission practices "overlook, bypass, and even reject outright many capable black students in favor of less-qualified students who fit a more fashionable stereotype." Professor Sowell charges that both qualified and unqualified black students are being victimized, in different ways, by ideologues for purposes of their own. To such "white allies of the race" black people "may mean much less . . . as human beings than as exhibits with which to indict society" *(67).*

These people do not want *square* black students, whatever their qualifications; they dismiss them as "middle class" even should their parents be laundry workers, as lacking the outlook of "authentic street types." On the other hand, unprepared black youngsters are "lied to" when they are assured, directly or tacitly, that they can be *given* a "quality education." They either become litigious and militant troublemakers or withdraw into a sense of confirmed inferiority. Professor Sowell does not, incidentally, advocate a sink-or-swim policy. He says that unprepared black students *should* receive special help and attention, not in the form of unearned degrees but precollege schools designed to rectify the deficiencies of their training.

The New Quotas

There are, then, contradictions and anomalies in the hip as well as the square approach to equality. The hip demand for proportional representation, to be imposed by government power, to some might appear odd in conjunction with the pronounced hip attitude of abiding distrust of all power. Moreover, for decades progressive thought denounced quotas as the rankest injustice, because they kept qualified individuals out; progressive thought now demands quotas as restitutive justice, because they bring unqualified individuals in.

They must bring unqualified individuals in. At present the pool of educated talent among Indians, blacks, Chicanos, and women is too small to satisfy the requirement of proportional representation in every school, business, and profession. And the question is never raised about how many individuals in these particular categories actually want to become college graduates, or doctors, lawyers, and engineers. There are, for example, many more Jewish doctors and professors than doctors and professors who are of Italian or Polish descent. Since prejudice and discrimination against all these ethnic groups is now minimal, that circumstance must have something to do with the special attraction to Jews of such employment.

Discrimination is no longer objectionable, at least in some circles, provided it favors selected categories of persons. But unequal treatment of that kind must be paid for with unequal treatment of other categories. Reverse discrimination must inevitably renew discrimination against former targets, such as Jews, and institute discrimination against those who never were its victims, such as WASPs.

If one person is admitted to college or offered employment on grounds other than those of individual ability, then some other person of higher ability must be discriminated against. Further, if the criterion for favoritism is membership in one category, then members of other categories must be discriminated against. And finally, if the doctrine of proportional representation were pushed to its logical conclusion, then favors would be officially withheld as well as granted on that basis. In that event, since American Jews for example constitute only about 3 percent of the national population, only 3 percent of American Jews could be admitted to college, only 3 percent could ever become doctors, or writers, lawyers, dentists, or businessmen.

It is conceivable that the economy could survive such a deliberate sacrifice of talent. But what we call democracy would surely be destroyed if one ethnic group were ever singled out for any such official persecution. The Nazi regime did last for more than a decade, but *only* Jews were singled out for deprivation of life chances. The new logic of proportional representation would also penalize WASPs and American Orientals, who compare favorably with

WASPs in socioeconomic status (68). The specific obverse of favored age, sexual, educational, racial, and ethnic categories comprises a small number of people—old, male, heterosexual, talented college-graduate WASPs—who would have to be singled out for special negative attention. If certain categories are to be raised to their fair collective share, by simple arithmetic other categories must be pushed down to their fair collective share (69).

The Main Ideological Dispute

We have been discussing the main ideological conflict of our time. It is true that the social problems of population growth and ecology are virtually unaffected by it. But poverty and race relations are very much affected, crime less so, by this issue of equal opportunity versus equal results.

There are sociologists who believe that this issue has already been settled. Daniel Bell says that the world of Locke, Adam Smith, and Jeremy Bentham is crumbling "and the political system is now being geared to the realization not of individual ends but of group and communal ends." We have come to the end of classic liberalism. "It is not individual satisfaction which is the measure of social good, but redress for the disadvantaged as a prior claim on the social conscience and on social policy" (70).

Nathan Glazer's mood is more somber, expressed in requiem. With equality of representation replacing equality of opportunity, he sees "America sinking—not rapidly, not insupportably, but inevitably. Nations do change in their capacity to produce and compete. Their values change, and clearly American values are today in large measure antagonistic to production and competition" (71).

Are "American values" in such a state? The key question is whether the changes of attitude noted by these sociologists are universal, or largely restricted to the hip contingent. Evidence cited here, mainly in the first part of this chapter, indicates a considerable majority adherence to those values of "classic liberalism" which Professor Bell says are outmoded, and as well to those values of production and competition which Professor Glazer says are moribund.

True, even squares are not so square as they once were. The welfare state—indeterminately imposed, indeterminately implored—unquestionably has eroded their will to work, their devotion to disciplined effort, their belief that strength of character determines success or failure, perhaps even their belief in success or failure *(72)*. Most of them now believe that failure is no total personal responsibility, and accede to collective help, if not for those who freeload, then for those who cannot or did not make it; indeed, they want assurance of collective help for themselves when and if needed.

At the same time, squares still believe that a kind of rough, approximate balance works out between ability and effort and accomplishment on one side, reward on the other, and, more important, that such a balance *should* work out. In short, they remain closer to Jefferson than to Professor Jencks, to the idea of deserved and rewarded merit than to the idea of imposed literal equality. And they are not likely to abandon their appreciation of prosperity and economic growth, their desired state of affairs which a really serious effort to equalize career results would destroy.

Their prejudices stand in the way of any such effort. The hypothetical average square has little if any knowledge about the great debate over the two versions of equality, because it has never involved him in a personal way, because reverse discrimination, redress for the disadvantaged, equality of representation, equal results have not directly threatened his own perceived interests. So far, surely no more than a few hundred squares have been denied a job because of their color or sex, or had to live with a son or daughter who was denied admittance to college, despite superior high school grades, so that the quota for "disadvantaged students," with low high school grades, could be filled.

As was pointed out in a previous chapter, trend lines do not march up and off the graph paper. There are short-lived intellectual as well as social-political fads. Only a few years ago there was excited discussion of the need to reinstate excellence and more rigorous standards of rewarded merit. Disenchantment with the as yet modest scope of attempts to replace equal opportunity with equal results conceivably might shift the present channel of intellectual discussion.

In either event, it is difficult to envision those attempts being pushed much farther. Too many vital, perceived interests would be visibly threatened in a way impossible to rationalize with other than divisive shibboleths. It is also difficult to envision how that version of equality could hold together a new and viable social order. Only a totalitarian solution could enforce the new version of equality upon an entire society, but whence would come the popular support for such a venture? Squares, after all, remain the majority, and any such authoritarian overturn of their traditional institutions appears highly improbable, even though, as has here been stated many times, the future meanders out of everyone's sight.

REFERENCES

1 Cited in Seymour Martin Lipset and Earl Raab, "The Election and the National Mood," *Commentary,* January 1973, pp. 43–50, p. 47.

2 Herman Kahn's estimates, and adjectives, are much less generous to the countercultural minority. "It's a very specific illness of a very specific group, less than 10 percent of the country." This "illness," he claims, does not afflict most college students: "Of the 8 to 8-and-a-half million young people in academia today, only 300,000 belong to the counterculture. There are 2 or 3 million who go along, but the average college kid is still quite square." Herman Kahn, "The Squaring of America," *Intellectual Digest,* September 1972, pp. 16–19, pp. 17 and 18.

3 William Watts and Lloyd A. Free (eds.), *State of the Nation,* Universe Books, New York, 1973, p. 252. This is an invaluable source, a compilation of data collected by the Gallup organization with many cogent interpretations appended. Included are the public's assessments of most of the social problems discussed in this volume.

4 Donald J. Devine, *The Political Culture of the United States,* Little, Brown, Boston, 1972, p. 105. Other material adapted from Devine can be found, in order, on pp. 193, 92, 150, and 204.

5 Watts and Free, reference 3, p. 21.

6 Watts and Free, reference 3. These distinctions, of minor scope in many cases, were found to hold up over a large range of public issues.

7 Devine, reference 4, pp. 270 and 279.

8 Watts and Free, reference 3, pp. 25 and 96.

9 Richard M. Scammon and Ben J. Wattenberg, *The Real Majority,* Coward-McCann, New York, 1970, p. 207.

10 Devine, reference 4, adapted from the table on p. 274. The CBS researchers accentuated the negative, "concluded that large minorities of American youth are 'sharply critical of our economic and political systems.'" This judgment, insecurely supported by their own figures,

both lends credence to those figures and illustrates a point made in the previous chapter: images, especially images of an ideological cast, are virtually impervious to "facts," in this case facts gathered by people who screened out the apparent significance of their own findings.

11 Lipset and Raab, reference 1, p. 48. The sentence which follows in the text is derived from the same source, p. 49.

12 Devine, reference 4, p. 275.

13 H. Edward Ransford, "Blue Collar Anger: Reactions to Student and Black Protest," *American Sociological Review,* **37:**333–346, 1972, p. 345.

14 On sex mores, see Devine, reference 4, p. 274; on use of marijuana, Lipset and Raab, reference 1, p. 44, and Watts and Free, reference 3, p. 58.

15 "Interview with Herman Kahn," *U. S. News & World Report,* Mar. 12, 1973, pp. 42–48, p. 45. These prophecies should be viewed with the skepticism justified in the discussion of prophesy in chap. 3.

16 Watts and Free, reference 3, adapted from the table on p. 323.

17 Devine, reference 4, pp. 261–264.

18 Lipset and Raab, reference 1, pp. 46 and 47.

19 Watts and Free, reference 3, p. 37.

20 Norman Podhoretz, "Between Nixon and the New Politics," *Commentary,* September 1972, pp. 4–8, p. 6.

21 George C. Kirstein, *The Rich: Are They Different?* Tower, New York, 1970 (originally published by Houghton Mifflin in 1968).

22 Tom Wolfe, *Radical Chic and Mau-Mauing the Flak Catchers,* Bantam, New York, 1971, p. 39.

23 Watts and Free, reference 3, pp. 101 and 102. It should be noted that whites tend to prefer white neighbors when the factor of socioeconomic status is held constant. At the same time, that factor remains a larger consideration than racial status.

24 Compare Theodore J. Lowi, *The End of Liberalism,* Norton, New York, 1969, especially p. 55; Louis Hartz, *The Liberal Tradition in America,* Harcourt, Brace, New York, 1955, especially pp. 57 and 210–211; Devine, reference 4, especially p. 65; and Seymour Martin Lipset, *Political Man: The Social Basis of Politics,* Anchor Books, Doubleday, Garden City, N. Y., 1963 (originally published by Doubleday in 1960), especially pp. 344–346.

25 There is a further complication. Those Americans who actually merit being called conservatives, those who associate themselves with a historic conservative tradition, are by no means philosophically one. In the century after Locke, two contemporaries, Adam Smith and Edmund Burke, staked out positions which accentuated one (individual

freedom: Smith) and the other (traditional restraints: Burke) of the two main emphases in Locke's thought. With or without conscious reference, the thought and attitudes of modern American conservatives quite markedly tend to reflect either Smith or Burke. Indeed the self-styled libertarians reject or ignore the Burkeian tradition. Like modern liberals and hip intellectuals, they place a virtually unqualified trust in human nature.

There is also a common vulgar assumption that conservatism and promoting big-buck profit by any means are synonymous. By no stretch of definition are most big businessmen conservatives. Some are of the hip persuasion. Many more are quite willing to sacrifice both individual freedom and tradition by acceding to or even demanding more government control, of a kind which will endow them with government contracts, favors, and protection from domestic and foreign competition.

26 Lipset and Raab, reference 1, p. 48.

27 Devine, reference 4, p. 196.

28 Nathan Glazer, "The New Left and Its Limits," in William P. Gerberding and Duane E. Smith (eds.), *The Radical Left: The Abuse of Discontent,* Houghton Mifflin, Boston, 1970, pp. 11–30, p. 19.

29 Compare Irving Kristol, "An Urban Civilization without Cities?" *Horizon,* Autumn 1972, pp. 36–41, and Herman Kahn, reference 2.

30 Again, an image cannot be disproved. Still, an "objective observer" might wonder at the apparent contradiction of enthusiasm which the square feels for welfare-state programs which benefit him. There are few of these beyond Social Security provisions, however, and he has been told, has come to believe, that he will receive only what is coming to him out of his own contributions. Unlike the conservative, the square does not view Social Security as a violation of the work ethic, and he also welcomes government intervention in the economy.

31 This particular square attitude is widespread, even among segments of the population not ordinarily associated with square attitudes. A survey conducted by the Yankelovich organization showed that 75 percent of college students regard collecting welfare to be immoral for anyone who can work. *Time,* Oct. 30, 1972, pp. 96–97.

32 Lipset and Raab, reference 1, p. 43.

33 Eric Hoffer, *The Temper of Our Time,* Harper & Row, New York, 1967, p. 47.

34 For a documentation of these views among blue-collar workers, see Ransford, reference 13.

35 Writing before the emergence of the counterculture and the hip phenomenon, Professor Lipset traced the egalitarianism and "leftism" of the American intellectual, which leads him to "attack the existing distribution of privilege," to the intellectual's own "self-image as a person of low status." He envies the "gratifying social deference" accorded intellectuals in many parts of Europe, but fails to note that *all* positions of high status are so treated in those countries. In short the intellectual "is really objecting to the equalitarianism of the United States, not to a lower evaluation of his occupation by its citizens." Lipset, reference 24, especially pp. 347–355.

Professor Kristol says that the intellectual demand for equality on the contemporary scene is really a self-serving bid for power. Social criticism aims at a disguised target. Concern expressed about a material inequality, which is of narrower scope in modern America than in any other time or place, is actually an attack upon "the spiritual egalitarianism of bourgeois civilization" with which the common man remains obdurately contented. Irving Kristol, "About Equality," *Commentary*, November 1972, pp. 41–47, p. 44.

36 These ideas are explicitly combined in Theodore Roszak, *The Making of a Counter Culture*, Doubleday, Garden City, N. Y., 1969. His proclaimed enemy is "technocracy," a social form which maximizes production, gadgetry, and "organizational integration." At the same time, "an economy of cybernated abundance" now calls forth a proliferation of alternative nonwork life-styles, an emergent development hindered by the "bourgeoisie" and its obsession with greed.

37 The so-called identity crisis is a hip and not a square phenomenon. It has been commonly misinterpreted. Anguish stems less from an unrewarded search for "Who am I?" than from the knowledge that one's ideas, shared with like-minded others, do not raise one's own social status or confer power of any consequence. The key question then becomes not "Who am I?" but "Why am I not as important as I should be?" Hip nonworkers are especially prone to the "identity crisis." Those who work establish an identity apart from their ideas and life-style.

38 Irving Kristol, "Urban Civilization and Its Discontents," *Commentary*, July 1970, pp. 29–35, p. 34. Continued affluence and tax-subsidized leisure, and escape from such major crises as economic slump and war of more than brushfire scope, might foster continued drift in the hip direction. Since square attitudes obviously have greater value for collective survival, however, any major crisis could bring about that square backlash the prospect of which Herman Kahn apparently relishes. See reference 2.

39 The question about how many squares hold an image of an enemy establishment opens up a gray area. Attitudes can be crudely ascertained with the polling technique, but not images. Since youth and educational attainment are highly correlated, though, young squares appear more likely than older ones to hold such an image, and disaffected working-class youth surely do, however inchoate the form might be.

Working-class youth outnumber college youth, although they are commonly ignored when the "youth question" is being discussed They do not want rapid change, but rather an opportunity to pursue modest goals in parental footsteps—a "good job," marriage and family, retirement with security. They see themselves as the chosen victims of programs designed to redress injustice to others and re-form existing institutions. They envision "an organized effort within which agents of government, the mass media and even the church are co-conspirators." And they do not have the alternative of dropping out—"there is no place to drop out to." William Simon and John Gagnon, "Working-Class Youth," in Louise Kapp Howe (ed.), *The White Majority: Between Poverty and Affluence,* Random House, New York, 1970, pp. 45–49, pp. 49–50.

40 C. Wright Mills, *The Power Elite,* Oxford University Press, New York, 1956. For some excellent assessments of Mills's thesis, see G. William Domhoff and Hoyt B. Ballard (compilers), *C. Wright Mills and the Power Elite,* Beacon Press, Boston, 1969, especially the piece by William Kornhauser, " 'Power Elite' or 'Veto Groups,' " pp. 37–59. Kornhauser agrees with Mills that bureaucratization and centralization have wrought institutional change and expanded the scale of events and decisions. "But centralization cannot be equated with a power elite. There can be highly centralized institutions and at the same time a fragmentation of power among a multiplicity of relatively independent public and private agencies" (p. 56).

41 M. Stanton Evans, *The Liberal Establishment,* Devin-Adair, New York, 1965.

42 *San Francisco Chronicle,* Dec. 3, 1972, "Sunday Punch" section, p. l.

43 *San Francisco Chronicle,* Apr. 16, 1973, p. 37.

44 Victor Lasky, "Ask a Liberal Where His Kids Go to School," North American Newspaper Alliance column of Dec. 5, 1971.

45 *San Francisco Sunday Examiner and Chronicle,* June 25, 1972, sec. B, p. 3.

46 Hip spokesmen have claimed, without being gainsaid, that square types predominate in the consumption of pornography. Hip types on average are younger, and in any case more likely to expend sexual energy in nonvicarious ways. But here as elsewhere, the ambivalence of desire and inhibition usually effects some kind of compromise. Many, perhaps most, square patrons of "adult movies" and dirty books would prefer that pornography be kept hidden, under the counter, surreptitious of access, in order to protect themselves as well as the public against those "coarsening effects" which disturb Mr. Wright.

47 Philip S. Foner (ed.), *Basic Writings of Thomas Jefferson,* Willey Book Company, New York, 1944, p. 150.

48 Gaetano Mosca, *The Ruling Class,* Hannah D. Kahn (trans.), McGraw-Hill, New York, 1939, p. 112.

49 For a list of the seventy most prestigious contemporary American intellectuals, derived from a questionnaire submitted to intellectuals, see p. 123 of Charles Kadushin, "Who Are the Elite Intellectuals?" *The Public Interest,* Fall 1972, pp. 109–125.

50 Helmut Schoeck, *Envy: A Theory of Social Behavior,* Michael Glenny and Betty Ross (trans.), Harcourt Brace Jovanovich, New York, 1970, p. 261.

51 Helmut Schoeck, "Individuality vs. Equality," in Felix Morley (ed.), *Essays in Individuality,* University of Pennsylvania Press, Philadelphia, 1958, pp. 103–124, p. 113.

52 See Roger Brown, *Social Psychology,* Free Press, New York, 1965, especially p. 142.

53 Andrew Hacker, *The End of the American Era,* Atheneum, New York, 1970, p. 31.

54 Devine, reference 4, p. 217.

55 Robert E. Lane, *Political Ideology: Why the American Common Man Believes What He Does,* Free Press, New York, 1962, especially chap. 4. The main citations are from pp. 61 and 77.

56 Christopher Jencks et al., *Inequality: A Reassessment of the Effect of Family and Schooling in America,* Basic Books, New York, 1972, p. 227. This variable, more accurately residual category, of "luck" is open to question. What enables individuals to innovate, to produce, to succeed has been determined by thorough research to be a "need for achievement," something apart from IQ scores, educational attainment, a drive to make money, or even being in the right place at the right time. See David C. McClelland, *The Achieving Society,* Van Nostrand, Princeton, N. J., 1961. For support of McClelland's work, based upon an examination of later research, see Brown, reference 52, especially p. 342. Luck does enhance the probability of success, but only if motivation is present.

57 Jencks, reference 56, p. 230.

58 Jencks, reference 56, pp. 75–76.

59 Daniel Bell, "On Meritocracy and Equality," *The Public Interest,* Fall 1972, pp. 29–68, p. 44.

60 Paul Seabury, "The Idea of Merit," *Commentary,* December 1972, pp. 41–45, p. 44.

61 The courts have also intervened. The Supreme Court has ruled against employer use of standardized intelligence tests when such screening for employment is not "related to job performance." That decision has been interpreted to mean that there can be no education requirement "without proof of its overriding business necessity." Elliott Abrams, "The Quota Commission," *Commentary,* October 1972, pp. 54–57, p. 56.

62 Abrams, reference 61, p. 55. On this same page Abrams cites the enabling legislation [Section 703 (j) of Title VII]: "Nothing contained in this title shall be interpreted to require any employer . . . to grant preferential treatment to any individual or to any group because of the race, color, religion, sex, or national origin . . . on account of an imbalance which may exist . . . in comparison with the total number or percentage of persons of such race [and so on] in any community. . . ."

63 Cited in Abrams, reference 61, p. 56.

64 *Wall Street Journal,* Oct. 10, 1972, pp. 1 and 18, p. 18.

65 Martin Mayer, "Higher Education for All?" *Commentary,* February 1973, pp. 37–47, p. 45.

66 Thomas Sowell, *Black Education: Myths and Tragedies,* McKay, New York, 1972, p. 135. The citation is from a Cornell Board of Trustees report.

67 Sowell, reference 66, p. 208. It has been similarly charged that by equality "mass intellectuals" really mean "*their* right to run society." They will never be satisfied with concessions granted to equal results "because the impulse is not, in the end, about equality at all but about the quality of life in bourgeois society." Irving Kristol, "About Equality," *Commentary,* November 1972, pp. 41–47, p. 44.

68 The average occupational status of Orientals in America is higher than that of the white population, and their educational status is much higher. Calvin F. Schmid and Charles E. Nobbe, "Socioeconomic Differentials among Nonwhite Races," *American Sociological Review,* 30:909–922, 1965, especially pp. 920 and 912.

69 Murray N. Rothbard, "The Quota System Must Be Repudiated Immediately," *Intellectual Digest,* February 1973, pp. 78 and 80, p. 78.

70   Bell, reference 59, pp. 48 and 58.

71   Nathan Glazer, "McGovern and the Jews: A Debate," *Commentary,* September 1972, pp. 43–47, p. 46.

72   Some more obscure reasons which have been offered to explain a supposed universal rejection of traditional American life include: loss of faith in personal immortality has destroyed religious justification of resignation to low status; waning faith in a collective secular destiny, of America a beacon of freedom and democracy to the world, has made private good an overriding concern; the near collapse of class structure has released envy from confinement within a given class and attached it to anyone who has or is something that another man lacks; and a sense of uncaring social isolation spreads with the burgeoning of bureaucracy, with the creation of faceless unidentifiable leaders who, unlike the old-fashioned boss, do not share the social environment of their status inferiors.

All these claims doubtless have some merit. But their sweep is too grand to afford much help in understanding the pull and tug of contemporary social life. Singly or in combination they will not explain why some elements in the population as vigorously defend certain traditional values as other elements attack them. On balance, the square retention of traditional values remains marked enough to maintain a qualitative difference between the two camps.

Social-Problem Explanation

Thus far we have dealt with social problems themselves, with particular stress placed upon a clash of attitudes expressed in the social struggle. In this chapter we focus primarily upon sociological problems of explanation. The next chapter unites both themes, and introduces some other aspects of social problems which have not hitherto been explored.

That social problems are essentially subjectivistic phenomena has remained our central thesis. Attitudes for or against a social-problem issue are held independently of how "bad" addressed conditions might be when those conditions are assessed with historical and statistical comparisons. Moreover, amidst continuous disputation the attitudes of nonsociologists create social problems. Therefore what any social problem *is* from one point in time to another shifts, contracts, expands, or even disappears.

While the attitudes of nonsociologists create and alternatively dispute the existence of social problems, social problems can be assessed by sociologists in a more systematic and "objective" way than by those who promote or deny them. Social problems remain essentially subjectivistic phenomena, but they as well as the attitudes which create them *can* be scientifically studied. And to repeat further, the sociologist's role is that of analyst, not activist, mover, or reformer. Only as objects of study are social problems the property of sociologists. What goals other men should pursue and what attitudes they should hold are not matters for sociology or any other science to adjudicate.

In this chapter we will first examine the main concepts which sociologists have used in social-problem explanation and classification, deviance and social disorganization. These concepts are shown to have limited scientific validity. Then an alternative way of approaching social problems is presented.

THE MAIN CONCEPTS

In the early part of the twentieth century many more people than is now the case unselfconsciously shared a common outlook and almost uniform prejudices. The baseline of what was right and wrong in action and attitude was, relatively speaking, firmly drawn. Again speaking in relative terms, departure from that baseline, whether viewed in statistical or moral terms, was slight.

Therefore, in the recent past what constituted departure from an assumed baseline could be fairly commonly agreed upon, within as well as outside sociological circles. The two main concepts developed by sociologists at this earlier time for the study of social problems, deviance and social disorganization, possessed an apparent objectivity which they lack at the present time. Only in recent years has the nonscientific character, the moral-judgment basis, of those concepts been revealed (1). Only later, when sociologists began to quarrel about where the baseline could be located, or whether it existed, was the dubious worth of the concepts disclosed. Sociological disagreement is now sharply registered on what deviance and social disorganization really are, how they can be isolated as objects of study, and finally how the two concepts might be kept separate.

The Two Sociological Camps

An ideological split in modern sociology divides those who are more or less in favor of the prevailing social order from those who are against it. The two camps strikingly differ in the attributions of deviance and social disorganization which they make, so that the nonscientific character of the concepts has been clearly revealed. One camp, the more or less traditionalist one, remains the larger despite continuing defections to the other. This larger camp retains a relatively "conservative" and "functionalist" cast (2). The members of it assume a continuity of present institutional arrangements; they tend to see each institution as making some essential contribution to a society viewed as being a more or less integrated social whole. The members of the smaller but growing one, the hip camp, on the other hand declare all institutions to be bankrupt, and they seek to justify efforts first to dismantle society entire and then to rebuild it.

Those sociologists who remain more or less on the traditionalist side have often been accused of holding a warped image of reality. They have been said to remain blind to the fractured social system which in fact has emerged. They have been described as holding onto an image of America past, with its relatively integrated social institutions, secure statuses and roles, and continuity of experience. And these sociologists, the indictment continues, blame those people whom they call deviants for what they call deviance, and name as social disorganization those very faults which are inherent in modern social organization.

These sociologists have been said to be displeased with nonconformity. "All approaches to social problems that define them with respect to the given society as the actor who is displeased, share a common ideological commitment to the established order. . . . The variation studied is in conformity or nonconformity to that order, and the factors associated with it. The bias is toward conformity" (3).

But by the same token the bias on the other, the hip, side is toward nonconformity and against the established order. No degree of permanence in the social structure is assumed, and therefore the concept of social disorganization is rarely employed, except when the entire social order is held to be in such a state. Here a conflict model of society replaces the integrative model. This conflict model is one of unrelieved antagonism, with little place for common loyalties, shared attitudes and convictions. In its starkest form, this model is one of ultimate conflict between good and evil.

The typical hip position is one which denies that terms like deviance and social disorganization refer to technical or objective criteria. These terms are said to be used to pass moral judgments upon issues of conflict. This is solid ground, however dubious the next steps usually taken may be: American society itself totally exemplifies social disorganization, and much more often the charge is made that those who "label" deviants are the source of the behavior they deplore.

Labeling

The original text of the so-called labeling school was written by Professor Howard Becker: "The deviant is one to whom that label has successfully been applied; deviant behavior is behavior that people so label" (4). Some of Becker's followers, like him, do take into some account the behavior of the person to whom the label is applied. But most of them do not, and for this school as a whole it can fairly be said that any behavior of the person who is labeled a deviant is ignored, and deviance is said to reside solely in the attitudes of, the rules and sanctions applied by, powerful others who define his behavior as deviance.

The point, up to a point, is well taken. Judgments by others of one's behavior determine how that behavior will be described, reacted to, and treated. But the point remains a half-truth. True, a pickpocket, for example, would not be a criminal if others refrained from labeling the act of picking pockets a crime. But even if they did so refrain, the pickpocket, and no one else, would be the person who picks pockets, and his acts would remain at least *statistical* deviance in the sense that most other citizens do not pick pockets.

The assumption that all deplored behavior is somehow the fault of those who do the deploring has taken some of Professor Becker's followers into paths he would surely avoid. For example: "Victim-blaming is cloaked in kindness and concern, and bears all the trappings and statistical furbelows of scientism; it is obscured by a perfumed haze of humanitarianism." This statement is not claimed to be based upon evidence, inferential or otherwise. Such a claim, though, is made for the following statement by the same writer: the "manic and mindless rock-throwing, and window-breaking, and bank-burning, and bombing" of the late sixties "seems almost too fortuitous, and much of it has such an aroma of irrationality that one is inclined to look for the spoor of the *agent provocateur*, the classical henchman of government repression" (5).

The value judgments of the labeling school, like any value judgments, are invulnerable to criticism on the grounds of evidence, but one theoretical claim they make is open to question: that with the adoption of a symbolic interactionist frame of reference, they have surmounted the crude environmentalism of earlier social-problems researchers. Crude environmentalism once held that slums, bad companions ("differential association"), poverty, and the like, *caused* deviance. Crude environmentalism in new, labeling, guise holds that attitudes of others wrongly define, blame, and make the so-called deviant.

Again, by no means do all sociologists affiliated with this school adopt a position of "hard" determinism. Some of them assign a certain degree of "freedom" to the labeled deviant, and explore some points of interaction between the labeler and the person labeled. The thrust of the school considered as a whole, however, is toward obscuring the identity of a fellow human being who might, like everyone else, perceive a total situation, interpret that situation, and then will to act, elect to choose what *he* will do.

We are still, as in the case of the older crude environmentalism, for the most part presented with a fictive automaton who is totally victimized by what is totally exterior to himself. The labeled deviant remains essentially a passive recipient of others' blame to which he can only react. He does not serially act after he continuously reassesses a shifting scene of interaction with others, which is only partly comprised of negative attitudes toward him. And the reactions of others to *his* subsequent actions are generally ignored by the labeling school. One might add that no attention has been paid the behavioral consequences for "so-called deviants" when their "alternative life-styles" are exculpated or even praised by publicists who studied labeling theory in college.

The Majority and Max Weber

The majority were defined in the first chapter as an unorganized nonmembership dispersed in space and lacking a self-conscious awareness of unified purpose, and whose cultural attitudes remain relatively traditionalistic. Their "way of life" is now much less articulated and consistent than heretofore. They tend to react defensively before the innovative ideas and programs of political-intellectual minorities, and since they lack much erstwhile support from figures of institutional authority, they do not possess social power commensurate with their numbers.

This situation, compounded by an increasing rate of social change which unhinges traditional statuses and roles, makes the concepts of deviance and social disorganization more than ever slippery to handle. Deviance and social disorganization, however defined, must be shown to depart from some baseline of comparison. That baseline can only be a total context of majority behavior, of established action and interaction, from which either a statistical or a moral departure is reckoned.

Majority attitudes alone will not suffice to form a baseline, for they often express resentment against changes taking place which the majority feel helpless to control. And most majority attitudes are mercurial; they shift within the public if not private personality with perceived winds of events, threats, propaganda, and faits accomplis. Majority attitudes, to be sure, are by no means unimportant epiphenomena. Those few which are widely shared and deeply felt circumscribe the will and actions of political-intellectual minorities, whose innovative attitudes for the most part create social problems. But at any given time the majority's public attitudes, essentially defensive attitudes, will not serve as a baseline from which *behavioral* departure can be described.

The majority can be said to share a common *way* of life much less than they share a common *view* of social life. The so-called postindustrial service economy, the varieties of expression sponsored by time-plan consumerism, high rates of mobility in space and status, the loosening of intergenerational ties within the family, and, most important of all, the growing tendency to identify self and others by job placement in a bureaucracy instead of by community and family affiliation—these and other crude (and admittedly tautological) factors have encouraged the promotion of alternative styles of life and ways of behaving. Thus when squares are compared with their opposite numbers, they may remain square, but they are not so square as they once were *(6)*.

The context of behavior from which departure can be assessed, then, has become less solid, less unified. That particular change has been unevenly recognized within modern sociology. In one extreme example, squares have been pictured as imposing uniform standards of morality upon "their infant children," as running about "censoring movies" and censuring others with an adamant intolerance (7).

Actually, the modern square is far more likely to tolerate, if not be tolerant of, divorce next door, pot smoking, the neighborhood kid returned from draft-encouraged residence in Canada, and pornography, if it is not too public. His neighbor's religious affiliation is not likely to interest him very much, or whether or not he attends church. His hatred can be, often is, unleashed, but typically when "they" are perceived as trying to put him down or threatening to destroy his own house of traditional culture, not when "they" are seen as discreetly doing their own not-so-different thing.

The square's toleration of those people whose conduct he does not approve of is no matter of conviction; it stems mainly from his feeling helpless to resist and control them. The market for converting his attitudes into action is not brisk. Moreover, his residual *in*tolerance is activated much less by anyone's "deviance" from his own chosen and by no means uniform path than by his profound displeasure at being held up to ridicule by his self-appointed betters, and from having to pay taxes for what are to him "radical" measures of reform.

A combination, then, of structural change and an inability of the majority to enforce standards of conduct they as much pay lip service to as live by, within a milieu apparently controlled by others, has narrowed any baseline from which departure can be effectively demonstrated. In short, new ways of life and styles of life proliferate independently of that cohesive set of cultural attitudes the majority still maintain.

A relatively fragmented social life has, then, emerged *(8)*. Like any other major social change, this one can be variously assessed, even with the same value commitment, such as that of preserving the "democratic way of life." Much of the unity upon which that way of life depends has been lost. On the other hand, a relatively fragmented way of life—at least in the short term—makes the imposition of totalitarian control difficult to imagine.

Nevertheless, while *1984* haunts the imagination of most other intellectuals, modern American sociologists generally remain captive to Max Weber's similar prophecy: the future will become more "rationalized," bureaucratic, centrally controlled, stifling of voluntary action and the human spirit. Weber further stated that the march of bureaucracy in the modern West cannot be stopped, that citizens will become more uniform in their acceptance of a common and imposed discipline. He failed to consider the possibility that social behavior might become *less* uniform, that the danger of the "iron cage" might be encroached upon by the danger of anarchy, and that at some further time large national units might break up instead of becoming further amalgamated.

The above is of course entirely conjectural. And in a consideration of all conceivable outcomes, Weber's prophecy *could* ultimately come to pass, and in that case departure or deviance from an *imposed* baseline will be readily demonstrable. But right now there is as much warrant for another guess, that no totalitarian regime will succeed in imposing a rigidly structured social life, that a relatively fragmented social life will persist into the near future, with the hip-square confrontation kept below flash point, and that departure from an assumed baseline will continue to be difficult to state and assess.

DEVIANCE

In the first part of this chapter a distinction was drawn between those sociologists who are more or less in favor of the prevailing social order and those who are opposed to it. The former were said to retain a relatively "functionalist" cast. For the sake of convenience the terms "functionalist" and "hip" are employed below in a shorthand way to refer to the two designated camps, even though most sociologists would doubtless deny that they could be so neatly cataloged, and in some cases with considerable justification.

In some ways the two camps are closer together than the arbitrary distinction used here implies. Deviance and social disorganization are commonly viewed as the main explanations as well as classification of social problems. There is a consequent strain upon both camps to assume a heavier baseline from which departure can be reckoned than the evidence will permit.

As for deviance, the two camps differ only marginally on holding "society" to be to blame for it. Beyond that point, however, some real differences do appear. Functionalists would have no basic quarrel with this hip sociological statement: a "deviant subculture" reflects "an ill or inadequacy in the social fabric itself." On the other hand, most functionalists at least imply the desirability of reincorporating deviants within a common social life, something of which no hip sociologist, including the one cited, would be guilty. For the extreme hip sociologist, the very notion of a common social life is anathema, a consequence only of control imposed by the establishment.

The majority, not the deviants, must change their ways. Deviance indicates the path of common redemption. According to the same source, sexual deviants "graphically point up the various deep-rooted sexual hangups of our society." In similar fashion, "the Black Panthers signify our racial inequalities and where they can lead." And, in the same vein, drug use serves to remind "how confining and 'soulless' our overtly rational and materialistic way of life may have become" (9).

The notion of a common social life, it should be noted, is totally dismissed only at the extreme hip end of the attitude range. The above quotations, for example, retain a faint nonhip tone by pleading for a change of heart on the part of the majority. The hope of rational persuasion is not abandoned nor are the majority summarily dismissed, as is the case in the following pure-hip sociological statement: "Applied sociologists" should help "members of subordinate marginal groups" to initiate change "from below." In this venture "drug addicts might be organized to alter laws concerning drug use; students might be organized to change the character of schools; and mental patients might be organized to change the way they are treated" (10). The target of the extreme hip sociologist is not only prevailing power distribution, but the very idea of authority.

Who Is Deviant?

As concept, classification, and explanation, deviance towers above everything else in the social-problems literature. But neither functionalist nor hip sociologist makes exactly clear who is deviant. The functionalist continues to regard the deviant as someone who violates socially approved behavior in a moral or moral-legal way, in an era when what is socially approved and what is socially disapproved have become somewhat murky and the means of punishing violation, outside of primary groups, quite attenuated *(11).* The hip sociologist locates deviance not in the "so-called" deviant but in the misguided behavior of those who might disapprove, which is even more difficult to ascertain.

Since majority attitudes still cohere about traditionalistic beliefs, the functionalist approach to deviance might appear to be still worthwhile, which would be the case except for two emergent circumstances. First, the social power of the majority has diminished, that of political-intellectual minorities has increased, and with the spread of higher education in company of a quasi-hip popular culture the means for transforming majority attitudes into unified action have been vastly reduced. Numbers provide strength only for occasional massive veto operations, not for the day-by-day enforcement of traditional rules of conduct upon others outside the circle of the personally known. For the most part, the majority *feel* like an unrepresented and voiceless minority. In large measure their attitudes are so many ineffective protests against a proliferation of alternative life-styles which are perforce tolerated if not actually approved.

Second, persisting traditional attitudes cannot reduce that role confusion which is endemic in modern society. No single and well-articulated moral code holds sway. What remains of traditional role requirements has been fractured. "The number of positions has increased; their role specifications have become narrower; consensus may have declined; the number of positions that can be achieved has increased; the size of position networks has tended to grow; and positions that formerly clustered in one person have been broken apart" (12).

Most married women, for example, now work outside the home

during one or more periods of their lives. The role of jobholder is somewhat incongruent with that of wife and mother. Even though the former may, like the latter, stress personal service, it contains requirements of competition and efficiency that are alien to the latter. In some lines of so-called women's work there is an enforced pattern of "being nice" to male clients or customers. These and many other violations of traditional requirements and expectations set the stage for interrole conflict, because the majority of modern American women still attempt to fulfill some semblance of the old wife-and-mother role, including some minimum of ritualistic subordination to the husband.

Many of them, of course, do not. The conflict of roles within the home itself, opening up choices among variations of housewife-and-mother, companion, and partner roles for the wife, makes any real fulfillment of the traditional housewife-and-mother role virtually as impossible as it would be distasteful, to many men as well as most women. Later ideological revolt by role-style leaders against "sexist" roles of any kind or degree, in the train of structural economic change, has almost legitimized ways of living which are nearly as free of man-woman interaction as definition. Those who disapprove lack the will, because they lack enough social power, to respecify arbitrary sex roles.

Given this sequence of pressures, contradictions, and perceived weakness, *who* is "more deviant," Gloria Steinem or a submissive, self-sacrificing housewife? A virgin at age twenty-five or an abortion-seeking unmarried girl? (That the first in majority opinion is still generally admired, the latter censured or pitied, is for present purposes beside the point.) A like sequence would apply to the question, Boy Scout or pot-smoking runaway *(13)?* And to that of "old-time darky" or Black Panther? Actually, the former is *more* deviant, in both a statistical sense and that of emerging moral approval of behavior, as the quasi-institutionalization of black militancy imposes more "responsible" limits upon action if not rhetoric.

One student at a Catholic university accepts traditional religious dogma and values. Another rejects both. Who is more deviant? It has in effect been argued that the former is more deviant. Of a sample of students drawn from a large Jesuit university, a statistical majority approved of marijuana use, student protests and strikes, sexual relations without marital intent, and occupations that afford "self-expression, creativity, and helping others, rather than money or status."

Close to half of the sample have left the parental religion, and more than half approve of "left-wing" politics. Most of them "tend to reject 'ethnic' identification, as well as aspiration toward the status, affluence, and 'moral propriety' of the WASP." Perhaps "espousal of 'countercultural' values is the final stage of acculturation for some college youth; 'ethnic' Catholic values have become as irrelevant as the 'dominant' WASP values. . . . Thus, it seems that for 'ethnic' Catholic college students, the counterculture is the final stage of acculturation" (14).

This last sentence is somewhat overstated. Data cited in Chapter 5 disclose that, on balance, attitudes of college students are possibly more square than hip. Perhaps the proportions listed in the two previous paragraphs more reflect temporary adoption of what is chic and fashionable in an enclosed social milieu than radical shifts of attitude.

However, the college square *is* "deviant" in the sense that the baseline of social conduct on campus is now set by prevailing hip fashion. The square in college has been more placed on the defensive than squares elsewhere, but for how long? Since no other stage in history has ever been final, the counterculture can hardly prove to be such. There appear to be signs that impassioned commitment to it has already waned, and any marked falling away would surely occur first among "ethnic Catholics." Their "acculturation" would then find another level of expression, although that would very unlikely be uniformly square. Nevertheless, it would be foolish at the present time to attempt to state who on campus is deviant from whom.

Deviance in the Hip-Square Arena
The attribution and denial of deviance have become part of the social struggle, in and outside books on social problems. Criminality is regarded by the majority, and in some social-problems texts, as the most obvious and flagrant type of deviant behavior. But hip

sociologists and the hip contingent in general claim that domestic military planners, corporations that resist installation of pollution-abatement equipment, and other "establishment" malefactors are far worse criminals than those individuals who simply rip off big and corrupt corporations or rob from other persons directly or even assault them physically. Such acts are relatively blameless. For example: "We must see that *covert institutional violence* is much more destructive than overt individual violence" (15). And hip sociologists muddle older distinctions between crime and political action. For example: "The rapidly rising crime rates indicate a further ambiguity in the traditional formulation of social deviance. It is of decreasing *sociological* importance whether 'crime' is perceived as an act of politics or deviance" (16).

This struggle provokes a great deal of "symbolic behavior"—in the special sense of protest action apparently designed more to state a position in the world than to achieve a specific objective. Temperance and antigambling crusades of the past have been discussed in this connection, when their respective proponents had no real hope of eliminating either. Since it should be obvious that gambling never has been and never will be eliminated, in Boston "the maintenance of a norm which defines gambling as deviant behavior thus symbolizes the maintenance of Yankee social and political superiority" (17). Zealots who oppose pornography, "con-porns" in the terminology of some sociologists, are said to realize they cannot put an end to smut, but their crusade goes on because their real goal is public affirmation of their own moral superiority.

Although "symbolic behavior" goes generally unremarked on the other side, it does occur there. The "Berkeley initiative" to estop enforcement of laws against marijuana possession and use was passed, but it was helpless to control the Berkeley police, who at that time were sworn to enforce California state laws against marijuana (18). Likewise, because of its ideological "moral righteousness" the recent college antiwar movement has been said to have been counterproductive. The majority solidly rejected the Vietnam war in its later stages, but only because that conflict was perceived as a military mistake which should be abandoned. "Disenchantment with the war [was] based on our visible lack of success in winning it." This change in majority attitude was accompanied by rising hostility toward antiwar college protesters *(19),* who failed in one real objective since the war ended for what was to them the wrong reasons, and they were left unvindicated.

SOCIAL DISORGANIZATION

The baseline of organization from which social disorganization departs is no more clear than the baseline of overt conformity from which deviance departs. In both cases value judgment rules, either the described value judgment of vaguely specified others or the unadmitted value judgment of the sociologist. These two categories do not constitute a classification of social problems, and as explanation they are sheerly tautological. "The sociological theories of disorganization and deviance . . . show . . . confusion over whether there is a causal or an identity relation between factors of disorganization and immorality. Factors of disorganization, anomie, and the like, are both defined in terms of immorality and used to explain this immorality" (20).

The terms "deviance" and "social disorganization" when used in sociological writing are often interchangeable. Social disorganization is often used to denote a failure of the socialization process, a failure to provide individuals with a status which incorporates conformity to assumed major values and beliefs. Social disorganization, in this sense, *is* indistinguishable from deviance. But alternatively, the term is used to refer to institutional breakdown, an assumed failure of one or more institutions to guide conduct for a total population.

As Failure of the Socialization Process

Professor Merton's hypothesis, that "aberrant behavior may be regarded sociologically as a symptom of dissociation between culturally prescribed aspirations and socially structured avenues for realizing these aspirations" (21), has become the most influential notion about social disorganization in the modern sociological literature. American society is said to lay upon *all* its members an absolute injunction to succeed, mainly in pecuniary terms. Widespread anomie, or "normlessness," is thus promoted, because the institutional means of achievement are denied to those near or at the bottom of the socio-economic scale. This state of social disorganization, of discrepancy between motivated ends and accessibility to means, is further said to have eroded traditional moral controls of striving behavior; hence, in company of mass frustration, crime is fostered.

It is within the family that this imbalance between pecuniary ambition and opportunity is viewed as first being imposed upon the child. While his parents may explicitly stress traditional standards of honesty, in subliminal ways he is cued on the greater importance they attach to making good over being good. They project upon the child their own unrealized aspirations. He must succeed where they have failed. Compensatory pressure upon children to make good is said to be heaviest within the lower strata, where access to means of high achievement is virtually absent. But this particular conjecture, about the distribution of compensatory pressure, is not borne out by empirical research *(22)*.

The above hypothesis, with the rising-expectations formula substituted for that of experience within the family, has been utilized to explain many instances of attributed social disorganization, including violence. The discrepancy between "societal forces" which stimulate personal aspiration and the limited means available for achievement "is one significant factor determining the level of violence in a society. If aspirations are escalated—by the movies, television, advertising, and modern secular education—while new jobs, income, and housing increase more slowly, violence will rise" *(23)*.

Although this and the original hypothesis retain persuasive verisimilitude, they will not encompass some counterindicative data. During the Depression of the thirties, when Professor Merton's hypothesis appeared in print, crime and delinquency rates were actually, comparatively, quite low *(24)*. In comparative terms, moreover, institutional controls of behavior remained consistent and firm. Finally, in the popular culture of that time was a celebration of wealth and conspicuous consumption which surpassed all that came before or followed. Money was a near monomania during the thirties. There was a brisk market for commerical fantasies about money, getting money, spending money in postures of monied elegance. Many of the movies of that era, which can be seen on the TV late-late show, are quite convincing on that point. The fictive life so lavishly displayed is not so much shocking as it is alien to contemporary sensibilities.

The overriding popularity of the success theme was almost a

distinctive characteristic of the thirties. It accompanied the frustration of a stone wall across the path. But at that time the essentially
contemporary notion that being deprived of anything one wants
must be someone else's fault was only beginning to find acceptable
public expression. Indeed, the popular culture of the thirties, by
stressing luck as the main line of separation between rich and poor,
with the ready chance of marrying a millionaire or getting a million
dollars from the random bequests of an eccentric tycoon, drained
off much of that sullen envy which tends to characterize protest
activity at the present time.

The state of anomie, which Professor Merton defines as one "in
which common values have been submerged in the welter of private
interests," has become more striking and widespread than ever it
was during the thirties. The pressure to succeed, however, appears
to be much less intensive. The very idea of success has entered "a
whirlpool of philosophical confusion." Public education seeks to
teach the child rather than subject matter, and educate him to his
own potential instead of exhort him to excel (25). Political-intellectual minorities tend to disapprove of and assign guilt to the successful individual who leaves others behind, and similar doubts about
the morality of a self-centered achievement which fails to "help
other people" are being expressed in the public schools.

Although Professor Merton has much company in his assertion
that everyone in American society is encouraged, and feels impelled,
to achieve the heights of success, that degree of emphasis may be
excessive. He does, however, for the most part restrict his assumption that the theme of success promotes anomie to a specific claim.
The poor, blocked from access to the means of success while impelled to seek it, are especially prone to crime and other manifestations of anomic behavior. Only in this particular setting, he adds,
does poverty "cause" crime. Poverty has no such consequence in
other societies where "differential class symbols of success" prevail.

Hard data are unobtainable in this area. Surely an "open-class
system" such as our own, in contrast to societies where status is
largely determined at birth, does fail to provide clearly marked
plateaus of achievement where dissatisfaction can abate when approbation is secured from one's own peers. That a difference exists
is beyond dispute, but the traumatic consequences of that difference
may not actually be all that severe in our own society.

There may be some danger of exaggerating career dissatisfaction in our society in comparison with that in more rigidly stratified ones. For most Americans, "success" has meant moving up and out from the material and career circumstances of an earlier point in the individual life cycle. We have no evidence that the majority, or most of the poor for that matter, ever suffered emotionally crippling frustration at failure to scale the heights. We really do not know that visible upward movement of modest scope, from the personal past and with reference to personally known circles, failed or now fails to bring some measure of satisfaction and contentment.

In any event, a further decline of the success theme appears probable. With the leveling out of the material base, any success which falls short of national recognition is difficult to register in one's own or others' eyes. As one probable consequence, most Americans at present appear to be more concerned with material enjoyment than about success, too busy living well to worry about making good. And college students, assured of affluence or at least subsistence, when they are surveyed from one year to another on average specify increasingly modest career goals. Such themes as serving others and seeking an interesting life are taking up much of the slack in the theme of success.

Professor Merton's hypothesis centers largely upon crime and the poor. Data cited in previous chapters show that the poor now have much readier access to means of legitimate advancement than heretofore—in education, in job opportunities and training, and through political intervention. The higher reported rates of crime and violence at the present time can thus hardly be explained as a combination of a ubiquitous success theme and denial of access to achievement. Like everyone else the poor are under less pressure to succeed than formerly, while means of access to achieve have been improved for them.

An Alternative Hypothesis

Another hypothesis than the one we have been examining may be more adequate to explain the measurable increase of anomic behavior since the Depression. It is based upon an intrusive factor which began to take shape at that time but since has become common coin in political-intellectual exchange. This factor is the new and popular idea that failure to receive (not achieve) high income and honorific status is to be blamed upon society or the power structure.

An earlier formula, which persisted throughout the Depression, in popular thought loomed far above fantasies of becoming rich through a lucky break. This formula stressed hard work, talent, and disciplined effort as the means, perhaps an almost sure means, of achieving success. In simplest expression: he who strives *will* succeed. This formula, that every individual is wholly responsible for whether he succeeds or fails, was cruelly naïve.

But the new formula may be equally cruel and naïve. While inciting resentment and envy, it fosters defeatism of another kind. It states that all categories of persons defined as suffering victims are helpless to affect any personal outcome. The poor, once charged with near total responsibility for their own plight, in certain quarters are now excused from any such responsibility at all. Many intellectuals, possibly most intellectuals, now argue that the poor are helpless because repression, suppression, exploitation force those at the bottom to remain where they are *(26)*.

No quarrel with that claim is being engaged, for exactly who is exploiting or repressing whom, like who owes what to whom, is a matter of images and their attendant attitudes, which are beyond proof or disproof. Situations defined as real nevertheless oftentimes do have real consequences, and the message continuously received by the poor, that their condition is totally explained by the evil machinations of others, can make that condition unbearable. The *experience* of frustrated desire is unquestionably more widespread and acute at the present time than ever it was during the Depression. And just possibly, as one instance, when the National Commission on the Causes and Prevention of Violence averred that the failure to provide the poor with a better life "continues to be a prescription for violence," it may also have been inviting violence.

Much intellectual and official moral justification has been conferred upon actions which at one time were universally labeled as being illegitimate. The assurance that important others are prepared to excuse violence and crime when certain desires are left unsatisfied merits consideration as one factor in any explanation of what Professor Merton calls anomic behavior. The received message that being where one is can acceptably be blamed upon the failure of society to grant what one desires could possibly exacerbate resentment and provide supportive rationalization for crime and violence.

Whether or not the message is "true" is essentially beside the point. True or false, it can become a calculation of weakness in others when a choice is made to act. Further, according to Professor Schoeck, lack of external opportunity to satisfy desires is much less an incitement to crime, vandalism, and violence than is the inner experience of envy, and envy "is in no way dependent upon the actual degree of existing inequalities" (27).

As Institutional Breakdown

Social disorganization as institutional breakdown shares similar difficulties with social disorganization as failure of the socialization process. In the first case the stated relationship between an assumed sovereign cultural compulsion to succeed and an assumed lack of legitimate means to improve one's lot remains uncertain. In this case there is no way to specify when social disorganization has actually occurred. Technical-objective criteria have not been developed for determining when a given institution has become "dysfunctional" in relation to the entire social order *(28)*.

We have already seen in Chapter 1 that much behavior generally described in the social-problems literature as social disorganization is actually highly organized and well articulated—organized crime, for example. Social disorganization, then, can be morally disapproved social organization. Much more often, however, the expression of such value judgments singles out one or another aspect of a social institution which is structurally inseparable from that institution.

Max Weber's important dictum—that we can never simultaneously maximize all our values—has important consequences for any claim that social disorganization can be assessed upon technical-objective grounds. If the failure to maximize one value within an institutional whole is termed a social problem of social disorganization, then an attempt to rectify the situation would logically require that some other prized value within that institutional whole would have to be sacrificed.

This kind of balance goes unrecognized in attributions of institutional social disorganization. Choice and sacrifice are neither made nor advised for others when the intrinsic relationship between desired and undesired aspects of social institutions remains unexamined. But the wanted change, even if it could be instituted, would demand a price, a price which is generally ignored.

What follows are judgments frequently passed in the social-problems literature. Appended to these judgments are the various and generally unreckoned prices which would have to be paid were each wanted change to assume overriding importance. Take, for example, disapproval expressed about a declared "alienation" from the job, said to result from narrowed, specialized, and repetitive operations within the modern division of labor. But there is an intrinsic relationship between job operations which are deplored and high levels of production which generally are not, because they in turn confer high levels of material consumption. Quite possibly a nation of craftsmen would be more contented with their work than one of specialists, but only if, given a total scale of values, they did not have to revert to near-subsistence living. The real price of a hypothetical recasting of the present division of labor would very likely be as unacceptable to a majority of the work force as it goes unreckoned by those who criticize "alienation."

Again, divorce is generally regarded as an index of family disorganization, and generally deplored. A high divorce rate, however, is maintained by values of individualism and hedonism, values which writers on social problems either endorse or take for granted, as Pitirim Sorokin and a few other sociologists have pointed out. In broader terms, most students of social problems state that a greater degree of stability and cohesion is needed in American society, but the freedom to exercise individual choice, which undermines stability and cohesion, is either assumed or praised.

Of some possible significance in this same connection is the institution of religion, which in the modern social-problems literature is rarely if ever referred to in discussions of social disorganization—no instances come to mind. But Max Weber, for one, was struck by the widespread and disruptive consequences of a loss of religious faith upon the entire social order. A failure to discuss the "social disorganization" of modern religion, an evident loyalty to the values of secular humanism, further indicates the primacy of value judgment in *selective* attributions of social disorganization.

War, on the other hand, *is* recognized as a social problem by all modern students of the subject. War is generally regarded as social disorganization and it is generally disapproved. However, not many sociologists, or many other American citizens for that matter, would be willing to accept conquest by a foreign power, or even sacrifice defined national interest in a hypothetical world-state.

(Bertrand Russell and a few other intellectuals *have* acknowledged that the price of unilateral disarmament would be conquest by a foreign power, and they have also declared themselves willing to pay that price in order to remove the threat of war.) One real or the other fictive price would ultimately have to be paid for that abandonment of state sovereignty which would inevitably accompany the decision to abolish the means of maintaining a military balance of power. The point is that the total context within which institutional social disorganization is invariably specified always contains inextricable elements of the highly valued and desired.

Reorganization and the Majority

There is another difficulty. Even were the analyst willing to pay the price for what he wants changed, how would he persuade others to follow his lead? Many sociologists, possibly most criminologists, plead for a total overhaul of the institutional structure in order to eliminate specified environmental causes of crime. But who will take action? Surely not the majority, who don't want vast institutional change engineered for any reason, least of all for the benefit of the criminal element, for whom they have limited sympathy. They reject the charge that they, or "society," are responsible for crime in the first place.

No majority have ever volunteered to take part in a plan to re-form their own institutions. And totalitarian regimes which emerge without their consent, such as those which followed upon the French and Bolshevik Revolutions, have been unable to succeed in their aim of creating a new and different institutional framework according to planned specification *(29)*. Even on a less ambitious scale of enlisting planned change to solve a specific social problem, intervening factors more often than not disclose an unacceptable sacrifice of certain values, and may bring about a redefinition of the social problem. Quite obviously, with or without democratic consent, no entire social structure can be changed for the benefit of one defined social problem and then be swiftly readapted to meet the requirements of a new definition of that social problem. The two main persisting controversies about the "world population crisis"—to encourage natality or birth control, to encourage modernism or no-growth—are notable examples.

During the thirties, here and abroad the social problem of

population was essentially described as one of too few births. Social critics and demographers demanded government action, chiefly that of granting subsidies to women in order to encourage them to have more children. During the sixties and seventies, the social problem of population was essentially described as one of too many births. Although very few Americans ever heard of either demand to modify their behavior, public policy did move in one direction and then doubled back. Intervening factors encouraged redefinition of a social problem, and several demographers have publicly sighed with relief that the institutional changes they once advocated to increase the birthrate were never adopted.

What the changing status will be of the second controversy, to encourage modernism or no-growth, is much less clear. Here and abroad, until about 1968, modernism—technological efficiency, capital investment, rationalization, expansion of production and distribution—was well-nigh universally regarded as desirable, as proof of progress. Since that time a vigorous attempt has been made to define modernism as a social problem, a lethal form of social disorganization which plunders the planet of resources and ultimately threatens to destroy life itself. But it is unlikely that the peoples of the world will turn themselves around hurriedly, not on the basis of conscious choice anyway.

This particular message makes no sense at all in the so-called underdeveloped nations, those with agriculture-based economies. They want more of everything which some people at a distance inform them they should not have, in the cause of planetary survival. The message is more favorably received in restricted circles of the United States, because a so-called mature economy already confers a high standard of living. Still, the few members of the majority in this country who have heard about the "crisis of growth" will doubtless continue to regard it with disfavor, for they, too, want more of everything.

Consider air pollution on one side, on the other the complex of highway networks, motel culture, proliferating suburbs, and with no exaggeration, millions of jobs—all entirely dependent upon the internal-combustion engine. If that engine represents "environmental social disorganization," it is nevertheless directly linked with material advantages most Americans are unwilling to sacrifice. Most of them now enjoy many activities and amenities which were once the prerogatives of the very few. The majority have access to automobiles, to energy-consuming gadgets, to a constantly rebuilt pile of convenient and disposable objects, to cheesebox jerry-built suburban housing which blights the open landscape, to overrun vacation resorts and crowded highways, and to national parks which they have turned into so many Coney Islands. It is this "democratization of privilege" which provokes the rancor of, indirectly provides much of the idealism for, that political-intellectual minority who insist that the ecological crisis is the overriding social problem. An elite attitude of distaste for the common man's failure to recognize the unobtrusive place assigned to him has in large measure created that social problem.

Really effective pollution control would enforce changes in the habits and expectations of millions of people who suddenly have come to know and enjoy affluence. Barring some unforeseen technological magic, and assuming present balances of political power and perceived interests, no "rational choice" seems possible—certainly not that of slowdown and no-growth. Only a series of compromises, tradeoffs between stated levels of pollution and accepted levels of inconvenience and unemployment, appear feasible or likely. And these tradeoffs will doubtless be arranged at a leisurely pace, when and as the majority and their political representatives redefine their own interests.

AN ALTERNATIVE APPROACH

The inadequacy of deviance and social disorganization concepts to explain social problems has been discussed. Further, attempts to classify social problems as either manifestations of deviance or examples of social disorganization were shown to provide little aid to understanding, analysis, or even separation. In common usage, the two terms are virtually interchangeable.

Unlike that approach to social problems, the one discussed below should provide some help in understanding why social problems resist solution on the terms most often stated by those people who define and address them. What follows is a classification—of chronic social problems, crises, and pseudoproblems. While chronic social problems simply persist in time, crises are quite different. They are suddenly brought to public attention, capture it, and then fade from attention, and that attention may or may not be renewed at a later time. Crises tend to lose their power of persuasion, at least temporarily, when one crisis replaces another in public attention, or when an apparent solution so outrages the majority in some way that a substitute social problem is formulated or that same one is reformulated. Pseudoproblems, on the other hand, never attract sufficient attention to become real issues.

Chronic Social Problems

Chronic social problems simply persist in time. Crime, for example, was a very serious problem in the seventeenth-century fishing town of Boston, and so it has remained. In late Colonial America such "vices" as drunkenness, gambling, and sex without benefit of clergy were also rife, and they also persist. But these practices were not the serious social problems they became, say, during the Victorian era, because in late Colonial America attitudes toward them were much less harsh.

Despite fluctuations in expressed attitudes, however, more or less general and persistent disapproval has been visited upon such indulgences as gambling, booze, and prostitution, as well as upon less condemned forms of nonmarital sex and drug use. All have been and remain chronic social problems. One of them may occasionally be raised to the status of crisis, as alcoholic consumption was during Prohibition. But whether they heave at the surface or continue their accustomed wont, all of them remain "more serious" problems in America than in most other Western nations because of the peculiar opposition of two traditions in this country. One is a latter-day residual Puritanism which demands laws, more laws, laws with teeth in them, to order others about and see that they do what they should. The other is that of the free, untrammeled pioneer, with his frontier disrepect and suspicion of all law and restraint, who will do as he damned well pleases (30). In this connection Henry Mencken, with some measure of sardonic exaggeration, once commented that a sufficient number of American citizens sobered up enough one morning to go to the polls and vote for the Prohibition they wanted.

There is a tilt point of popular noncompliance which, at least for some time, renders ineffective any legal penalties applicable within this general area of behavior. That point was reached years before Prohibition was repealed. It has now been reached in the case of pot smoking; this social problem, too, may become less serious as usage becomes more widespread. As for nonmarital sex, the law itself is backing off rapidly, and oddly enough more so in the case of homosexuality than prostitution, despite a greater popular disapproval of the former. Does an erstwhile illicit personal indulgence that becomes more tolerated in law and public attitude cease to be a social problem? Not altogether, but it is then relegated to a virtually nonactionable level of public concern where it will remain unless, which often does happen, condemnation of the given practice again rises.

Toleration of a practice at a low point on a range of specific behavior makes action across the range more problematic. "Bingo Tonight at St. Matthew's Church" lends an air of unreality to "Federal Agents Threaten Crackdown on Mafia Gambling Lords." Little can be done about alcoholism (which is treated as "deviance" in some social-problems textbooks) on any appreciable scale when consumption of alcohol is almost universal and goes unquestioned. Hard drugs are in similar relationship to marijuana *(31)*. When only the extreme end of a range of behavior which includes accepted and tolerated usage is condemned, both popular support for action and the probability of implementing it are weakened across the entire range. Practices such as these are never "solved." Their scope can only be temporarily reduced when public opinion becomes solidly raised against them.

Crises

Very different are crises, which appear when effort is mobilized in a moral crusade. They are instigated by some political-intellectual minority, but to achieve full status they must attract some measure of majority support, whether active cooperation, audience applause, or mere bystander acquiescence. Social-problem-as-crisis is almost a distinctive American culture trait, with a long historic tradition *(32)*. There is a characteristically American interest in problems, in defining problems and "attacking" or even "making war" on them.

Professor Berger has generalized that our country is "dedicated to the proposition that no evils are ineradicable, no problems insoluble, no recalcitrance beyond reconciliation, no ending need be unhappy; we are a most un-Greek democracy" (33). When large numbers of the majority have been swept into quasi-messianic hope, as during the early days of Prohibition and at the founding of the United Nations, subsequent disillusionment has only temporarily quelled potential enthusiasm for the next crusade. That generalization may not continue to apply. Several attitude studies have revealed an apparent recent waning of optimism in social-political affairs. We do not know if this trend will continue to develop, or whether it will prove to be a temporary relapse of the peculiarly American historic pattern.

Some social problems are crises, or critical problems, from their very inception. Of the five social problems chosen for special consideration, that is clearly characteristic only of ecology. Crime, race relations, and poverty throughout most of American history have been chronic problems, although they too from time to time have been raised to the status of critical problems. On the contemporary scene, ecology, crime, race relations, and poverty are at different stages of crisis, discussed below.

Crises may be viewed as catastrophes of steady deterioration or as catastrophes approaching a doomsday climax, or as both, depending upon the image of the viewer. They may also be seen as in process of being resolved. The majority assess environmental pollution as deterioration, some minorities as doomsday climax. The present majority view is that crime has reached climactic proportions. Some political-intellectual minorities now assess race relations and poverty as being climactic, while the majority believe both are being alleviated or require no immediate remediable action. The so-called population explosion became climactic for a minority during the late sixties, but concern was so restricted to an alarmed few without an appreciable audience that it can almost be described as a pseudoproblem.

The Crisis Cycle

A history of anyone or anything is a chronicle of particular events, and so is the history of any one crisis, or critical social problem. Nevertheless, a crude sequential pattern does emerge when the histories of several crises are compared. The following schema of the crisis cycle, however Procrustean, does afford some insight about the possible lines of development in future crises. The schema is mainly derived from two sources *(34)*.

1 Recognition Conditions deplored as unconscionable are usually more objectively apparent—insofar as measurement can be taken—*before* effective attitudes create a given crisis. And whether the given crisis is created depends largely upon who has access to the channels of public communication. In this selective process, powerless groups without access cannot gain attention for whatever they may find deplorable. In any event, a sufficient number of people of sufficient social power must perceive the crisis as such and then promote it, or it does not emerge. For recognition to occur, to repeat an observation made in Chapter 1, expressed concern must also have a narrow focus and provide some hope of remediable action.

2 Enthusiasm and Legitimation For a crisis to survive the stage of recognition, alarm must spread in company of conviction that something can be done about it in a short period of time, by means of a moral crusade. This heightening of awareness and enthusiasm requires social endorsement and encouragement by the press, church, school, civic organizations, and finally, officialdom. These agencies certify and legitimize the crisis. But why one concern is thus elevated and another fails to make the grade is often, in the term William Graham Sumner applied to the origin of the mores, "lost in mystery."

Some but not all crises at this stage, the one prior to realization of what costs will be exacted, run into the beginning of opposition on sheerly ideological grounds. On the other hand, ecology at this stage was almost unanimously greeted in a favorable way. Unlike the War on Poverty, for example, ecology could be persuasively depicted as being in the common interest, as something which would benefit everyone.

3 Action and Perceived Cost Various organizations are formed to "attack" the crisis; at first usually private-voluntary ones, then local agencies, and finally national organization comes to dominate and coordinate the total effort. Before national organization becomes solidified, crisis propaganda tends to verge upon rhetorical totalism. Potential foot-draggers are warned that imminent disaster threatens, such as a barren planet, unless unified social action is immediately taken. Later, the audience is invariably assured, usually from official sources, that the crisis can be overcome at minimal cost, with no need to change the social order in any fundamental way.

But as officialdom takes over to coordinate the work of scattered ad hoc committees and organizations, and comes to direct the entire crusade, inevitably are costs unanticipated by some groups—perhaps higher taxes imposed upon the entire public—spelled out. After official programs have been operating for a short while, a sharp recognition of those costs and of the years of effort or compliance required to reach the stated goal tends to dampen enthusiasm. Conflicts of interest now become painfully apparent, and direct political opposition hardens. Officialdom then begins to formulate modified or even substitute goals, mainly in response to rising conflict over the initial means employed. Ecology and race relations are now at this stage. The reader should keep in mind, however, that these or any other crises can in the near future move up or down in the scale of attention and effort.

4 Decline of Interest If a given crisis fails to move back to a previous stage, the originally proposed or modified solution for it moves farther into the future, a solution which becomes ambiguous in light of earlier confidence. Perceived costs run much higher, including that of potentially fundamental social change. Some people are discouraged; others feel threatened. Meanwhile, some new and dramatized crisis is bidding for public attention. The majority, who never were actively engaged in the previous crusade, simply shift or are shifted to a novel and more interesting claim upon their short attention span. Something new is offered, to be consumed as entertainment or denounced with moral, if futile, outrage.

The crisis may then disappear, like the problem of under-population in the decades which followed the thirties. More often it recedes to a lower level of social action along with reduced public attention. Once a crisis has been lodged within bureaucratic officialdom, action programs can persist almost without public awareness and with original goals entirely superseded, as has happened with agencies still in operation which were designed to encourage natality during the thirties. Alternatively, a receding crisis may revert to the status of erstwhile chronic social problem. That happened to poverty—now at this stage of crisis—when the War on Poverty was tacitly abandoned.

Pseudoproblems

There are, finally, pseudoproblems, those which fail to leave the ground when they are launched. With the notable exception of crime, it is true that social problems invariably are the products of the minds and will of political-intellectual minorities. Nevertheless, recognition of a specific problem requires some degree of majority concern about and interest in the issue addressed.

Pseudoproblems stem from the media, or from some official bureaucracy, or from academia, or from some combination of these sources. They arouse no concern in the general public and provoke no interest. They never become a topic of conversation among the majority. Examples include leisure, physical unfitness, anti-intellectualism, and an undeveloped level of taste in the audience of public entertainment. Population growth, labeled a crisis by its promoters, shows evidence of reverting to the status of pseudoproblem, if it ever was otherwise. Two subsidiary issues, abortion and contraception, remain genuine social problems. On the other hand another subsidiary issue, no-growth in the economy, accompanies the issue of a clear and present danger of too many Americans as a quasi-pseudoproblem.

Limits of the Alternative Approach

What has been presented in this section is more useful for classifying social problems than for explaining them. No substitute for such facile and misleading explanations as deviance and social disorganization has been offered. The range of social problems is actually much too wide, the factors involved too various and complex, to accommodate easy and encapsulated explanations.

No apology should be inferred, for none is intended. The reader was cautioned in the first chapter that the descriptive content of the very many concurrent social problems cannot be reduced to interchangeable propositions of common explanation. That stated limit cannot be exceeded, here or elsewhere.

Any empirically defensible explanation of social problems can be arrived at only by a circuitous route. Such a journey requires an abundance of historical materials, social-psychological analysis, constant reference to comparative data, and a sparing use of taxonomies. No final answers are thereby vouchsafed. But what may eventuate is an improved understanding about social problems, what they are and how they got to be what they are.

REFERENCES

1 There is one school of thought which holds that in or out of sociology positive statements and value judgments are only analytically, never contextually, separable. In the case of deviance and social disorganization concepts, however, analytical separation is impossible since the concepts themselves are value judgments of the same kind.

2 The term "conservative" is used in a limited sense indeed. Most sociologists are no more conservative than they are square or hip. They are liberal in the modern sense; that is, they favor institutional change of a kind and degree which far surpasses anything acceptable to either squares or conservatives. But at the same time most sociologists retain some allegiance to the prevailing social order, upon which hip sociologists heap contumely.

   Whether conscious adherents of functionalism or not, most sociologists as yet continue more or less to accept the values implicit in functionalist theory. For a brief but excellent discussion of functionalism, see Walter L. Wallace, "Overview of Contemporary Sociological Theory," in Walter L. Wallace (ed.), *Sociological Theory: An Introduction,* Aldine, Chicago, 1969, pp. 1–59, pp. 25–28. Unlike hip sociologists, functionalists are not conscious bearers of ideology. Functionalist theory, however, does imply a continuation of the conservative tradition in which sociology was founded.

3 Kenneth Westhues, "Social Problems as Systemic Costs," *Social Problems,* **20**:419–431, 1973, p. 422.

4 Howard S. Becker, *Outsiders: Studies in the Sociology of Deviance,* Free Press, New York, 1963, p. 9.

5 William Ryan, *Blaming the Victim,* Pantheon, New York, 1971, pp. 6 and 234.

6 There do remain thousands of dusty little towns in the West, back-

woods towns in the North and Southeast, which retain a close nexus of community relationships, gossip, near-uniform way of making a living, and mutual pressure to conform within narrow limits. But they continue, steadily, to lose population, and they are known as the boondocks, even to most squares.

On the other hand, how sweeping the scope of social change has become remains elusive of general statement. It is well to view with skepticism all claims of new sovereign or catastrophic social changes carrying an entire population into a "greening America," or "future shock," or a "postindustrial world," alternatively a "post-Christian world." Many exciting discoveries made by intellectuals are unheard by most people and, more important, leave those people with their established habits and beliefs undisturbed.

In short, while ours is indeed a "period of rapid change" in a relative sense, much does not change or changes slowly. Moreover, the high-level abstractions cited above, as well as those listed in the text paragraph referred to, point to no ineluctable goal of change. Any number of emerging intervening factors, as yet unassessable, might cancel any grand scenario, even change the rate of change itself.

7 J. L. Simmons, *Deviants,* Glendessary Press, Berkeley, Calif., 1969, p. 6.

8 In one opinion: "America is a more fragmented . . . and autonomous set of parts than revolutionary theory would admit." Joseph R. Gusfield, "The Student Revolt: Afterthoughts and Prospects," *Contemporary Sociology,* 1:9–13, 1972, p. 11. The assumption of a highly articulated social order is shared by most sociologists and other intellectuals, devotees of revolutionary theory or not.

9 Simmons, reference 7, pp. 133–134.

10 Irving Louis Horowitz and Martin Liebowitz, "Social Deviance and Political Marginality: Toward a Redefinition of the Relation between Sociology and Politics," *Social Problems,* 15:280-296, 1968, p. 285.

11 For some obscure reason the concept of deviance persists in sociology long after the concept of adjustment, the inverse analogue of deviance in social psychology, has steadily fallen into disrepute since its salad days of the 1940s.

12 Milton J. Yinger, *Toward a Field Theory of Behavior: Personality and Social Structure,* McGraw-Hill, New York, 1965, p. 129.

13 A kind of "deviance" can depart from an earlier baseline of the *same* described category. The Boy Scouts themselves are not so Boy Scout as yesteryear they were. Theft, once a solid no-no in the *Handbook,* has entered a twilight zone. According to the eighth edition, what should you do if some friends of yours take your sister's bike? "Just remember

to look at both sides. Listen carefully to the arguments and then do what you believe to be right." Cited in *Time,* Sept. 4, 1972, p. 61.

14 Lauren Langman et al., "Countercultural Values at a Catholic University," *Social Problems,* **20:**521–532, 1973, p. 531. Other quotations appear on pp. 528, 529, and 530.

15 Alexander Liazos, "The Poverty of the Sociology of Deviance: Nuts, Sluts, and Preverts [sic]," *Social Problems,* **20:**103–120, 1972, p. 111.

16 Horowitz and Liebowitz, reference 10, p. 288.

17 Joseph R. Gusfield, "Moral Passage: The Symbolic Process in Public Designations of Deviance," *Social Problems,* **15:**175–188, 1967, p. 182.

18 *San Francisco Chronicle,* Apr. 19, 1973, p. 4.

19 Howard Schuman, "Two Sources of Antiwar Sentiment in America," *American Journal of Sociology,* **78:**513–536, 1972, especially pp. 519 and 535. Skewering the opposition is another major consideration in "symbolic behavior." The following passage will not endear the authors to the "conventional sectors" of those cities which are less hospitable to deviance than San Francisco, the model of conduct approved by them and ostensibly being promoted: "Despite the wide range of visible freakiness, the citizenry takes it all in stride, without the fear and madness that permeates the conventional sectors of cities like Detroit, Chicago, New York, Washington, D. C. and similar centers of undaunted virtue." Howard S. Becker and Irving Louis Horowitz, "The Culture of Civility," *transaction,* April 1970, pp. 12–19, p. 15.

20 Jack D. Douglas, "Deviance and Respectability: The Social Construction of Moral Meanings," in Jack D. Douglas (ed.), *Deviance and Respectability: The Social Construction of Moral Meanings,* Basic Books, New York, 1970, pp. 3–30, p. 21.

21 Robert K. Merton, "Social Structure and Anomie," in Walter L. Wallace (ed.), *Sociological Theory: An Introduction,* Aldine, Chicago, 1969, pp. 162–183, p. 164. This piece originally appeared in the *American Sociological Review,* **3:**672–682, 1938.

22 The "achievement-motivation" mean scores of sample school populations in the Northeast compared as follows: Greeks, 10.80; Jews, 10.53; Protestants, 10.11; Italians, 9.65; French Canadians, 8.82; and Negroes, 8.40. The mothers of the subjects were questioned about what occupations would satisfy their own ambitions for their children, and the mothers of Jews, Greeks, Protestants, Italians, French Canadians, and Negroes ranked in that order of diminishing insistence upon high-status occupations. Bernard C. Rosen, "Race, Ethnicity, and the Achievement Syndrome," *American Sociological Review,* **24:**47–60, 1959, pp. 48 and 59.

23 Amitai Etzioni, "Violence," in Robert K. Merton and Robert Nisbet (eds.), *Social Problems,* rev. ed., Harcourt Brace Jovanovich, New York, 1971, pp. 709–741, p. 723. Professor Etzioni apparently assumes that there is a direct relationship between escalation of aspiration in media depiction and escalation of aspiration in consciousness. But raising or not raising one's own aspirations does not accompany in any exact way the extent to which themes of success and high living are presented by the media. And much more to the point, such media themes were more prevalent during the thirties, when the rate of violence was lower than it is at the present time.

There has surely been a general raising of expectations, which is discussed in the next chapter. There is, though, a question about how much the media have been responsible for it, and how much rising expectations *in themselves* have caused an increase in violence. The increase in violence can more plausibly be attributed to the "alternative hypothesis," discussed later in the body of this chapter.

24 For documentation of this critical point, check reference 4 of Chap. 3, p. 110.

25 Richard M. Huber, *The American Idea of Success,* McGraw-Hill, New York, 1971, especially p. 368.

26 See, for example, the works cited in references 5, 7, 10, 15, and 28.

27 Helmut Schoeck, *Envy: A Theory of Social Behavior,* Michael Glenny and Betty Ross (trans.), Harcourt, Brace & World, New York, 1970, p. 225.

28 This entire section has little relevance for the position of hip sociologists, who eschew any consideration of functionalism. When the hip sociologist refers to social disorganization, invariably he indicts American society entire itself as *the* social problem. For example: "Social disorganization exists because capitalism favors the capitalists." D. M. Azimi and Joseph A. Scimecca, "Social Disorganization and the Economic System," mimeographed paper to be published in *Social Problems,* 14 pp., pp. 5–6. The reasons why this kind of judgment has no legitimate place in a discussion of social problems were discussed in Chap. 1.

29 By 1815, when the French Revolution was said to have completed itself, the result was quite different from what had been planned. "Instead of a rational, well-organized, international order, governed by sage assemblies, people were in the grip of acute nationalism—irrational and divisive passions which the Revolution was against." Announced goals of liberty, equality, fraternity produced instead reaction and military conscription throughout Europe. Isaiah Berlin, "The Hazards of Social Revolution," in Aaron W. Warner et al. (eds.), *The Environment of Change,* Columbia, New York, 1969, pp. 1–27, especially p. 5.

30 Roscoe Pound, *Criminal Justice in America,* Holt, New York, 1930.

31 Several critics have pointed out that programs designed to "eliminate the pushers of hard drugs" are self-defeating once the demand for drugs has reached a high level, an inelastic demand which does not slacken when supply runs short. Since pushers run additional risks when police and narcotics agents are seriously trying to apprehend them, the street price of hard drugs goes up, a price which will be met, if need be financed by crimes of mugging, shoplifting, and burglary. There is no evidence that periodic attempts to crack down on the drug traffic have ever resulted in the reduction of drug use, or, except sporadically, affected the total supply from outside the country. During periods of heightened official interdiction, foreign suppliers work more diligently, and ingeniously, to get drugs into the country and take advantage of a higher street price. It is a lesson in classical economics.

32 Some time ago Tocqueville took note of an impatience he said was quintessentially American, a determination to reduce complex issues to simple moralisms, a fondness for still another crisis demanding still another crusade. This tendency, he failed to note, is more striking among intellectual minorities than the majority; nevertheless, to some extent an enthusiasm for defining and addressing crises *is* widely shared, leading to ad hoc efforts which invariably have been disappointed.

33 Bennett M. Berger, "Suburbia and the American Dream," *The Public Interest,* Winter 1966, pp. 80–91, p. 87.

34 Herbert Blumer, "Social Problems as Collective Behavior," *Social Problems,* **18:**298–306, 1971; and Anthony Downs, "Up and Down with Ecology—the 'Issue-Attention Cycle,' " *The Public Interest,* Summer 1972, pp. 38–50. Mr. Downs regards crises as a distinct category among social problems and Professor Blumer apparently does not.

Chapter 7

Can Social Problems Be Solved?

Social problems are never solved, at least not in the terms set out in a proclaimed goal. A combination of expressed hope, adopted means, and compromises made, always results in an ambiguous state of affairs which discloses much that was unanticipated and unwanted. We deal with a tangled web of wish, delusion, resentment, cross-purpose, disappointment, and then renewed hope—with social life itself.

Many people will resist efforts to address this or that social problem because their perceived interests are adversely affected, while others whose office it is to expedite solutions may hedge for fear of losing influence and power. Many "solutions," indeed, are politically engineered for other than announced reasons. A clear majority may believe, or be led to believe, that they want some social problem solved, and then lose heart when the price tag is uncovered. And even if a few hardy souls should announce that a given social problem had been resolved, which has never happened, that hypothetically announced state of perfection in retrospect would have lumps in it.

PRICE

We do not get rid of the lumps for many reasons, the most obvious being that which Weber pointed out: we cannot simultaneously maximize all our values *(1)*. This particular dilemma is a truly ancient one. During the process of organic evolution a marvelous solution to the species problem of boredom appeared—sex; it exacted only one unalterable price—death. Likewise, when solutions to more transitory social problems have been sought, a price has always had to be paid.

There is no harmony of all interests, not in the world, nor in one nation, group, family, even soul. For every choice made or imposed, some other potential good is sacrificed. Equality, as one instance, is a uniformly relative and never an absolute condition. When a basis for some new equality is established, some other inequality is perforce imposed. The real question, as Professor Frankel has pointed out, is never equality in the abstract, but *which* equality, at what price of some new inequality. "The victory of those who say that women cannot have equality so long as marriage, home, and family are perceived as their primary goals puts the young woman who wants just such roles at a psychological and educational disadvantage" (2).

Pareto's Utilities

Vilfredo Pareto rummaged throughout history for examples of a constant theme, although not expressed in the following words: for every choice made or imposed, some other potential good is sacrificed. He was especially impressed by the price which individuals as individuals, or individuals as representatives of some collectivity, have to pay when one or another utility is emphasized. A military power, for example, protects its citizens from the danger of conquest and enslavement, but its posture of "strong defense" will endanger the careers and even the lives of many young men who might otherwise have lived out their private lives.

Pareto's summary term for divergent and individuated interests of the latter kind is "utility for a community"—the personal, subjective short-term advantages and satisfactions enjoyed or anticipated by individuals and groups within a society. Against that utility he posited "utility of a community"—collective strength and determination, a capability to survive in a hostile world *as* a collectivity. He cautioned that the two utilities are not and cannot be made uniform.

Incongruence between the two is especially marked in a long span of time. It has been argued, says Pareto, that the rudimentary technological base of the ancient world made slavery an economic necessity. In either event, the absence of slavery in Greece would have precluded the emergence of that minority whose leisured intellectual pursuits were to determine much of the Western cultural tradition. If one considers only "a problem of maximum utility *of* species," then slavery of Greek by Greek might be viewed as having been of incalculable benefit. But another person who "envisages nothing but the utility of the human beings who [were] reduced to slavery" can hardly reach the same conclusion (3). The uncertain moral can be drawn that future generations as well as present exploiters can benefit from the misery of others. It can likewise be said that utility *for* a present generation can lack coherence with utility *for* and *of* future generations, as in the case of consuming irreplaceable natural resources in order to maintain a present high level of living.

Various Prices

The prices exacted by attempts to solve most social problems do not appreciably affect utility *of* a community, except as they may promote conflict within the society. Much more visibly do such attempts provide utilities *for* some people at the expense of utilities *for* others. Examples drawn from crime, poverty, race relations, population growth, and ecology follow.

The perceived interests of most citizens are best served when protection from criminal depredation takes precedence over protection of the rights of the accused. The public pay a price when the rights of criminals weigh more heavily in the courts than the right of protection (4). As for poverty, political efforts to reduce it require higher tax levies or result in more inflation via government indebtedness and expansion of a cheapened money supply; either citizens pay now or their children and grandchildren pay tomorrow.

Discriminatory enrollment of academically unqualified representatives of favored ethnic and racial minorities bars some more qualified youngsters, black as well as white, from access to higher education. Zero Population Growth, Inc., whose crusade for a stationary native population apparently is becoming self-liquidating, at a recent national meeting voted to promote reduction of immigration. The present law, the Immigration Act of 1965, is designed in part to afford political refuge to victims of oppression abroad. The ZPG shift from one to another means of reducing total population size could force many foreigners to pay the price of continued submission in their native dictatorships.

Pollution abatement, if made an overriding consideration, carries the price of reduced energy consumption, high unemployment, and a drastically lowered material level of living. In expanded perspective, efforts to protect the environment within highly industrialized nations have already begun to reduce availability of credit to the "underdeveloped nations." They must pay part of the price for ecological concerns their spokesmen say they cannot afford in their own countries.

UNANTICIPATED CONSEQUENCES

The result of political action or social reform, said Max Weber, always stands in "paradoxical relation to its ultimate meaning." Efforts of either kind are invariably accompanied by unforeseen and usually by unwanted consequences. Such efforts, once embroiled in the social struggle, eventually shift the meaning of the values they were originally designed to promote or defend.

The Reasons Why

There are many reasons for unanticipated consequences, here reduced to a few summary statements. Conflict can force modifications in social-problem definition and disposition, as in the hip-square confrontation discussed in Chapter 5. But our attention now turns to the nonconfrontational aspects of failure to achieve results according to plan or expectation. They fall into two main categories.

First: every human society remains in an unstable state of

dynamic equilibrium. Any introduced change of a certain magnitude will disturb the prevailing and ever-temporary balance of social forces, and bring about subsequent changes by ramifying throughout the social structure. Even established trends may be affected, in one direction or another.

The kind of introduced change in which we are interested is consciously designed. Technological innovations and attempts to solve social problems are the notable examples. Such consciously designed changes combine with parallel trends, and they bring about modifications in trends which are not congruent with them. Therefore, consciously designed changes foster subsequent unplanned and unforeseen changes, unanticipated consequences which invariably differ in character and scope from the initial, planned change (5).

Parenthetically, many far-reaching unanticipated consequences are not the ultimate result of a consciously designed innovation at all. Instead, they "are the social resultants of a great many individual or group actions directed to quite other ends but together conspiring to bring them about" (6). For example, businessmen, labor unions, and politicians may all pursue a common goal of economic prosperity, but the conjuncture of their separate efforts may instead produce economic slump. Likewise, a conjuncture of individual choices within a nation at one time to raise large families, at another time to reduce family size, will ramify and affect all other institutions, education most obviously, but also the division of labor and even the state of the military establishment. But however important for other analytical purposes such conjunctures and their unanticipated consequences may be, our concern here is mainly with consciously designed change.

Second: peoples' attitudes, values, even their perceived interests, do not remain constant in time. Sartre said that in middle age he was astounded to recollect what he believed he wanted and thought worth striving for when he was a young man. Collective aspirations and images of the world are equally transitory. Although the hope never dies, no generation has ever been able to ensure that its own deities, instead of strange and new gods, will be venerated by the generations to follow. And within the time span of a single generation, if some social problem is addressed in terms of a prevailing balance of power and ascendant attitudes, then very soon shifts in power or attitudes or both bring new goals and purposes to public attention. The new ones then redefine the original *projected* goal and lead to a reassessment of the concrete result which differed from that projection.

Examples of unanticipated consequences are almost embarrassing in their abundance. Every social problem carries and is accompanied by them. Only a few are listed below, and only for a few social problems.

Crime

Action taken against certain criminals may increase the incidence of crime, or at least of other crimes. When suppliers of narcotics have attracted heightened police attention and court prosecution in recent years, the supply of drugs has been reduced and the retail price raised. Rates of burglary, shoplifting, and mugging have then gone up when junkies required more money to finance their habit.

Again, our sumptuary laws against gambling and prostitution as well as drug use remain on the books mainly because of residual puritanism. More permissive attitudes (some of the "strange new gods" alluded to above) have not uniformly displaced older censorious attitudes. But retention of sumptuary laws, *in combination* with widespread and growing infraction of them, undermines respect for law and reduces police time for seeking out violent criminals.

Another combination of circumstances has much graver implications. Modern technology, especially that which provides means to move about rapidly, and the depersonalized secondary-group organization of modern urban civilization reduce the scope of personal acquaintance and the application of informal controls. The resultant growing difficulty in identifying and thus apprehending criminals has played a part in the rise of popular demand for *more* immediate identification and apprehension of criminals.

If this demand is met by determined police action in the modern milieu, then the price of more intensive surveillance of the entire population probably must be exacted, with phone taps, computerized life histories, luggage searches at airports, and the practice of wholesale fingerprinting. We may be faced by a dilemma which, given a balance of contradictory values, may be unresolvable. Any hope of reducing the crime rate apparently requires further incursion upon individual liberty. If that price is unacceptable to the majority, then they may have to live with a relatively high crime rate.

Poverty

Millions of people have directly benefited from programs addressed to the alleviation of poverty. Some of these programs, however, have served to perpetuate poverty among their beneficiaries, and others have not directly benefited them. The several programs of urban renewal, for example, on balance have created further slums. One reason for that unintended result was the practice of demolishing ruined apartment houses whose renovating could not be financed. Displaced slum dwellers were forced to move elsewhere, and they founded new slums.

This chain of events goes back to two loan programs which were instituted after World War II, FHA and the GI housing bill. These programs facilitated the issuing of loans against the purchase of new houses, but not old ones. Issuing loans for the renovation of older multiple-dwelling properties, such as apartment houses, was made even more difficult. New single-dwelling unit construction was stimulated, and deterioration of old neighborhoods encouraged. And because most of the new home construction took place outside of city limits, "this old-new disparity has accelerated the exodus from the city to the suburbs" (7).

A kind of "rural renewal" also had unanticipated consequences. Programs formally designed to "rescue the small farmer" instead promoted corporate agribusiness on the land *(8)*. Much of the erstwhile need for hand labor was then eliminated, which in turn led to a flight of displaced Southern farm workers to the Northern cities. Pushed by one circumstance, they were pulled by another, the availability of higher welfare payments in the North.

When they got there, fewer of them were able to get jobs than might otherwise have been the case. However laudable the intent of minimum-wage laws, they do create difficulties for many people in finding employment. The productive capacity of most unskilled, uneducated youngsters, and of many adults as well, will not cover the labor costs of potential employers when they are forbidden to pay them market-determined wages. Formally designed to improve the lot of the poor, minimum-wage laws price many of the poor out of the job market. They "mock their legislators by increasing unemployment among the least skilled and the lowest paid." Such laws especially discriminate against black youngsters, "who desperately need jobs and on-the-job training," but who are only too often "barred from working by punitive wage fences"(9).

On the other hand, as is shown in the next chapter, the total effect of all poverty programs has probably been to redistribute income downward in some measure. But there are countercurrents. Those people who officially work to redistribute income downward constitute a new and large well-to-do "class." According to Daniel P. Moynihan, the working if not the nonworking poor have been penalized by this circumstance. "As the public sphere expands in the announced quest for greater equality, the almost certain outcome is greater inequality deriving from the transfer of income from lower to higher income levels" *(10)*. Each new program requires a further expansion of government personnel, of administrators, supervisors, technicians, and clerks; low-income people are then taxed to pay the salaries of more people with higher incomes than their own.

Population Growth

Partisan rhetoric aside and taking only measurable comparisons into account, the "threat" of population growth in the United States is quite manageable. Such is not the case, however, in much of Asia, Africa, and Latin America. Largely because of population growth, by 1974 starvation was endemic in many nations, notably in a famine belt stretching across the countries on the southern fringe of the Sahara desert. There and elsewhere around the globe, a grim price in unanticipated consequence is being paid by the present generation for the humanitarian impulse which led the United States and other Western nations to intercede and lower the high, stable death rates of previous generations.

The West has sent technicians, engineers, physicians, and wonder drugs to such areas and cut death rates dramatically. Death control is relatively easy to achieve. Resident populations are quick to cooperate; they will line up by the thousands for inoculation and they will volunteer to drain swamps. But because of custom, religion, and politics, they are not at all quick to lower traditionally high birthrates. Also, birth control of remedial scope requires disciplined and intelligent action by millions of people within a very private area of their lives, while they need only passively accede to a death control that is paid for and managed by others. And quite simply, there are more people who want to live a long time than who want to have few or no children.

The imbalance is both new and quite pronounced. To take one instance, during the period 1911–1921 in India the birthrate was 48 and the death rate 47 per 1,000. Comparable figures for 1970 were 42 and 17, respectively. If such an enormous gap is maintained between birthrate and death rate, India's population will double in a quarter century, and so will that of Latin America, which has the highest annual rate of growth in the world. In the "developing countries" neither offsetting growth of agricultural and industrial production nor changes in habits and social outlook are in the immediate offing. Unless these circumstances change, and in the imperative short term, the Malthusian check of famine will soon rule over most of the globe. This particular warning from those who advocate measures to reduce population growth has provoked very little if any disputation.

Ecology

Certain measures to preserve the environment led, by a circuitous route, to an increase in arms sales by the United States in the recent past. The connection between the two can be traced to the end of an era of cheap energy. Energy became more expensive for many reasons, including dwindling reserves and a government policy of setting consumer prices below market-clearing levels, which encouraged more consumption of gasoline and natural gas, and discouraged exploration for new sources of energy and expansion of power facilities. In the short term, though, the success of ecological pressure groups in halting some of the strip mining of native coal and deep mining of coal with a high sulfur content, in protesting the erection of nuclear plants and stateside oil refineries, had more impact *(11)*.

Given these circumstances, the oil-rich Persian Gulf came to be regarded as the indispensable, the only consequential remaining source of cheap energy available. But purchase of that oil was aggravating this country's unfavorable balance of trade. The tangled skein was partly unwound by sales of more arms, a decision reluctantly taken in 1970 as a necessary means to repatriate more dollars.

By 1973, United States arms sales had tripled, to $4.5 billion a year. These sales were scheduled to jump another $900 million in fiscal 1974 (12). The Persian Gulf happened to be the most lucrative market for arms sales. But then the resumption of Arab-Israeli hostilities in October of 1973 prompted a drastic revision of policy, which included compensating arms shipments to Israel. Arab resentment of United States policy to some extent determined later developments in 1974, when the entire industrialized world was apparently placed in temporary thrall to the so-called oil sheiks.

Good-Bad Means, Good-Bad Ends

That the character of results is determined by the character of the means employed to achieve them is an ancient and honorable idea which has been refurbished by good men in every succeeding generation. The idea may very well be true, in some higher ethical or philosophical sense, but it will not apply very well to the tight context of social interaction with which we are here concerned. The proposition that bad means inevitably produce bad ends and conversely that good means always produce good results is not one which can be supported with direct accounting procedures, even when the stipulations of good and bad are accepted as given. The employment of means described as good can have undesired unanticipated consequences, and the use of means described as bad can have desired unanticipated consequences (13).

That described good means can go awry has been amply demonstrated with illustrations already cited in this chapter. The converse relationship was well stated by Nathaniel Hawthorne, who observed that the advantages of human effort on a grand scale are never more than incidental: "Man's accidents are God's purposes. We miss the good we sought, and do the good we little cared for."

The problem of unemployment in the Great Depression was "solved" only with the emergence, at the time of America's entrance into World War II, of that military-industrial complex which was later widely denounced. Negro intellectuals Ralph Ellison and Bayard Rustin have said that black participation in this nation's wars has done more for integration, reduction of interracial prejudice, and black economic progress than all the programs specifically designed to achieve those ends. "The tangible rewards to Negroes in the form of command over goods and services grew most rapidly in absolute and relative terms during World War II, during Korea, and during the expansion of the war in Vietnam" (14).

The well-nigh universally deplored energy shortage of 1973–1974 is already having consequences which some ecologists have declared to be desirable. The situation remains equivocal, since the initial reaction of pollution-control agencies and legislators was to lower abatement standards for automobiles and industry. But later, as the prices of fossil fuels broke through one government ceiling after another, industry found that the cost of installing pollution controls receded in comparison with those rising prices. Many company treasurers were converted to pollution control, not by environmental idealism but by economic pressure. Moreover, as prices of other materials rose in company of fuel prices, the recycling of paper, tin cans, and bottles became more economically feasible, and so did reclaiming much of the sulfur which had been spewed into the air.

Economists are in virtual agreement that the brief era of cheap energy has come to an end. In that event, nonideological pressures to "improve the environment" will doubtless continue. Conservation would then become a matter of economic necessity, more an unwitting than a deliberate good deed. Heartily detested rising prices are apparently more persuasive than earlier rational appeals proved to be, those warnings of threatened energy scarcity voiced by several conservationists, oil-company executives, and government researchers.

There may be other benefits achieved by means which most Americans do not want. If those people who are unable to afford or find gasoline for driving on casual errands decide to walk, if they have to exert manual effort as power-driven gadgets become too expensive to run, they might become more physically fit. If they keep their thermostats at lowered levels, they run less risk of contracting respiratory troubles. And quite possibly within large cities there will be a revival of public-transport systems, the most economical, efficient, and cleanest mode of short-distance travel.

SOLVE ONE, CREATE ANOTHER?

To say that efforts to solve one problem automatically produce another would be to oversimplify. In appearance that may be so, but only if intervening changes of interests, attention, and, most important of all, attitudes are ignored. The interstate highway program, for example, in one way *did* solve a defined problem; it met a perceived need for linking all parts of the country together with means of rapid automotive transportation. It was only later, when ecological concerns mounted, when new attitudes designated the automobile and all its ancillary products as an air-pollution menace, that a solution became part of the "cause" of a new problem.

Vietnam and the Draft

With a revision of attitudes we can in a sense create a problem we do not want and "solve" one already addressed in ways which afford little satisfaction. Perhaps no piece of legislation was ever greeted with so much civilian enthusiasm as that which abolished peacetime conscription. This measure, proclaimed to end the possibility of "any more Vietnams," found Senator Barry Goldwater and what remains of the New Left making strange common cause. Some emerging consequences have been recognized, especially that of an army disproportionately made up of poor black volunteers, because very few white "middle-class" youngsters can be tempted to enlist, no matter how eager the "New Army" may be to "join you," no matter how high the pay and how low the Mickey Mouse profile. For several different reasons this result is disliked, by many "old army men" on one side, many black and white social reformers on the other.

What have gone generally unrecognized are the implications of creating a large *professional* standing army, something as alien to the American tradition of the citizen soldier as was peacetime conscription. Anyway, reluctant non-career types, and more significantly, resentful antimilitary dissidents, are now in process of being eliminated from the New Army. These people, and their families, will no longer serve as a political brake on potential decisions to send troops abroad. In at least this *one* dimension, the way to "another Vietnam" has been made not more difficult but easier.

Collective Expectation

One important reason why social problems are never solved, or if in surface appearance they are solved another similar or variant social-problem definition emerges, is the constant raising of sights by the attitudes which constitute social-problem consciousness. As one instance, poverty never can be "solved" when the ranks of the poor by previous official definition thin out, and those ranks are then replenished by raising the poverty-defined income level. Likewise, when professional black athletes come to be as readily hired as white ones, questions are then raised about the number of black coaches and team managers (15). And, too, when automobile assembly lines were stopped during the Great Depression, the "problem" was unemployment. Later, when men on the line averaged about $14,000 a year, the "problem" became the putatively meaningless, stultifying, repetitive, and demeaning nature of their employment.

Professor Maslow has developed a thesis within individual psychology which, with caution, may be applied to collective expectation. He says there are five universal goals which deserve the name of basic needs: physiological, safety, love, esteem, and self-actualization—arranged in a hierachy of prepotency. Each need will, in sequence, monopolize consciousness and organize the capacities of the organism until it is gratified. When "a need is fairly well satisfied, the next prepotent ('higher') need emerges, in turn to dominate the conscious life and to serve as the center of organization of behavior, since gratified needs are not active motivators"(16).

Maslow warns that his schema is a statement about general tendency, and it will not reveal how or why an individual acts as he does. It will not, for example, explain why some men deliberately choose martyrdom and thus sacrifice all physiological needs; Maslow suggests that martyrs may have had all their physiological needs fully gratified in earlier life. All he insists upon is that an individual will want the more basic of two needs when he is deprived in both.

Even so, this thesis begs further qualification. Those modern people who are in a position to gratify the more basic needs of physiological gratification, safety, and "love" without effort, challenge, or risk may find attainment of such higher needs as esteem and self-actualization in that degree rendered more difficult. The muting of the success theme, noted in previous chapters, may thus in part be explainable.

Nevertheless, a Maslow-type thesis could actually have as much and possibly more application in collective behavior than individual psychology. Many social problems, notably those of poverty and race relations, have dramatically shifted attention from narrowly defined material welfare to emotional-psychological gratification in material terms. The drive to redistribute income, and access to goods and services, is inspired more by a desire to rectify putative ego damage in an equality of results than merely to relieve physical suffering. Deprivation has come to mean far more than material want, and thus social problems which bear historic names have taken on new dimensions.

The rise of collective expectation can be stated with a formula: as conditions originally deplored get better, they are interpreted as worse. What has come to be known as the "Tocqueville effect" makes possible the statement of a tentative principle: confrontation politics disregarded, a people will accept social problems (or permit social problems to be defined for them) as extensive and expensive as they believe (or are told) they can afford. Thus, to repeat, school dropouts—now about 10 percent of the school-age population—are a serious social problem, which they were not at all at the turn of the century when a majority of youngsters dropped out of school.

The inflationary spiral of collective expectation accompanied diffused affluence and optional leisure. Maslow's "self-actualization" is no longer, as once it was, almost solely associated with meaningful work, that is, productive effort which others as well as the self might regard as essential to serve an image of the common good. Especially among the liberal arts segment of the college young has the work ethic fallen into disrepute. A growing tendency to justify self with social idealism instead of success-striving is in this quarter most pronounced. Those investigators of the counterculture who are sympathetic to it, such as Keniston and Roszak, agree that a search for some new way to self-fulfillment is the true source of its motivational drive. Or, in somewhat less sympathetic assessment, feeling good may take precedence over doing good—but that same judgment was made by critics of eighteenth-century humanitarianism.

In any event, a risk of disappointment must be run in any such approach to the outer world. First, as has been demonstrated above, purity of intention will not guarantee defined good or even desired results. Second, countercultural idealists must run a risk of coming to see that certain aspects of modern civilization which they deplore really constitute the ultimate means of achieving certain changes they want made. Such goals as more leisure, better medical care, more educational facilities, pollution control, more subsidies for the poor all depend upon what is anathema in the counterculture—uninterrupted prosperity and hence more consumerism; mounting production and further technological advance; and a highly integrated, specialized, and supervised division of labor. This statement, of course, has uncertain application to those who seek less to improve the world than to renounce it.

THE FALLACY OF CONTEXTUAL CHOICE

What we now explore by indirection prevents social problems from being solved. The fallacy of contextual choice is the mistaken assumption that ends and means which are or were appropriate in one setting can be selected and applied intact to a different setting. Cultural anthropologists have established one manifestation of it which lies outside our present focus of attention: the belief that elements of culture and social organization from one society can readily be transmitted to and engrafted upon another society which is alien in thought, tradition, and social values. With the exception of the final example, the fallacy of contextual choice is restricted here to our social system in its own historic perspective.

Subtype 1

No institution or collective habit or basic orientation of the past can be revived in such a way as to duplicate the setting in which any of them once thrived. The national physical fitness program of the fifties, as one instance, converted very few citizens to a strenuous way of life. The physical fitness of an entire population is apparently at optimum when there is enough affluence and knowledge to check debilitating hunger and disease, but also privation sufficient to *require* a great deal of physical exertion out-of-doors. Modern Americans simply ignored an invitation to volunteer to do what at one time they had done of necessity.

The President's Committee on Juvenile Delinquency and

Youth Crime once underwrote local plans to furnish rafts that would drift groups of teenagers down the Mississippi. This apparent attempt to make Huck Finn delinquents out of modern delinquents is matched by the square image of returning to the law and order of a previous time with a policy of handling suspects summarily and punishing them severely. In relative terms, what is lacking at the present time is the supportive consensus, institutional integration, ideology of personal responsibility, and guilt-free punishment procedures which at another time made use of such procedures an infrequent occurrence.

Modern laws against sumptuary indulgences cannot make sovereign a morality which no longer reigns. Again, morning prayers in public schools were once a manifestation, not a cause, of strong community religious sentiment. The movement to reinstate what the Supreme Court has frowned upon, if successful, would do little to revive strong community religious sentiment. At a more material level of being, providing modern welfare families with the means to acquire a private house does not recapture for them the fierce pride of ownership, the will to mow lawns and spend long hours in painstaking maintenance work, shown by the progeny of turn-of-the-century immigrants once they had made it out of the ethnic slums.

Subtype 2

The fallacy is made nakedly apparent when a fusion of images selected from past and present is projected into the future. Several "Goals for America" issued during the Eisenhower years, for example, combined for tomorrow all of the Jeffersonian-agrarian virtues and a futuristic technology. Most of our politicians say and most of our citizens apparently believe that something traditionally known as "free enterprise" will coexist in the future alongside a government control over all economic activities designed to placate the political demands of separate and competing special-interest blocs.

The appeal of modern Chinese agrarian life for many young American communards accompanies a vision of rural, essentially solitary and totally unfettered, ancient arcadia. But their Chinese imagery of a march into the future ignores such signposts as "the social control of promiscuity, the banning of pornographic literature, the arrest of drug users, and the putting of all personal choices about career, work place, or life-style into the hands of the state"

(17). When examined, the fallacy of contextual choice indicates that you can neither go back home again nor live at a selectively packaged tomorrow.

DRIFT OF ATTENTION

The drift of attention robs some social problems to pay others. In Chapter 6 perceived crises were traced through a cycle, ending with a decline of interest as attention centers upon some new perceived crisis. But the drift of attention has long-term as well as short-term dimensions.

The chronically sick, the disabled, and the mentally disturbed are now granted less publicized concern than they received in the late nineteenth century. While on balance their plight may be somewhat less severe than it was then, they have ceased to be fashionable social problems. They have become the stepchildren of the welfare state, in Sweden as well as in the United States (18).

Much more interest in them was shown when virtually all charity effort was channeled through voluntary organization. Humanitarian expression in the late nineteenth century, in and out of government, was almost exclusively directed toward the chronically sick, the disabled, and the mentally disturbed—along with widowed mothers of small children. In short, those who were defined as helpless took center social-problem stage. They have since been shunted into the wings by more powerful constituencies and their ideological supporters.

The decline of attention granted the genuinely helpless can be traced to two factors. First, various political-intellectual minorities now virtually monopolize the allocation of attention to this as compared with that social problem. These minorities display relatively little humanitarian concern for those categories of the "unfortunate" who by conviction support the given social order or who because of sheer physical helplessness cannot be enlisted in crusades to change it. Therefore, political-intellectual minorities celebrate the plight of the vigorous young, whether they be young blacks, young women, young Indians, young poor, or young homosexuals. These categories of persons can be relied upon to protest, in a dramatic way, any grievance which is defined for or by them.

Second, virtually all social-reform effort is now channeled into the governmental apparatus. Being relatively helpless and immobile, the chronically sick, disabled, and mentally disturbed do not constitute powerful constituencies. Government officials, bureaucratic as well as elected, are oriented to the last and the next election, and powerful constituencies *are* heeded. The squeaking wheels of organized insurgence and organized voting blocs thus get the grease of attention and appropriations. Social problems which deal with the collective rights and privileges demanded by special interests for ideological reasons as well as those of material advantage become centrally located in the political process *(19)*.

The drift of attention has also moved away from the aged, although to a lesser extent than from the chronically sick, the disabled, and the mentally disturbed. The old have no hip spokesmen at all, and various political-intellectual minorities now display little interest in manipulating pathos for their political benefit. The majority, on the other hand, in part because of their own personally valued stake in the Social Security program, are very much interested. The old, then, retain considerable political clout, and no politician would risk any word or act which might make him vulnerable to the charge of "being against the old folks."

But the mounting accent on youth in our culture erodes the remaining place of the aged. The aged tend to be isolated in modern society, relegated to a shelf, a circumstance as much revealed as relieved by federal financing of segragated "senior-citizen" housing and entertainment centers. The continuing shift from real family property to consumer property in the economy is another consideration, as well as that from independent to hired status in the division of labor. Also, previous gains made in tax-paid subsidies of various kinds for their benefit have reduced potential claims of the aged upon the humanitarian impulse. For whatever set of reasons, the social problem of old age is now much less fashionable than it was during the thirties, when the Townsend Plan threatened politicians at the voting booth.

Some of the subsidies granted to and wrested by the aged have been accompanied by restrictions interpreted in some quarters as unjust. Wealthy oldsters may derive any amount of income from interest, rents, or corporate dividends, with no reduction of their Old Age and Survivors (Social Security) checks, while the checks of poor ones are reduced if their wages paid for work exceed a stipulated amount. On the other hand, the aged have been conferred one kind of equality which many of them, poor as well as rich, do not want. The state and private corporations generally reserve the "right" to terminate employment at age sixty-five, with no regard for demonstrated competence, physical and mental vigor, or the very unequal rate at which the biological time clock is set from one individual to another.

GOVERNMENT AND UNANTICIPATED CONSEQUENCES

Government organizes attempts to solve a multitude of defined social problems. The sheer size and complexity of this intervening unit inescapably becomes associated with unanticipated and unwanted results of like magnitude. Particularly within the federal government are social-problem decisions made, modified, or recast in response to a great many conflicting pressures within and outside of government.

Part of the pressure from outside stems from the considerable faith retained by the majority that the federal government is the appropriate instrument to set all things right. To be sure there has been some slippage of erstwhile public faith in government. But remaining faith in big government is bolstered by a greater public distrust of big business. Thus a number of surveys taken in the first half of 1974 showed that American families held the oil companies to be more to blame for the energy shortage than government officials and planners.

What follows is not intended as a criticism of government operation. Recall the proposition that the sociologist, in his role as sociologist, is not licensed to state what goals other men or an entire society *should* pursue. As a social scientist he can only assess the adequacy of the means employed to secure a given goal. Our purpose in this section is to state what some of the unanticipated consequences have been of the means adopted by government to solve certain social problems. There is no quarrel, here, with anyone who, like economist John Kenneth Galbraith, holds an image of the good society as one in which "the public sector" is expanded at the expense of "the private sector." He and like-minded others cannot be proved wrong, or right for that matter.

Neither is what follows a plea to dismantle bureaucracy. As

Max Weber pointed out, modern democracy and bureaucracy arose together; they are inextricably intertwined. The historic extension of democratic rights could not have been achieved without the introduction of new bureaucratic regulations. But those regulations in a sense can also become "undemocratic." They inevitably foster the growth of a bureaucratic officialdom who develop interests of their own, and in some degree assume an autocratic position. " 'Democracy' as such," said Weber, then comes in some measure to oppose "the 'rule' of bureaucracy, in spite and perhaps because of its unavoidable yet unintended promotion of bureaucracy."

"Democracy," at least in its present stage throughout the West, generates special-interest groups which are accommodated by a further expansion of bureaucracy to administer and serve programs designed for those special interests.That is one important reason why the governmental means employed to solve a given social problem so often are at loggerheads with governmental means employed to solve another social problem, why the different directions which are discussed below appear. This particular development, parenthetically, Weber did not foresee. He conceived modern bureaucracy as an ineluctably pervasive and monolithic control, increasingly "rationalized" in time with ends and means calculated with ever-greater efficiency. His projection has not been borne out in the case of modern America, as is also shown below.

Different Directions

In contrast to the Weberian model of bureaucracy, separate agencies and bureaus in modern America have tended to become independent of one another. They pursue different and in some cases conflicting goals, so that the means separately adopted do not coalesce. Different directions appear at high as well as low levels of policy determination. The Employment Act of 1946, for example, remains the law and charters the federal government through many different bureaus and departments to make overriding considerations of production, employment and income. On the other hand, the National Environmental Policy Act (NEPA) of 1969 has empowered the Environmental Protection Agency (EPA) to issue directives which are irreconcilable with the 1946 act.

The EPA itself shares responsibility for environmental protection with many other agencies, including the Water Quality Administration (WQA) and the National Air Pollution Control Administration (NAPCA). From time to time the NAPCA has ordered copper mines to cut sulfur dioxide emissions, and the WQA has moved to prevent the dumping of resultant increases of sulfuric acid into streams and rivers. But that WQA action, in turn, produced temporarily undisposable hills of solid waste. This particular tangle then wound up in the courts, where for a time legal action was taken against NAPCA and EPA to lower their standards for sulfur dioxide emissions. A perceived economic necessity to utilize all materials, pointed out in a previous section, may untangle that situation.

In pursuit of unreconcilable goals, the federal government itself has become a notable source of ecological malpractice and pollution. To protect domestic suppliers of oil from foreign competition, the oil import system restricted the importation of low-sulfur oil needed by domestic refiners to help reduce air pollution. That restriction was lifted in 1973, not for ecological reasons but to meet the "energy crisis."

Dumping grounds for discarded automobiles litter the countryside from coast to coast. Possibly the main reason why most of that scrap metal remains unreclaimed is the action of the Interstate Commerce Commission (ICC) in setting higher freight rates on scrap metal than on ore. Thus recyling the automotive hulks of usable steel has become an economically marginal operation. But why the freight rate differential? Most of the railroads are in financial straits for many reasons, including the airline and trucking subsidies dispensed by other agencies which reduce the competitive potential of railroads. The ICC attempts to recompense the railroads in part by setting lower freight rates on iron ore than on scrap metal. Large shipments from the single collection points of mines cost the railroads much less to handle and haul than scrap metal from dispersed loading points.

The interstate highway program did fulfill its assigned purpose of building highways—and drove through parks, destroyed scenic areas, divided towns, and fostered suburban development. This particular development has made one subsequent solution to automobile air pollution now being promoted, that of mass transit designed to link outlying suburbs with central cities, almost economically impossible. Housing sprawl in outlying suburbs has become too thin to provide collection points at mass-transit stations. In the near future, only large metropolitan areas themselves can readily accommodate new rapid-transit facilities.

The Department of Agriculture has often subsidized the export of one or another product in order to maintain high food prices in this country, while the State Department has equally often promoted reduction of agricultural exports to those nations whose domestic price levels it has sought to raise. The Office of Defense Mobilization has the responsibility of dispensing much of the information that the Atomic Energy Commission is charged to protect as classified. The Department of Public Health is legally empowered to discourage cigarette smoking, while the Department of Agriculture continues to promote the sale of American cigarettes abroad, aided by a federal export subsidy.

Some federal agencies seek to preserve endangered animal species; others finance predator-control programs which endanger some of the same species. The blame for going in different directions, if blame is called for, is not assignable to "stupid bureaucrats," but to a combination of two factors. First, the bureaucrats of an all-emcompassing but essentially fragmented state are unable within their separate fiefdoms to evaluate and choose among the multitude of special-interest (including ideal-interest) pressures they must severally and separately try to accommodate.

Second, some of the same as well as different sections of the public demand that action be taken in opposite directions. For example, many citizens by legal and other means resist the location of power-generating plants, especially nuclear facilities, in their own communities, and these same citizens also clamor for an expansion of power capacity. Thus some agencies seek easements for immediate power-company locations, while other agencies simultaneously set higher pollution standards and oversee requirements for multiple safety permits, compliance with which in some instances has taken as long as a year to complete.

Programs designed to go in one direction can become equally bogged down. New legislated programs are invariably added to, not meshed with, previous and similar programs. The Eighty-ninth Congress alone passed twenty-one new health programs, seventeen new educational programs, and four new manpower-training programs. Each of them created a new bureau, agency, or unintegrated division of an existing bureau or agency. Senator Robert Kennedy, for one, pointed out at the time that no one in or out of government really knew which outfit was empowered to handle what sphere of responsibility.

Who Benefits?

The main announced intention of the various programs of welfare administered by the federal government has been to redistribute income and services downward. This goal has in some measure been achieved. Nevertheless, on balance the means utilized have been of questionable efficiency and to some extent even contradictory.

That is why the Family Assistance Plan or any of its variants, whose essential purpose is to dispense federal money directly to the poor, has attracted support across the spectrum of political ideology. One reason for this state of affairs is a growing awareness that the means of the "service strategy" funnel off much and possibly most of the money expended upon welfare programs to various categories of the nonpoor. In short, there are many other beneficiaries of the so-called welfare state than the poor themselves.

Despite the absence of any direct accounting procedures, many of the well-to-do outside of government, certainly the well-to-do within government, have benefited more than the poor from welfare programs designed for the poor. Further, many of the well-to-do outside of government have secured or been granted "welfare programs" of their own. There are three categories of well-to-do beneficiaries—the well-to-do as consumers, the well-to-do as business participants in welfare programs, and the well-to-do as administrative and service personnel in welfare programs.

The poor are not ordinarily consumers of high culture. Only the well-to-do, or rather a minority of them, attend art shows, the theater, and ballet performances, all of which are subsidized by the federal government. In a similar way, our state and national parks are maintained by all taxpayers for the benefit of the relatively well-to-do (20). Again, the poor do not ordinarily travel by air; the fares of those who do fly are subsidized in part by the federal government. And various federal aid-to-education programs mainly subsidize families in the middle- and upper-income brackets, notably so in the case of higher education; the same can be said of "free college tuition" in those states which offer it.

Special-aid bills passed by the Ninety-second Congress for the benefit of Lockheed Aircraft, the Penn Central Railroad, and several pesticide manufacturers were of dubious benefit to the poor. The multibillion-dollar farm program, originally designed to "rescue" the poor farmer, aids not the poor or marginal farmer but the operator on huge mechanized holdings, because federal bonuses and subsidies are granted according to capacity to produce. A 1973 study prepared for the Joint Economic Committee of Congress revealed that 7 percent of benefits from the federal farm commodity programs go to the poorest 41 percent of farmers, while the richest 7 percent receive 32 percent of those disbursements. Former United States Budget Director Charles Schultze has estimated that consumers would annually save $4.5 billion in food prices if all farm subsidies were abolished.

The business participants in welfare programs also do rather well. Most of every dollar paid in federal aid to education goes to increase teachers' salaries, which are much higher than the earnings of the average taxpayer. Urban renewal has forcibly displaced citizens from their homes, destroyed low-rent housing, fostered commercial developments and expensive high-rise apartments for upper-income occupancy. Urban renewal has benefited politically favored contractors and downtown businessmen at the expense of taxpayers and the poor (21). And in the first year that Medicare and Medicaid were in effect, the rate of increase in physicians' fees tripled and the rate of increase in hospital fees quintupled (22).

The chief beneficiaries of welfare programs, however, may very well be the professionals who direct and service them. The cost of all federal income maintenance provisions and Great Society programs went from $30 billion in 1963 to $110 billion in 1973. And in 1973, of the approximate $100 billion paid in personal income taxes, about $64 billion went to employees of the federal government in salaries and benefits *(23)*. How much of that $64 billion in turn went to personnel directly or indirectly engaged in welfare programs is not known exactly, but most of it probably did, based on the circumstance that HEW alone—with a budget of $111 billion in fiscal 1973—is funded at a higher level than the Defense Department.

The administration of Indian affairs is possibly the most extreme example of welfare-money absorption into bureaucratic salaries, which again can be stated only by inference. The federal government annually spends a sum that averages over $8,000 for every Indian citizen in the country, while the average Indian *family* receives only a fraction of that amount, in direct and indirect cash benefits. With government aid supplemented by earned income, Indians remain the most severely impoverished ethnic segment of the population.

Bureaucratic Drag

The persistence of bureaucratic drag is one important reason why government social-problem intervention produces consequences which are unanticipated. In turn, while these consequences may be unanticipated by the general public, at least some of them are fabricated by bureaucratic officials or lower-level personnel in order to serve their own ideal or material interests, or both. Bureaucratic drag is manifested in two ways: opposition by some level of officialdom to majority wish, legislative act, or executive decree; and the adoption of protective mechanisms to maintain a bureaucratic constituency.

The sheer size of governmental bureaucracy fosters inefficiency and waste *(24)*. Our main concern, however, is with those postures and decisions which are internally generated, regardless of how wasteful or inefficient the results may be. But note should first be taken that certain beliefs held by the general public can sway those internally generated decisions. As one instance, the amount of time spent in school is commonly believed to be the primary means to reduce poverty (25). Empirical research has shown that making opportunity available to acquire job skills is a more promising strategy. Nevertheless, in the name of raising the status of the poor, academic education still gets more federal aid than occupational training, even though in recent years the latter has received increased attention and funds.

The public are also convinced that antitrust laws serve their own interest. Some of the ways those laws are administered may very well be in the public interest (the validity of any interest definition is beyond proof or disproof with evidence), but there have been some consequences of those laws which the public would doubtless define as being against their own interest. For example, financial columnist Sylvia Porter has pointed out that grocery man- ufacturers, wholesalers, and retailers continue to use different pallet sizes for transporting food "because of concern about the antitrust laws." If they felt free to use uniformly sized pallets, which is their common wish, they could increase productivity and reduce consum- er prices. Porter quotes Edgar Weinberg, of the National Commis- sion on Productivity, as saying: "Standardization of pallet size is probably more of a labor saver than the electronic computer!" And encouragement of productivity affords the only long-term means of alleviating poverty. That, at least, is the opinion stated by most economists who have addressed the issue.

When polled, the public consistently endorse price controls. They continued to do so in late 1974, when the Ford administration stood adamantly opposed to price controls. Herbert Stein, Chair- man of the President's Council on Economic Affairs, has said that the price freeze of 1973 was reluctantly imposed, in response to popular desire. A certain amount of disillusionment then set in. George Meany, President of the AFL-CIO, joined with the Nation- al Association of Manufacturers in demanding that all price as well as wage controls be scrapped. But enough public faith in price controls remains to perpetuate or retain the official threat of some of them, along with their administrators and investigators, notably in the case of "sensitive" commodities such as gasoline.

Bureaucratic drag is much less often abetted by the entire pub- lic, however, than by particular segments of it. When any welfare program is legislated, for some section of the well-to-do as well as of the poor, its funding is invariably scheduled' to expand in subse- quent years. A new voting bloc emerges, one which shares a mono- lithic interest and frequently organizes to demand ever-more subsi- dies. The ad hoc bureaucracy created to administer the new pro- gram is thus empowered to perpetuate itself on grounds other than proven effectiveness in solving a social problem, since legislators have much more to fear from any organized voting bloc than from the much larger, but unorganized and relatively uninformed and apathetic, general public. All politicians endorse "reduced spend- ing" in general, but not for this or that program in particular.

Bureaucracy, Its Own Constituency

The general public and even special interests within it remain relatively minor factors in bureaucratic drag. The main one is bureaucracy itself. Modern bureaucracy constitutes its own chief constituency. Personnel within it often mobilize to advance and protect their own special interests, which include the perpetuation of old programs and the engendering of new ones.

In paraphrase of a famous general, old programs rarely ever die, they only slowly fade away. Public-assisted urban housing has been declared a scandal-ridden disaster by several top officials who have been defeated in their efforts to manage it. The many agencies which are empowered to "solve" this particular "problem" on a long-term basis have achieved an apparently invulnerable position. Then, too, a conjuncture of certain business interests and bureau interests serves to protect anything other than superficial aspects of already institutionalized programs from being dismantled.

The Office of Economic Opportunity has survived even greater troubles. In September of 1972, OEO Director Philip V. Sanchez declared that the War on Poverty "didn't happen"; it was, he said, a "massive fraud." After his resignation, efforts made by the executive branch to scuttle the program were successfully resisted by members of Congress, who in turn faced the concerted pressure of organized civil servants.

While the directing of policy may be in the formally constituted hands of top administrators who act under a combined executive and legislative mandate, a program once put into the pipeline filters down to subaltern levels, where personnel have a large if officially unacknowledged independent sphere of operation. These are the people who work on details, who *execute* policy and thus can thwart changes in officially announced policy. When bureau functionaries write the specific implementary regulations of legislation passed on the Hill, congressional intent can be, often is, transformed into something quite different.

Max Weber anticipated the growth of power at lower levels of bureaucracy, but not the degree of independence which has emerged. According to Donald Zoll, he did not foresee "the likelihood that bureaucracies within governmental frameworks would in time develop their own internalized value-systems and procedural doctrines." A structurally protected and quasi-insulated position enables bureaucratic personnel from time to time to impose their own definitions of what policy should be. At lower levels of bureaucracy ideology and action can negate "the will of the designated organs of policy formulation" *(26)*.

The government bureaucracy has become the largest and most powerful special-interest bloc in the country. That under civil service rules it is virtually impossible to terminate the job of any minor bureaucrat, barring criminal act, is a minor consideration. Of salient importance is another: "The social legislation of the middle third of the century created 'social space' for a new class whose privilege (or obligation) it is to dispense services to populations that are in various ways wards of the state" (27). This "new class" share common interests, and for the most part a common ideology.

Thirteen million people are presently employed at all levels of government, more people than the total number employed by all the durable goods manufacturing industries. Unlike workers in private industry, government employees have a common interest in keeping public expenditures at high and preferably advancing levels, especially in dispensing "services to populations that are in various ways wards of the state," in which dispensation a majority of government employees are directly or in some ancillary capacity engaged. And "unlike workers in private industry, those in government sit on both sides of the bargaining table. Through their unions and associations they can press their managers for increased wages, and as voters they can threaten ungenerous officials" (28).

This particular voting bloc dwarfs any other, whether labor union, racial, ethnic, business-interest, or whatever. Its size, common interest, and more or less unified purpose will surely not explain why old programs which are heartily endorsed by the majority are retained, such as Social Security. But the longevity of such popularly discredited programs as OEO can in large part be explained on this basis.

New programs are engendered as well as old ones perpetuated. A social problem can be created in order to justify a solution. The OEO Community Action programs were no response to popular demand. They came to be administered by bureau and agency personnel *after* the expenditure of much effort and money had failed to change the life or attitudes or performance of the physically able nonworking poor. "If no solutions were available and no one had the foggiest notion of how to do anything, it *was* possible to increase the demand for solutions, to create pressure from below that would effect the release of ever increasing amounts of federal money" (29).

In recent years there actually have been only minor increases in the total amount of direct-cash disbursements to aid recipients. But during that same period, as a result of "administrative entrepreneurship," social services spending has been a different matter. "Enterprising consultants, program analysts, state budget planners, and other officials . . . have sought to redefine and regroup programs so as to take advantage of open-ended sources of federal aid." With no appreciable growth of social dependency, "such services spending has disappeared into the existing state budgets" (30).

Established Expectations

Bureaucratic drag may very well be internally generated, but it is protected by the perceived interests of the present majority. Some operations of the bureaucracy may be resented, but other operations are generally regarded as indispensable. And given the scope of recent structural change, continued and massive government operations of all kinds are inevitable.

In little more than a decade a geometric increase in commitment by the federal government to a multitude of welfare programs has, at least in the intermediate term, irrevocably changed the society as well as the economy. These programs have become not only a vested interest to those who benefit from them, but also a basis for planning the rest of many lives. They provide a ground for critical decision making, whether to prepare for or renounce a career, work or loaf, take out life insurance or not, go into business or accept employee status, save or depend upon the promise of government protection from contingencies of ill health and old age.

Individual adaptations made by millions of citizens to government intervention continue to expand that intervention. There can be no decision to turn back. Nevertheless the means, the open-ended financial scope of the means, employed in trying to solve many of our social problems have built into the economy an unmanageable rate of inflation (31), which at some future time popular attitudes may define as the supreme social problem.

SOCIAL PROBLEMS CANNOT BE SOLVED?

The numbered chapters can be reduced to as many propositions. First, social problems are the result of attitudes and not the comparative seriousness of deplored conditions. Second, the attitudes which create social problems have a cultural and historic context. Third, the "same" social problems nevertheless are redefined in time. Fourth, social-problem definitions and programs incorporate a clash of interests, a power struggle, and the creation and promotion of subjectivistic imagery. Fifth, the ideological struggle between hip extremists and militant squares over what social problems are and what should be done about them is the main arena of conflict on the contemporary domestic scene. Sixth, in part as a result of this struggle, neither "deviance" nor "social disorganization" is of much aid in classifying or analyzing social problems. Seventh, in this chapter the difficulty, indeed the impossibility, of proceeding along a straight line to the solution of social problems has been explored.

Only with the unified purpose of totalitarianism, a total political control of decision making, can a society move in a straight line to solve defined problems. But democracy is a process, not an achieved result, a process which remains poised in uneasy tension between the human desire to maintain difference and the human desire to make everyone alike. Freedom or liberty—or whatever similar inadequate and imprecise concept is equally impossible to define—thrives on mess, muddle, paradox, and false starts in many directions.

If a commitment to democracy is assumed, then the inefficient handling of defined social problems by modern American bureaucracy confers some unanticipated consequences which are not altogether deplorable. A successful because unchallenged application of directly efficient means to social-problem goals would in all likelihood promote changes of attitude in two opposite directions, toward subservience and intransigence. Such changes of attitude could in turn create many new social problems, in retrospective assessment possibly "worse" ones than now hold public attention.

One conclusion, anyway, is not derivable from the above numbered propositions: that nothing can be done since nothing has been done. To hold the idea that effort has proved useless would be to confuse utopia with the scene before us. While no specific social problem has ever been solved in terms of hope and plan, the total enterprise has been a different matter.

Victory may have been denied in all of the separate battles, but some kind of war was somehow won in the course of the last two centuries. The total enterprise has fostered a new consciousness and sensibility. A sense of shared responsibility for the welfare of distant others is one of the great achievements of the modern West. It is shared by hip and square, however at loggerheads they otherwise may be.

This view of the world is beyond objective judgment. Many critics have nevertheless essayed that task, and noted shortcomings, even failures. The vision, some say, is narrowly materialistic, one in which social achievement is reckoned not in philosophical, ethical, or religious terms, but primarily in physical terms. The West shares with the Communist world a consequent and similar stunting of the human spirit. Others say that physical welfare, even widely shared physical welfare, has failed to correct, may even have exacerbated, discontent, emotional unrest, and spiritual malaise. Man does not live by physical welfare alone, and a price has been paid for neglect of higher levels of human experience and aspiration. We are, continues this indictment, more confused about the meaning and purpose of life than were people in distant times.

Aristotle, Saint Francis, Dante, Shakespeare, even the Founding Fathers, would have found our outlook alien and bizarre. Several ancient manifestations of human experience—the sense of cosmic being in a world suffused with divine purpose, awe, transcendent beauty, honor, loyalty, devotion, sin and redemption, the classic image of the ordered and examined life and the romantic image of exceeding one's grasp— have all receded. Kindness has emerged as the supreme virtue, the alleviation of others' material and physical if not spiritual suffering as the most laudable goal. The expression of kindness has become an almost distinctively modern culture trait, and an important means for declaring worth of self in the world. The ways of the past were quite different. But quite simply they are not ours *(32)*.

Nevertheless, because of the factors analyzed in this book our way has not solved any of the social problems discussed. Of the two main reasons, one is the persistence as well as inconstancy of opposed images, attitudes, and interests amidst incessant change. The other is the sheer magnitude of our defined social problems. Hence an axiom: the wider the scope of the problem posed and addressed, the more will unanticipated consequences, recalcitrance and jobbery, intervene—checking, modifying, distorting original ends and means; and thus the less certain will any concerned individual be of achieving an end result which will resemble his projected goal.

Fortunately, that axiom has a corollary: the more reduced in scope the problem posed and addressed, the fewer intermediaries and agents need be involved; and thus the more certainly can means be applied to projected goal in order to achieve the wanted end result. Many young people today are developing this insight into a way of life, some in religious and others in secular terms.

REFERENCES

1   Weber had in mind social decision making, but precisely the same difficulty has arisen throughout history in the unceasing albeit essential efforts of moral philosophers to inculcate the standard virtues. Unfortunately, they are not altogether consistent; some of them are mutually contradictory. For many centuries moral philosophers have propagandized, cajoled, educated, and exhorted others to be cooperative, altruistic, forgiving, kind, and nurturing, while they have also exhorted others to be independent, self-reliant, ambitious, patriotic, realistic, and loyal to one divisive cause or another.

2   Charles Frankel, "The New Egalitarianism and the Old," *Commentary,* September 1973, pp. 54–61, p. 57.

3   Vilfredo Pareto, *The Mind and Society,* 4 vols., Andrew Bongiorno and Arthur Livingston (trans.), Arthur Livingston (ed.), Harcourt, Brace, New York, 1935 (originally published in 1916), vol. 4, p. 1473.

4   This generalization is qualified below as the point at which surveillance of the public itself is extended in the name of protecting the public.

5   The automobile was introduced in order to provide cheap and rapid private transportation and also, of course, to make a profit. It thus cohered with such trends as expanding markets, growth of cities and population. But it also provided improved means of criminal escape. Further, while the automobile was not a cause, it was a necessary basis

for ultimate unanticipated changes in courtship practices and attitudes toward leisure. And the automobile later became intimately associated with the problem of air pollution.

6   Robert M. MacIver, *Social Causation,* Ginn, Boston, 1942, p. 20.

7   James S. Coleman, "Community Disorganization and Conflict," in Robert K. Merton and Robert Nisbet (eds.), *Social Problems,* rev. ed., Harcourt Brace Jovanovich, New York, 1971, pp. 657–708, p. 700.

8   Under the farm-subsidy plan launched during the Depression, the only politically feasible basis for making a series of direct and indirect payments to farmers was retained acreage, the larger the holding, the higher the subsidy. The big operators got enough money from other taxpayers to mechanize and to buy out hundreds of thousands of small inefficient farmers who could not compete in the new government-sponsored market.

9   Leo Rosten, "A Lesson in Politics," *World,* Feb. 13, 1973, pp. 8–11, p. 11.

10   Daniel P. Moynihan, "Equalizing Education: In Whose Benefit?" *The Public Interest,* Fall 1972, pp. 69–89, p. 87. Only private enterprises can fail. Public enterprises operate outside the discipline of the open market and its price system, and any supposed failure becomes an argument for yet more resource allocation in the same place. "This view, that the general good is served by advancing the interests of the public sphere, is apparently the dominant social view of the time, and is terribly hard to argue against with any success" (p. 84).

11   For an expanded discussion of the points covered, see Marc. C. Roberts, "Is There an Energy Crisis?" *The Public Interest,* Spring 1973, pp. 17–37. Mr. Roberts holds improvement of environmental quality to be an eminently desirable goal, and he argues that while "environmental pressures" have hindered utility companies, we could have energy maintenance *and* cleaner fuels if we were willing to pay enough to defray the increased costs.

12   *San Francisco Sunday Examiner and Chronicle,* July 29, 1973, sec. C., p. 14.

13   A similar generalization applies to motives, especially political motives. See Arnold W. Green, "The New Morality," *Modern Age,* Summer–Fall 1970, pp. 293–304.

14   Albert Wohlstetter and Roberta Wohlstetter, " 'Third Worlds' Abroad and at Home," *The Public Interest,* Winter 1969, pp. 88–107, pp. 98–99.

15   For example: "We are certainly not among those . . . who believe in any sort of racial quota. We believe color should be irrelevant, but we wonder why managers' jobs have not been offered to the likes of Frank Robinson, Elston Howard, Bill White, Larry Doby and others." *Wall Street Journal,* Oct. 3, 1973, p. 14.

16 A. H. Maslow, "A Theory of Human Motivation," *Psychological Review,* **50:**370–396, 1943, p. 395. This theory has been challenged on the ground that it exaggerates the extent to which "change comes from within and to this process of self-actualization man owes his first allegiance." Alan L. Mintz, "Encounter Groups and Other Panaceas," *Commentary,* July 1973, pp. 42–49, p. 48. But it was only in Professor Maslow's later work that he made "self-actualization" a prescription, with implication of the right to ignore the rights of others.

17 Sheila K. Johnson, "To China, with Love," *Commentary,* June 1973, pp. 37–45, p. 45.

18 Staffan B. Linder, *The Harried Leisure Class,* Columbia, New York, 1970, p. 132.

19 Special interests have always received special political consideration and will continue to do so. But like much else, privilege and graft, formally legitimate or otherwise, have been democratized and rendered sensitive to intellectual ferment. Special interest is no longer a near-private reserve of the rich and their political henchmen. In paraphrase of Edward C. Banfield, the talk-filled room of the "conscience constituency" is becoming larger at the expense of the smoke-filled room of the boodlers.

20 Arnold W. Green, *Recreation, Leisure, and Politics,* McGraw-Hill, New York, 1964, p. 26.

21 Edward C. Banfield, *The Unheavenly City: The Nature and Future of Our Urban Crisis,* Little, Brown, Boston, 1970, p. 16.

22 Fred Anderson, "Paying for Health," *The New Republic,* Feb. 7, 1970, pp. 17–19, p. 17.

23 Taylor Branch, "Taxpayers' Eve," *Harper's,* April 1973, pp. 70–71, p. 70. "Together with eleven million state and local employees, federal workers now comprise more than one worker out of every five in the United States" (p. 71).

24 There is a common complaint that business corporations exemplify inefficient and wasteful giantism. The charge may have some merit, but in nonideological comparison big government must be assigned first place. As one instance, from 1932 to 1974, the charge for mailing a first-class letter went from 3 to 10 cents. In this same period AT&T, a popular target of criticism, increased some phone services by a relatively trifling amount, reduced others, and provided rather obviously better service than the governmental mail monopoly.

AT&T is by no means the best comparison which could be cited, because it is itself a quasi-monopoly (*all* monopolies either are government operations or result from government charter; a monopoly can be created on no other basis). Most business corporations are not even quasi-monopolies. They cannot dissuade consumers from choosing alternative products or services if prices fail to meet the competition of the market, and all of them must hold down costs or go out of business. There is no such discipline which controls government operations, including expansion of personnel.

25 Lester C. Thurow, "Education and Economic Equality," *The Public Interest,* Summer 1972, pp. 66-81, p. 66.

26 Donald A. Zoll, "American Government: A Byzantine Predicament," *Modern Age,* Winter 1973, pp. 62–70, p. 67. Presidents Kennedy and Nixon vowed to curb the bureaucracy. Neither succeeded.

27 Moynihan, reference 10, p. 83, underscored in the original.

28 James H. Kuhn, "The Riddle of Inflation—a New Answer," *The Public Interest,* Spring 1972, pp. 63–77, p. 76.

29 Aaron Wildavsky, "Government and the People," *Commentary,* August 1973, pp. 25–32, p. 26.

30 Martin Rein and Hugh Heclo, "What Welfare Crisis?" *The Public Interest,* Fall 1973, pp. 61–83, p. 64.

31 Kuhn, reference 28.

32 These "ways," theirs and ours, should be understood to be primarily different aspirations and not contrasts of overt behavior. In any epoch, ideals tower above performance. Such historians of morals as Lecky, Brinton, and the Durants have demonstrated that morality, expressed in action, neither improves nor retrogresses appreciably from one century to another. Possibly most eighteenth-century citizens were no more honorable than most modern citizens are kind. Nevertheless, ideals like ideas do have consequences, and one of them is the application of collective attention upon what a given society of people will try to do as well as affirm.

Some Possibilities and Contingent Prospects

We cannot simultaneously maximize all our values, for many reasons. Ideal values are often inconsistent, as was pointed out in the previous chapter (see reference 1 of Chapter 7). Program values, such as social reforms, always disclose practical as well as logical incompatibilities within and among them. Within the social struggle, overt conflict prevents and latent conflict undermines the realization of one value at the expense of others. Even when widespread attitudes support a given value with little dispute, the price exacted by the means proposed to achieve it may be deemed too high by recalcitrant groups and parties. And all values, including desired social reforms, are subject to transvaluation by convergent trends, unanticipated consequences, and shifts of collective attention.

With these considerations in mind, we now turn to a final assessment of the five social problems which have been our main focus of attention. This will not be history or summary, nor prophecy of what will be nor antisociological prescription of what should be; instead, we will make contingent statements about what *could* happen. If certain trends should continue or combine in specified ways, if certain ascendant attitudes wax or wane, if attempts are made to push given values to their logical conclusion, then, cautiously, this or that intermediate outcome is possible. It is an exercise in speculation and conjecture.

CRIME

Daniel Patrick Moynihan has said that we really don't know anything about crime. In a very limited sense he is wrong. We know that crime rates go down during slumps and up during periods of economic boom—at least they have done so in the past. We know something about the statistical probability of criminal behavior according to sex, age, race, economic status, and some other criteria. We also know that incarceration or any other form of punishment "rehabilitates" very few, if any, criminals. On the other hand, newer programs "like increased staff for probation, or half-way houses, or intensive prison counseling, or liberalized bail" have been shown by research to be no more successful "in reforming the criminal or lowering recidivism rates" (1).

But Moynihan is quite right in exactly what he does mean. "We" (presumably those of disinterested scientific or scholarly bent) do not know what to do with the knowledge available. It does not tell us *why* some men, and not others, commit crime. To the exact point, no one, whatever expertise he may have or claim, knows how to prevent crime or reduce its occurrence—within extant practical and logical incompatibilities.

Free Will and Determinism
The chief manifestation of these incompatibilities in the social problem of crime remains the controversy over free will and determinism. It is an old one which will never be settled because ideology, not science, provides the opposing arguments. The points debated by St. Augustine and Pelagius centuries ago remain unresolved in modern forensic psychology, law, and criminology, which incorporate both deterministic and free-will assumptions.

The weight of modern intellectual opinion, however, is heavily on the side of determinism—in a somewhat biased way. As often as criminal behavior is excused because it is determined, retaliation against criminal behavior, official or otherwise, is disapproved on moral grounds. Criminals are said to be helpless to refrain from behaving as they do because antecedent environmental influences determined their behavior. We are told therefore that determinism exculpates the "so-called" criminal, exonerates him from blame, or that prisons should be abolished because they fail to rehabilitate the criminal, that is, determine his behavior in a new direction—or both.

Antecedent environmental influences which determine criminal behavior, the argument continues, stem from malformed social institutions which should be totally recast. The incompatibilities of that proposal are impressive; it faces three unsurmountable obstacles. First, no institutional framework has ever been destroyed and built anew, even when such a decision has been supported by totalitarian power. Second, in no society will the majority ever accede to revolutionary social change designed for the special benefit of any segment of the population which is under popular disapprobation.

If the first two incompatibilities should magically disappear, and if the assumption of absolute determinism is accepted, there is in the third place no method in science, and surely not in law, of tracing exactly how all the antecedent factors combine to produce a given decision, such as in one case to commit a crime and in another to refrain from so doing. In any event, all modern legal codes, whether American, Chinese, or Russian, are founded upon the assumption of legal responsibility (or "free will"), whatever mitigating circumstances such as "legal insanity" and age of defendant may be admissible.

While determinism has become ideologically associated with lifting blame from criminal behavior, there is no such logical affiliation. In the eighteenth century Holbach endorsed rigorous determinism in the cause of dissuading men from crime. "Penal laws," he said, "are ways of offering to men strong motives, to weigh in the scale against the temptation of an immediate personal gratification."

It is Professor Matza's opinion that our modern juvenile courts do not offer delinquents any such strong motives. They instead

encourage commission of further infractions because "the incre-
ments of sanction are sufficiently slight and administered gradually
enough so that each appears not much worse than the one preceding
it." Matza argues further that the rhetoric of determinism, or personal nonresponsibility, is employed in the delinquent's presence by
judges and social workers. But since these people detain *him* in an
"honor camp" or place *him* under the surveillance of probation and
not the antecedent causes they blame, their ideology of child welfare
confirms the delinquent's own "conception of irresponsibility, and
it feeds his sense of injustice. Both support the processes by which
the moral bind of law is neutralized. Both facilitate the drift into
delinquency" *(2)*.

Two mutually hostile demands have simultaneously become
more insistent. That of prison abolition, based upon a selective
humanitarian concern for the "so-called" criminal, faces that of
more and longer sentencing, based upon a rising fear of violent
crime. Two very different images of the "criminal" are therewith
invoked. Any trend toward majority compliance with the first demand is difficult to imagine. The argument of determinism is basic
to this generalization.

Individual Responsibility

The controversy over free will and determinism actually has no
essential bearing on the existential universality of individual responsibility. The argument that the criminal's behavior or anyone else's
is determined requires neither answer nor rebuttal. Even assuming
that position to be correct, in social life we do go on holding ourselves responsible for our own actions and holding others responsible for theirs.

The meaning of the term "responsibility," however, must be
clarified. Those people who mean by responsibility personal control
over individual destiny, after demonstrating to their own satisfaction that no man is master of his own fate, believe they have excused
criminals from being held accountable for their actions. As used
here, on the other hand, responsibility does not refer to free will, but
to accountability itself.

Parents hold children accountable for keeping clean, for keeping quiet under certain circumstances, for getting grades in school

which will bear scrutiny. Children hold one another accountable in some ways that most adults would approve and in others that fewer adults would approve—such as the schoolboy code against squealing when a companion has cheated in class or broken a window. When those children grow up they will in turn hold their own children accountable in the same or similar ways, and possibly in different ways: children being raised in communes are often held accountable for renouncing the "stereotyped sexist roles" of the conventional outside world, and for being "spontaneously creative" in their play.

We are held accountable, we hold others accountable, at home, in the street, on the job, even in the tavern. By tacit understanding a man in his cups is permitted minor liberties, but he is expected to respect the distinction between being amusing and making a nuisance of himself. He may have read about someone else who got away with literal murder on a plea of irresistible impulse, but he usually keeps several of his own impulses in check because others hold him accountable.

We know that this or that person will invariably act thus and so in a given situation, because if he should depart markedly from the behavior that is expected of him he would be disadvantaged in one way or another. He would, in short, be punished—by withdrawal of affection, by ridicule, by destruction of his reputation, or, in extreme cases, by expulsion from the group in which his disruptive behavior occurred. To the majority it simply makes no sense in justice, no logical, ethical, or practical sense, that those who have maximally flouted the rules they themselves reluctantly accept should be maximally exempted from their application by special dispensation.

The present wave of prison reform, including proposals to abolish prisons altogether for the indisputable reason that they fail to rehabilitate those incarcerated, is thus likely to retain a low priority among the electorate. In commonsense rebuttal, violent criminals such as muggers, rapists, and murderers are at least prevented from following their trade while they are locked up. It is protection from violent criminals which has a high and decisive priority among the electorate.

The Criminal-Justice System

To be sure, the majority are not being very well protected. The criminal-justice system apprehends and processes many more petty than violent criminals. Those ultimately incarcerated are mostly inept misfits of crime. By a long chalk most criminals and delinquents will never be sent to an "honor camp," a jail, or a prison (3). But very few noncriminals are aware of this situation, and the majority in any event can be depended upon to insist that all criminals *should* be locked up.

A continuation of their scorn for the idea that society is responsible for crime also appears to be a likely prospect. The majority are part of society, but so are criminals, and if criminals are not to blame for crime, then they, the law-abiding majority, must be to blame for crime. Such dubious logic has small likelihood of becoming more persuasive than it ever has been. This is not to say that the majority are keenly aware of logical fallacy, only that they are prone to address the outer world with specific and concrete instances, not with the intellectual's reified abstractions.

And yet, however defined, the "crime problem" is not likely to be "solved" with the simple, direct measures which appeal to the majority. Like other institutions, legal systems have a long history and once entrenched are not amenable to a sudden shift in course. Criminals are handled summarily in the French legal system, as the American majority would like to see criminals handled in their own country. But in France the main concern has been and remains whether a crime was or was not committed, with such matters as how evidence was gathered and protection of the accused from judicial error granted much less consideration (4). On the other hand, traditional American legal procedure incorporates a concern with these two matters which overrides the question of guilt or innocence.

Thus the "innovations" of the Warren Court which so aroused square hostility—some which expanded the scope of procedural delay and vacillation in the courts, others which "handcuffed the police" in gathering evidence—more fulfilled legal tradition than departed from it *(5)*. Although the Burger Court in 1974 modified the ruling which had excluded evidence obtained without a search warrant, and granted prosecutors some leeway in using evidence gathered in a more flexible way, the entrenched philosophy of protection for the accused was hardly abandoned. Given this entrenched philosophy, which is not even vaguely understood by the majority, their demand for more police and more arrests is not likely to achieve the goal sought—that of reducing the crime rate. Indeed Judge Bernard Botein has argued that increased police activity can only make a bad situation worse.

Additional police manpower and equipment would be "largely wasted" because other agencies in the criminal-justice system are already hopelessly bogged down in unprocessed cases. The majority, and the politicians who represent them, go on endorsing fattened police budgets, but not concomitant budget increases for courts, judges, prosecutors, defense counsels, probation officers, and places of incarceration. What good are more arrests when little can be done with those already arrested? By 1970 the backlog of cases in New York City criminal courts reached 500,000.

"Of the millions of criminal cases instituted each year in the nation's criminal courts, relatively few—perhaps three or four percent—proceed through trial" (6). Most of the rest are disposed of with what is known as plea bargaining. Deals are worked out between the prosecutor and defense counsel, sometimes with the judge's participation, for a mutually acceptable plea of guilty to a lesser offense—such as "possession of burglar tools" in a case where a man was caught without tools but with positively identified loot in his possession. Lack of facilities and personnel, combined with the burden of proof placed upon the prosecution in American law, including the inadmissibility of much evidence such as incriminating statements made in the absense counsel, leaves the criminal-justice system with no other recourse. Through plea bargaining, 90 percent of all convictions are secured by admission of guilt to lesser, fictitious charges (7).

Images and the Crime Problem

Disinterested and enlightened discussion of the crime problem is notably rare. Images held are too diverse and too exclusionary to provide much room for minds to meet. An angry shouting match continues, as it has for decades, over the apparently simple proposition of exactly who is victim and who perpetrator. Intransigent emotional and ideological convictions stand in the way of concerted action.

Even Judge Botein's modest proposal to increase nonpolice budgets in the criminal-justice system will have hard going against the grain of majority attitudes. The majority retain an image of themselves as victims of crime, not as potential defendants in court or as imprisoned felons. That is why the all-or-nothing rhetoric so often directed at them—for example, injustice visited upon one prisoner places all of us in jeopardy—remains less than persuasive. They will doubtless continue to place their faith in the police to arrest dangerous criminals, most of whom will not be processed any further, and in the law to apply more severe penalties, which the law is unable to exact.

The "facts," even when agreement may be reached about what one of them is, afford no basis for concerted action. The majority view the crime rate as rising, and quell their humanitarian sentiments with a demand for more severe punitive measures to reduce it. Many hip spokesmen, within and outside the criminal-justice system, also accept the "fact" of a rising crime rate, and then conclude that prisons should be abolished. "The empirical test is simple," Dr. Timothy Leary has said. "If the crime rate is rising, the penal system is unjust" (8).

Whatever the crime problem may be, it will continue to resist solution, as has been the case throughout history. How on balance it will be addressed as well as defined will depend upon the drift of effective attitudes along the hip-square range. Given the total context of modern social life, prevailing square attitudes are not likely to promote measures that will markedly reduce the crime rate, not, anyway, in terms which the majority would consider to be acceptable.

The majority have not begun to appreciate the price that would have to be paid to achieve that goal, a rigorous surveillance of the total population discussed in the previous chapter, a kind of surveillance which would virtually destroy our political system and surely would destroy our traditional legal system. On the other hand, hip attitudes are not likely to prove any more effective. It is difficult to foresee any circumstances under which the majority would ever accept reform measures designed to exempt criminals from account-ability.

POVERTY

The entire noncriminal population want something done about crime, whatever lack of consensus may persist about what that might be. The social problem of poverty differs in a salient way: by no means do all the nonpoor in the population want very much of anything done about poverty, except for those people who are phys-ically helpless and a few other categories of the "deserving poor." Then, too, criminals openly challenge the social order with their own acts, while it is the passive failure to act on the part of the "undeserv-ing poor" which brings them to public attention, a recognition not generally perceived as requiring an immediate and all-out response.

Further, while who is and who is not a criminal may be disput-ed, the distinction in commonsense terms is not difficult to make. The dividing line between poverty and nonpoverty is much more elusive. Expanding expectations as well as inflation move the line upward, at least by official determination. On August 7, 1973, the Labor Department set the poverty line at $4,300 a year for a non-farm family of four, $100 above the line set in December of 1972.

Income Distribution

At the present time, people in high-, middle-, and low-income brack-ets receive about the same proportion of all personal income which those same categories received at the end of the Second World War. The poorest 20 percent of families continue to get about 5 percent of the total income, the richest 20 percent about 40 percent. Once a high level of industrialization is reached, apparently income distri-bution stabilizes and is little affected by political efforts to redistrib-ute it. Strictly comparable data are unavailable; however, income distribution appears to have become stabilized in a similar way in France, England, Germany, and Russia.

On the other hand, while measures of income distribution are more reliable than those of rates of crime, they too can be mislead-ing. Cash income, which is the only measure taken in determining the poverty line, excludes benefits like food stamps, Medicaid, subsi-dized housing, school lunches, and graduated income taxes *(9)*. At the other end of the scale, cash income of the well-to-do does not take into account those "welfare programs" designed for them (which were discussed in the previous chapter), in which the poor do not participate; also left unconsidered are capital gains, realized or unrealized.

On balance, however, Sanford Rose says that there has been a trend toward income equalization in recent years, a trend hidden by reduction of "family size" at lower income levels which income data ignore. Ironically, diffused prosperity has resulted in an overcounting of "poor" households, those of single young residents and of retired married couples. In less affluent times most of these people would have continued to live in larger "primary family units," contributing to those units small incomes like part-time earnings and Social Security checks. But since so many of them can now afford to live apart, and in the case of young people receive checks from home which are unreckoned in census data, a real trend toward income leveling is disguised. The number of "households" at the lower end of the income scale has been vastly increased. By 1970 the income of the poorest 20 percent of households supported an average of three people, while that of the richest 20 percent of households supported an average of four people. It is the distribution of income *per family member* which has become more equal (10).

Majority Attitudes

Available data on income distribution may be somewhat misleading, but no matter how figures and definitions are juggled, some people do remain poor, others rich. And attitudes of the majority toward the former remain somewhat ambivalent. Some degree of humanitarian concern for the poor is accompanied by perhaps a greater degree of resentment, tinged with hostility, for poverty programs. Phrased differently, "most Americans are not much interested in poverty, and not at all interested in poverty programs" *(11).* An implication of greater interest than does exist may be fostered by the requirement to answer yes or no to opinion-poll questions devised by strangers. Anyway, the logical and programmatic contradictions which appear in responses to questions on poverty indicate a division of mind if not lack of interest or concern.

During a time of persisting affluence, most Americans accepted an expanded public obligation toward the poor. Yet when a national cross section of Americans were asked if a person's being poor results from lack of effort or circumstances beyond his control, only one-fourth chose the latter alternative. "Three-quarters pointed either to lack of effort, or a combination of lack of effort and circumstances—both of which, of course, placed the stigma of blame on the poor for their own condition."

There is a seeming inconsistency in the willingness of 42 percent of respondents to endorse a federal "guaranteed annual income" for families without a worker, as well as for those with a worker at very low wages—when that finding is juxtaposed with another. As between "a less expensive" scheme of simply having the government give cash payments to poor people without requiring them to work and "a more expensive one" of government training, job finding, and where necessary, providing care for children in the absence of the worker, 81 percent opt for the more expensive system, 9 percent for the less expensive, and 10 percent can reach no conclusion (12). Quite simply, the majority do not want others to get something for nothing, and they are willing to spend more money to ensure that they don't.

It would probably be an error, however, to conclude that the majority of Americans are more punitive than humanitarian in their attitudes toward the poor. What we are dealing with here is something basic and universal, which is absorbed during the socialization process. Within the family, in all societies and periods of time, children are motivated to accept social rules by being told, again and again, that only "good" children are rewarded.

Adults, socialized in the same way when they were children, also wish "good" behavior to be rewarded, or, having lost the child's initial faith, they may wish that it always were rewarded. This particular outlook is most marked in those people who view themselves as having obeyed the moral imperatives of should and ought and responsibility to others. Thus it is that adults, especially within the family, tend to regard moral rules as being *mutually* binding.

Any sacrifice of impulse expression to should and ought and accepted responsibility by adult family members is rationalized by a principle of mutuality. Allegiance, duty, loyalty—all cut both ways; and if parents accept obligations of nurture and protective care to their children, they are in turn led to expect obedience and respect from them as their due *(13)*. At any time or place in history, and presumptively for many thousands of years prior to history, human beings have accepted moral obligations to others with the belief or at least the hope that in one way or another they would be rewarded.

The rules which support moral obligation differ considerably in content from one society to another. In our own historic tradition they have tended to stress application, disciplined effort, and deferral or sublimation of impulse gratification. These exactions laid down by parents and parental surrogates are notably severe. The child seeks assurance of reward for his reluctant acquiescence, and equal assurance that others are penalized for noncompliance or rebellion.

The child's envy and resentment lead him to search for counter-evidence of others in the same or similar family situation who may receive love and appreciation or are only ignored when they fail to comply with what is demanded of him. He can readily find many such instances, and if, as usually happens, he continues to identify with parents and parental surrogates, he turns rejecting affect upon the lucky children. If virtue is indeed its own reward, at deep levels of subliminal consciousness lies a demand that it *should* be more solidly rewarded. Those who obey the rules should be rewarded, but not the others.

The adult with this emotional outlook, the outlook of possibly most people in the majority, is not very far removed from the nursery he once knew. Criminals, who have flagrantly violated the rules, *should* be punished. The "undeserving poor," believed to have flouted the rules, should not be *too* well treated. These attitudes are incorporated in the historic myth of the social contract, which stems from the deep-lying wish of the "good child." He should be rewarded, but those others should be punished, or deprived of reward, or at least made to realize the gulf of contractual responsibility which separates him from them. Only those perceived as being helpless and deserving are exempted, on the grounds that they were unable to fulfill the "contract."

This is the heart of the matter, why it is that the humanitarian sentiment is invariably compromised in efforts to alleviate the plight of the poor. The majority are ambivalent. They will doubtless continue to drag foot in accepting some antipoverty programs and continue to reject others outright. They remain suspicious of those people who quell any ambivalence of their own with an assumption of superior knowledge and social conscience, and of those who materially benefit from such programs, whether clients or government intermediaries.

Conceivable Shift in Attitudes

Before attitudes of the majority could be made to veer appreciably in the direction desired by social reformers, it seems reasonable to assume that one or the other of two changes in circumstance would have to occur. The effortless ease forecasted in some quarters as an imminent result of cybernation and automation would surely erode the ancient relationship between judged performance and sanctioned reward. Were everyone exempted from a perceived need to exert disciplined effort, envy of and hostility toward those now— fairly or unfairly—regarded by the majority as parasites would doubtless disappear. But such an essentially magical solution of more social problems than that of poverty is an unlikely prospect, for reasons discussed in previous chapters.

On the other hand, within the range of possibility is a massive educational program designed to soften public resistance. It could not, at least at first, afford to be wholly candid. "Workfare not welfare" was the slogan adopted in the first and unsuccessful round of President Nixon's guaranteed annual income or Family Assistance Program. Unlike some representatives of top officialdom, the majority no more now than before are prepared to accept a permanent "underclass" of physically able nonworkers as an irremediable reality. It is, however, conceivable that over a long period of time practical demonstrations might persuade an increasing number of taxpayers that cash subsidies are cheaper than the "service strategy." But if most American taxpayers now prefer spending more money for a service strategy, which has notably failed to reduce unemployment among the able-bodied poor, to spending less money on direct handouts, then the techniques of persuasion utilized could hardly be "rational" ones.

If by whatever means a permanent underclass of the poor came to be legitimized as well as recognized, the long history of American effort to eliminate poverty would come to at least a temporary close. In that history punitive and humanitarian attitudes combined inextricably. The most positive affirmation of this combination has been a belief that poverty *could* be ended by helping others to help themselves, and the present willingness of the majority to spend more money on job training and similar measures than on direct subsidies for the poor should be viewed in this light.

A new consensus, that the poor cannot be helped to help themselves, could possibly emerge. It would exact some kind of price from the poor, perhaps the unanticipated consequence of depriving them of full citizenship. There is a conceivable danger that, no more than American Indians could during that long period when they were legally wards of the government, would the poor be allowed to exert control over the circumstances of their own lives.

RACE RELATIONS

Poverty and black America are often, and mistakenly, held to be synonymous. While a higher proportion of blacks than whites are poor, there are more than twice as many poor whites as poor blacks, and most blacks, two-thirds of them, in 1972 lived above the official poverty line. Moreover, only one-fourth of all black families in 1971 received public assistance *(14)*. And as was indicated in previous chapters, the improvement in overall black economic status, relative to the white, has been quite rapid in recent years, at least in nonideological terms.

This achievement has been shadowed for most Americans by a publicized failure to redistribute income appreciably through various antipoverty programs. A far greater achievement has gone generally overlooked—that of full citizenship for black Americans. Social reform, insurgent demand, and legal authority have destroyed interference at the voting booth and categorical denial of jobs; have promoted black access to elected as well as administrative office; have wiped clean all the demeaning harassment of separation in motels, restaurants, barber shops, buses, stores, and public libraries. Much more important, full and equal citizenship is now universally accepted, almost as much endorsed, by the white population.

Black and White Attitudes

Something else has gone generally ignored, the emergence of a large black "middle class" who have obtained above-average income and occupational status, who are motivated to defer gratification, plan for the future, and work hard to achieve an independent life. There is a common failure—shared by many blacks as well as whites—to differentiate between these people and the approximately equal number who are below, at, or near the official poverty line, people who more often than not are oriented to the immediate present and hedonic impulse expression. There are, to be sure, many hard-working, future-oriented poor blacks, and also many well-to-do sybaritic ones. But while the line of separation drawn above is by no means sharp, it does not falsify a general tendency. What that line does fail to do is to separate political attitudes. On both sides of it are blacks who seek to maintain separation of the "black community" from the white, others who want to encourage greater unity between the two.

The answer to the following allied questions could determine the immediate future of race relations in this country. Assuming a continuation of the present drift in white attitudes, will cultural commonality instead of racial separation come to have a greater appeal to upwardly mobile blacks? Will their attitudes accommodate greater acceptance of a widening differentiation within the black community?

If the answer should prove to be affirmative on both counts, they would probably then repeat the immigrant experience: individual achievement by some immediate descendants made their way of life virtually integral with that of other "middle-class" Americans. In short, will the traditional American way be followed, or will most blacks cling to racial solidarity and make an overriding priority of seeking changes uniformly applicable to all blacks? To some extent this issue will be determined by the kind and extent of cooperation they receive from whites, but not in the total way that many blacks assume.

The cause of black-white unity might well be served by black success striving, on an individual basis. Much of what goes by the name of race prejudice is actually "class prejudice." Studies previously cited indicate a growing white willingness to accept black neighbors, provided "they are like us"—in outlook, behavior, and life-style. The white flight to the suburbs has been much less an escape from blacks than from urban criminals, prostitutes, and dope addicts. Most well-to-do blacks are similarly motivated. That any abatement of race prejudice requires social acceptance of *all* blacks, when whites are little less exclusionary in attitude toward other whites with whom they have little in common, is, upon close examination, a curious assumption.

It is true that such a development would not "solve the race problem," as this is commonly posed. But perhaps also a form of racism is revealed when 22 million Americans are addressed as if they were indistinguishable from one another. White "friends of the race" as well as bigots do not ordinarily use phrases like the "white problem" or the "white," while both evidently do tend to hold an indiscriminate image of all blacks, whether in favorable or unfavorable lineament.

And such a development would exact a psychological price from able hard-working blacks—that of sacrificing, to a greater degree than in recent times, racial to "class" identity. Any willingness to pay such a price will receive no encouragement from some whites. Eric Hoffer, a militant square, and many white liberals stand together in advising successful blacks to go back into the black slums and help those left behind. Another form of racism is thereby revealed, since no appeal of that kind can be recalled as ever having been made to the successful grandchildren of white immigrants, even though some them did *volunteer* to do just that.

At the present time there is a great deal more elbowroom for black action, economic as well as political, than perhaps most blacks believe and certainly many whites will acknowledge. Any people with a history of being oppressed are not likely to exaggerate a recent widening of the area of freedom and self-determination. And yet while the following implied advice may be somewhat gratuitous, it is also germane: "To constantly explain away one's failure as a product of one's environment, or worse, of another race's or class's doing, either directly or through the system it controls, is to reduce oneself to the level of an object, and further to prolong one's dependency on that other group or environment" (15).

Affirmation of black independence does remain, of course, to some extent hostage to white opinion, especially that which feeds residual prejudice and discrimination. In the perspective under consideration, persisting white attitudes of a different kind are also counterproductive. There are well-intentioned whites who have a psychological stake in seeking to perpetuate that kind of black dependency Professor Patterson alludes to in the above quotation. Expiation of guilt is a motive cherished by those people who feel more comfortable with a black whom they can commiserate and publicize as a victim than with a competent black who merely wants to make his own way without serving as an involuntary therapist *(16).*

Which Direction?

It seems unlikely that continued promotion of collective white guilt can be counted upon to diminish racism. An assumption of collective responsibility, black and white, might better serve *(17).* Movement in that direction has been hampered by cross-purposed goals. On one side, an apparent majority of blacks and whites are either willing or anxious to see economic, educational, and political integration completed. On the other, a minority of blacks and whites advocate racial separation; the white contingent, ironically enough, includes "friends of the race" as well as bigots, who promote separation for different material and ideological purposes.

Both goals might conceivably be sought concurrently, in movements toward integration in some areas and separation in others. Still it is difficult to see how energy could be effectively mobilized, black-white cooperation forged, within so clouded and confused a prospect. The assimilationist impulse is directed against social discrimination. The benignly segregationist one promotes educational, job, and other quotas, and welcomes separate facilities designed to affirm racial pride and consciousness. But the effects as well as implications of these latter choices, however laudable the intent, interfere with any possible continuation of a movement *toward* one society.

But what do terms like "assimilation" and "integration" signify? If to fulfill the specified condition of integration a state of total unselfconsciousness must be attained in which visible race differences are entirely ignored on both sides, then in the light of all past history it never will be achieved. In various kinds and degrees, categorical exclusionary attitudes have been and remain universal, attaching to perceived differences of age, nationality, social class, sex, and religion, as well as race. "If there is a conspicuous societal religious minority, there is religious prejudice. If there is a conspicuous racial minority, there is racial prejudice" (18). Although largely correct in pointing a general tendency, that statement will hardly explain a demonstrable waning of prejudice against a "conspicuous racial minority" in this country while that minority grew in size.

At Home and Abroad

The charge that much more could be accomplished cannot be refuted. But any inference of complacency which might be drawn from a recounting of what *has* been accomplished is well balanced by the common practice among many American intellectuals of dismissing any movement toward a domestic improvement they themselves advocate because that improvement fails to realize a proclaimed ideal. Such a rigorous standard is rarely applied to other contemporary societies. Little has been made of the evidence that anti-Semitism is incalculably worse in Russia than in the United States, that antagonism toward whites runs higher in mainland China than antagonism toward Orientals in this country, that antagonism toward whites is markedly severe in the new African states in comparison with white antagonism toward blacks in America.

Exclusionary attitudes do not require racial differences for their formation and expression. Negative attitudes toward a defined out-group can flourish without any present or historic imputation of social inferiority. And contrary to a widely held view, close personal knowledge of out-group members, experiences shared with them and thus presumably a greater "understanding" of them, can in some circumstances exacerbate those attitudes.

The harijans, or "untouchables," of India are racially one with all other castes; yet neither the Indian Constitution nor the Untouchability Offenses Act of 1955 has secured them from continuous persecution. Over 200 of them die each year in "caste murders," and the police in most cases refuse to investigate. Brazil, frequently cited as a bastion of prejudice-free social life, has witnessed a decline of its once estimated 2 million Indian population to about 100,000.

They have been systematically hunted down and killed, for "sport" as well as land.

Ibo and Hausa tribesmen in Nigeria hate one another. The convulsions among neighbors in Northern Ireland rarely fail to be reported on the front pages of American newspapers. The Walloons and Flamands in Belgium do not get along at all: the source of their quarrel is linguistic, whether French or Dutch shall predominate in the schools and public life. The Chinese living in Indonesia would tolerate only commercial relationships with the natives, until they were virtually wiped out in racial mass murder.

Hopi and Navaho Indian, Greek and Turk, Arab and Jew, Hindu and Muslim in India, are in each case indistinguishable on racial grounds; they live side by side, share many common elements of culture—and harass one another. Still, it would be impossible to demonstrate that the incidence of antagonism, whether justified with race, ethnicity, language, or whatever, has either increased or decreased. What does appear to happen, in macroscopic view, is an endless shifting of targets and an endless waxing and waning of prejudice in hostile action.

Citizenship

There is one reason to assume, however, that the historic periodicity of race relations may be arrested in this country. In none of the foreign countries mentioned above does citizenship provide so firm a bond as does American citizenship. A quite diverse people, Americans never shared a common origin, ethnic identification, or religion. What they did share was American citizenship, almost perforce made the primary mark of overall social inclusion. Once American blacks—through a combination of legal enactment, insurgence, and dramatic changes in white attitudes—achieved full citizenship, a further drift toward social inclusion inevitably followed. It was through assumption of full citizenship that most of the recent major black gains were secured, particularly the right of equal access and thus in large measure that of equal opportunity.

The danger that wish may father thought must be guarded against. Still, largely as a result of full black citizenship, there are indications of a twin movement toward greater differentiation within the black community and of greater black-white cooperation. It was local black leadership in Atlanta, Georgia, for example, which in 1973 ended a fifteen-year school desegregation controversy. The compromise: White and black students are to be enrolled in their neighborhood schools, with the proviso that half of the top positions in the Atlanta school administration will be reserved for blacks. The black middle class wanted racial unrest stopped, black and white parents assured that their children would not be bused out of their neighborhoods, and an end to the flight of white families into the suburbs, which had endangered Atlanta's economic prosperity.

Any continuation of the movement toward integration, a common social life, nevertheless has probable limits. What blacks always resented most, according to several black spokesmen, was a categoric restriction upon the right to make choices of their own. Were fully integrated access to the public forum, to all services, all jobs, all competitive statuses to be attained, blacks, like whites, would probably continue going pretty much their own way in private and intimate relationships. There is no historic precedent for a disappearance of racial identity—nor of white-ethnic identity for that matter. Supposedly melted down, white-ethnic identity has, if anything, become more affirmed than was the case a few decades ago. From neither of these identities is the Republic in any danger— so long as the identity of common citizenship is preserved.

POPULATION GROWTH

At 0.8 percent as of 1973, the United States had one of the lowest rates of annual growth in the world, slightly above that of Europe (0.7), far below that of Africa (2.5), Latin America (2.8), and Asia (2.3). Moreover, the birthrate in this country continues to plummet, so that a ZPG rate has been achieved—discounting, of course, the possibility that the birthrate might soon reverse its present direction. Again, in comparative terms the rate of population density in the United States is quite low. But since ours is a highly agglomerated population, that is, crowded on a small amount of the land surface in compacted strips, environmental wastage is exacerbated as well as the sense that "there are too many people." Nearly three-fourths of the people live on 1.5 percent of the land; apparent overcrowding results from individual decisions to cluster in cities and suburbs.

Numbers and density of themselves do not "cause" pollution and other oft-cited ills like crime and racial strife. The Netherlands, for example, has the same annual rate of growth as the United States and a population density eighteen times higher, but also much less air and water pollution as well as less "deviance" and "social disorganization." Affluence, in combination with high density and large numbers, can work both ways. It can provide a broader tax base and more effective technology, potential means of abating pollution associated with high resource exploitation, and potential means of promoting research for new materials.

Much of what is regarded in some circles as intolerable population growth (read: agglomeration) and resulting higher pollution levels can be usually traced to a resentment of urbanization itself and to the affluence of what at one time were the "lower classes." These people have been consuming more; moving to the suburbs and spreading farther; crowding parks, beaches, and other amenities that were once reserved for the elite; getting their "fair share" of energy, as exemplified in the purchase of various electrical appliances, such as television sets and air conditioners, and thus compounding the "energy crisis." With some justification, ecological crusaders have been charged with prejudice against the "masses" and their new high standard of living. Somewhat more recklessly, advocates of ZPG have been accused of secret warfare upon the poor in general and blacks in particular. That argument is farfetched and possibly tinged with a degree of paranoia: most proponents of smaller or childless families express a range of attitudes which includes special concern for the poor and blacks (19).

In any event, those who seek to promote a social problem of population growth have enlisted a very small following. In continuing surveys taken between 1959 and 1972, open-ended questions about national hopes failed to elicit any recorded response on the issue. In 1972 5 percent so responded to questions about national fears, but none did in the previous years noted. On the basis of *personal* hopes and fears, no responses about population growth for any year were recorded *(20)*. A vast majority of Americans either have never heard of this issue or take no interest in it. It is, therefore, a pseudoproblem.

A Possible but Unwanted "Solution"

In previous chapters the claim, often made, that the United States faces a present danger of population growth was questioned. It appears unlikely to get any worse, in part because a newly emerging problem has become widely recognized. At least in terms of attention and concern, a quantum leap in the so-called energy crisis occurred in late 1973 when an embargo was placed upon oil shipments from the Persian Gulf. Less energy will be available—in terms of politically acceptable price levels and with immediately available technology—than has hitherto been consumed. The era of *cheap* energy had been drawing to a close anyway; the oil sheiks less precipitated a crisis than they provided the shock of recognition.

At this writing there is no way to judge whether national apprehension about recession or depression is justified. A great deal of sober, informed, nonalarmist opinion holds that it is. In that forecast an accelerating energy shortage will forge a chain of high unemployment, reduced levels of consumption, higher prices, inevitably more inflation, and surely an economy operating in lower gear. Curtailment of food production is part of the dreary scenario. At present about 80 gallons of gasoline are needed to produce an acre of corn. Farm machinery requires oil, and so do trucks which bring produce to market and to the food-processing plants which in their turn use oil.

Doomsday is not in prospect, and quite possibly search for new domestic oil sources, as well as expansion of nuclear-power facilities and development of presently economically unfeasible sources of energy, may ease the shortage. Nevertheless, the long era of widely diffused affluence appears to be threatened by interlocked dislocations. Hard times *are* an undeniable prospect in the immediate term.

If hard times should return, then pressures similar to those which motivated people during the Great Depression to reduce family size, drastically, would operate once again. Prior to recognition of the energy shortage, birthrates had already fallen below those of the thirties. A new period of economic dislocation would, in all probability, accelerate the prevailing downward trend of the birthrate. If that should prove to be the case, further population reduction *as a social policy* would be deprived of plausible justification.

ECOLOGY

At least temporarily the ecological crusade was sidetracked by the energy shortage. Attention massively shifted to newly defined priorities. Hitherto intolerable levels of pollution suddenly became tolerable to a minority, and virtually desirable to a majority. The matter of the Alaska pipeline, which had been held up in the courts, was cleared without debate by a frightened Senate, which also decreed an end to further delays of litigation, of judicial review of its environmental impact. The Department of the Interior once more sanctioned, more, encouraged, offshore drilling for oil. The Environmental Protection Agency issued regulations which further extended the time for meeting standards set for automotive emissions and further relaxed those standards. An overriding concern made starkly evident the power of immediate interest to suppress ideal and long-term interest.

Environmentalists did not quit the field, but except for occasional sniper fire they settled—by tacit or declared understanding—for a temporary cease-fire. One spokesman, Thomas L. Kimball, head of the National Wildlife Federation and an ardent conservationist, said that the "environmental movement" must for a time compromise with the energy shortage, accept the prospect of dirtier air, polluted rivers and streams, and a landscape scarred by strip mining. Nonpolluting energy sources such as solar power plants and safe nuclear reactors "probably [can] not be put into effect until the year 2000." In the short run, high sulfur oil and coal will be used to generate power. "I'm worried that we'll raise generations of people who have never seen clear air or clean water, and that we'll never be able to get back"(21).

A Narrowing Vista

On the other hand, we may be able to get back at least part of the way. It was pointed out in the previous chapter that a continuing energy shortage, possibly more than ecological idealism, is serving to reduce some kinds of pollution and waste of resources. That continuing shortage may also serve to curtail economic growth.

Anyway, the prospect is dim for indefinite continuation of the unrestricted *homo faber* theme in the American experience, unlimited expansion for its own sake, sheer exuberance in conquering the environment. Unreflective dynamism, build, wreck, build again, keep moving, never pause or look back, will doubtless continue to face discouragement and thus revision. The drive to expand, though, is less likely to be abandoned than to be curbed.

Those intellectuals who advocate a national, indeed an international, policy of nongrowth will continue to find little support among the majority. The perceived interests of the latter are immediately and visibly threatened by such a goal. Worldwide mass expectations have been carried upward by a vision of material progress; there is no conceivable way to replace wish and hope with the promise of stagnation. Possibly the world could be driven into such a state, but not led into it *(22)*.

Nevertheless, and the possibility of our being caught in irremediable catastrophe aside, the American ethos is likely to turn farther away from feverish expansionism. The long crusade to make the world over in our own image reached a climax in the period from the Second World War to the abandonment of the Vietnamese misadventure, and collective self-confidence diminished. Opinion polls indicate that apprehension about the state of the nation continues to deepen.

At least temporarily, faith in American institutions, especially their leadership, is on the wane. That mood reinforces, in turn is reinforced by, an uneasy sense among the majority that we live in a finite world, a world of limited horizons, one in which the promise of uninterrupted onward and upward no longer beckons. By this prospect Professor Burch for one is heartened rather than discouraged: "Like the British who found the loss of Empire had its gains in relaxation and a chance to explore their humanity, we may find that the limits to exponential growth will provide us with the chance to ignore our machines and discover ourselves" *(23)*.

Whatever our reaction might be to what we discovered about ourselves, a combination of imposed environmental limits and value change is likely to move the majority in the direction of ecological concern. In small measure, a change has already occurred. Perceived self-interest, though, undoubtedly assumes first place, a situation revealed in a Gallup poll conducted for the National Wildlife Federation which found 51 percent of those interviewed to be "deeply concerned" about environmental problems. But the "over-

whelming majority placed emphasis upon discovering technical solutions rather than limiting production and consumption. It would
seem that conservation has yet to find its place in the hearts of the
democratic masses" (24).

But a Larger Vision

And yet, if by barely perceptible degrees, a new and larger vision
does appear to be forming. What cannot be measured, can only be
inferred from sportsmen's publications as well as from more idealistic sources, is a growing realization that man is no longer—if ever
he was—lord and master of the earth, that he is a creature who for
reasons other than his own survival must treat the delicate balance
of natural forces with more respect. Once the narrowed focus upon
the energy shortage lifts, themes of accommodation to and cooperation with the natural environment will probably be reasserted at the
considerable expense of those of conquest and expansion.

In that event, limited specific aspects of economic growth
would be traded off for environmental protection. Immediately
prior to the "energy crisis" a growing number of small towns, in
reversal of erstwhile universal practice, had removed the welcome
mat to corporations seeking new locations for branch offices and
factories in order to preclude further air, water and noise pollution.
In Oregon and Vermont *state* policy had shifted to one of limited
economic growth.

But any voluntary abandonment of economic growth *as such*
is a most unlikely prospect. Long-established habits, wishes, drives,
expectations, and attitudes of the American people can no more be
jettisoned than by fiat they can be suddenly reconstructed. Any
hope of soon converting most Americans to the Hopi world view of
harmonious cooperation between man and nature would be a futile
exercise in the fallacy of contextual choice.

Finally, and again, we cannot simultaneously maximize all our
values. Those social critics who are unwilling to accept the prospect
of graduated compromise, who demand instantaneous adoption of
ecological totalism and a policy of nongrowth, have probably failed
to reckon a real price of their hypothetical victory. Of the major
social problems we have discussed, that of poverty most obviously
requires continued economic growth to furnish the means for con-

tinued efforts to solve it. The costs of a totally pollution-free environment, of severely restricted resource use, of "ignoring our machines," in short, of completely repudiating the theme of expansion, simply will not square with the goal of raising the material welfare of the poor to a predetermined and high level.

REFERENCES

1   David J. Rothman, "Prisons, Asylums, and Other Decaying Institutions," *The Public Interest,* Winter 1972, pp. 3–17, p. 16.

2   David Matza, *Delinquency and Drift,* Wiley, New York, 1964, pp. 188 and 98. Professor Matza has unveiled a paradox: rhetorical use of determinism can *determine* further criminal action. On the other hand, no argument should be inferred that condign punishment would appreciably lessen present crime rates. That naïve idea invokes the fallacy of contextual choice. The present balance of conflicting attitudes will neither support nor implement severe and conscience-free punishment procedures.

    While the threat of legal punishment *does* control behavior, it operates indirectly and in a sense upon the wrong people. The hypothetical average citizen much less fears the law's threat to fine or imprison him than he fears a loss of reputation, what his family, his boss, his associates would say and think if the law's threat were carried out. In other circles the law's threat is experienced directly, but as a limited and calculated risk. Muggers, bookies, prostitutes, burglars, dope peddlers have little else to lose than time and income if they are sent up.

3   James Q. Wilson, "The Crime Commission Reports," *The Public Interest,* Fall 1967, pp. 64–82, p. 78.

4   Carol J. Harris, "Crime and the Treatment of Criminals in France," unpublished manuscript in writer's possession, p. 3.

5   "Delay is a heritage of 19th-century Jacksonian democracy—the attitude that the parties and their counsel control the process of litigation, and that the judge's function is solely that of a referee who hands down specific rulings at the request of the parties." Macklin Fleming, "The Law's Delay," *The Public Interest,* Summer 1973, pp. 13–33, p. 19. During and since that time the judge has been stripped of most of the authority which inhered in his office under English and Colonial law. In American law delay is viewed as a positive good, an indication that "due process" required by the Constitution has been fulfilled. An American judge is almost helpless to render a decision that will stick

in any important criminal case; that decision will inevitably be de-layed, before and during trial, and subsequently be appealed if sen-tence is passed.

6 Bernard Botein, *Our Cities Burn,* Simon & Schuster, New York, 1972, p. 95.

7 Botein, reference 6, p. 132.

8 Cited in Charles McCabe's column, *San Francisco Chronicle,* Oct. 23, 1973, p. 43.

9 In fiscal 1972 the federal government alone spent about $27 billion to aid the poor. Only half of this amount took the form of direct pay-ments, the kind of transfer acknowledged in census data. "The other $13.5 billion or so consisted of in-kind transfers, the largest of which was in the form of medical assistance." Noncash transfer payments nearly doubled from 1968 to 1972. Census failure to include this type of payment overstates prevailing income inequality. Sanford Rose, "The Truth about Income Inequality in the U. S.," *Fortune,* December 1972, pp. 90–93, 158, 162, 167–169, and 172, p. 167. On the other hand, Rose fails to estimate how much of those noncash transfer payments was absorbed in bureaucratic salaries.

10 Rose, reference 9, p. 172.

11 George F. Will, "Nixon, The Great Society, and the Future of Social Policy," *Commentary,* May 1973, pp. 57–61, p. 58, underscored in the original. Will is a self-styled conservative, and like many such, as well as many economists of every political hue, he advocates direct income support for the poor, the "guaranteed annual income." He bases his stand on two claims: conservatives are helpless to dismantle the wel-fare state they abhor, and government subsidies are now a major determinant of virtually all personal or family income. Equity and morality, he says, demand a redressing of the total subsidy system which on balance continues, he says further, to penalize the poor.

The difficulty—a large one—is that the majority are neither as knowledgeable nor as sophisticated as Mr. Will. Nor are they as pre-pared as he to accept public acknowledgement and legitimization of a permanent "underclass" to be maintained, as they see it, at their ex-pense. At this writing a variant of the Family Assistance Plan is being taken off the shelf where the original, and popularly contested, version was placed.

12 William Watts and Lloyd A. Free (eds.), *State of the Nation,* Universe Books, New York, 1973, pp. 171, 173, and 175.

13 Idealized responsibilities cited here and elsewhere in this section are surely departed from more often than they are met. But the majority

are tradition-oriented, and tend to view themselves, however inaccurately, as being exemplary models of traditional cultural ideals.

14 The old wheeze about interpretation of measurement intrudes: is the glass half-filled with water, or is it half empty? That black poverty and enrollment on welfare predominate over white is not being denied. Only 9 percent of whites lived below the official poverty line in 1972, and 95 percent of white families received no public assistance in 1971. The racial disparity *is* wide; still, the popular image of poverty and public assistance as more or less characterizing the entire black population is unsupported by evidence.

15 Orlando Patterson, "The Moral Crisis of the Black American," *The Public Interest,* Summer 1972, pp. 43–62, pp. 52–53.

16 Thomas Sowell, *Black Education: Myths and Tragedies,* McKay, New York, 1972, p. 165. White researchers of the black scene especially irk Professor Sowell. He says their work has a built-in bias, in favor of the unusual, the lurid, the pathological, "both in terms of its inherent interest and its potential benefit to the researcher." In his assessment of the case, no sociologist has an audience for writing about black men and women who work hard to make an independent life for themselves and their children. Research findings are biased in another way. Sociologists "prefer to work in the daytime, which means interviewing the kind of people who are around in the black community during the day while most adults are off working somewhere" (p. 163).

17 "Racism" is an omnibus term with a built-in prejudice of its own. It can form a bludgeon for use against anyone, black or white, who disputes the value of any measure or program on the grounds of probable counterproductivity, such as "busing," racial quotas, or the exoneration of black criminals *because* of race. And an imputation of "racism" protects the accuser from having to acknowledge the complex, mercurial shifting of attitudes which continues to occur.

What, for example, is "racism" in these findings? A Gallup-poll comparison of 1963 and 1973 responses showed a growing opposition by white parents to "busing." But in that same period, objection in the North to sending one's own child to a school "where a few are Negroes" dropped from 10 to 6 percent, in the South from 61 to 16 percent. "Where half are Negroes" elicited a rise in Northern response, from 53 to 63 percent, and a drop in Southern response, from 78 to 36 percent. "Where more than half are Negroes," a rise from 53 to 63 percent in the North, a drop from 86 to 69 percent in the South. *San Francisco Chronicle,* Sept. 10, 1973, p. 7.

18 Donald J. Devine, *The Political Culture of the United States,* Little,

Brown, Boston, 1972, p. 340.

19 See, for example, Eleanor Holmes Norton, "Population Growth and the Future of Black Folk," Population Reference Bureau Selection 43, October 1973, 4 pp. The author is chairman of the New York City Commission on Human Rights.

20 Watts and Free, reference 12, pp. 257–260. As of 1972, the four greatest national fears were recorded in the following order: war, lack of law and order, economic instability, and national disunity and political instability (p. 258).

21 *San Francisco Chronicle,* Nov. 15, 1973, p. 7. Mr. Kimball is unduly pessimistic. Air, soil, and water are renewable resources. And so is timber, the brightest part of the resource picture: more trees now stand in the United States than at the turn of the century. Fossil fuels, like oil, coal, and natural gas, on the other hand, are not renewable.

22 A belief that the world could be so led is entertained by the "Club of Rome" (Donella H. Meadows et al., *The Limits of Growth,* New American Library, New York, 1972). They also warn of the danger in projecting exponential curves, and they then drive their own extrapolations of population size and resource exploitation off the graph paper.

In another view, adaptations to critical challenges will continue to emerge, as has been the case in previous eras. Energy and material shortages at home, as well as population pressure in some overseas areas, *could* be rectified by unforeseeable conjunctures of present with future trends, as well as by individual and collective decisions yet to be made, which escape the programming of today's computers. The Club of Rome, for example, ignore such technological possibilities as solar energy and pay no heed to a more homely detail—only a trifling proportion of the world's coal reserves is liable to depletion by the year 2000, even with more intensive mining than at the present time.

23 William R. Burch, Jr., *Daydreams and Nightmares: A Sociological Essay on the American Environment,* Harper & Row, New York, 1971, p. xi. Professor Burch may have somewhat overstated his case. A British writer says his own countrymen have paid a high price for "exploring their humanity": "The experience of Britain would suggest that a non-growth society can produce as many and as unpleasant stresses on the social and political economy as industrial growth can impose on the ecological and natural resources of the globe." Rudolf Klein, "Growth and Its Enemies," *Commentary,* June 1972, pp. 37–44, p. 43.

Likewise, if in this country we should "ignore our machines" in order to "discover ourselves," the price would be high and the likely unanticipated consequences drastic. No one, for example, has suggested how current levels of pollution and other ecological distortions can be remedied without more and improved technology, except by a policy of economic contraction which is unacceptable to the majority. Compromise of economic expansion, not its abandonment, is the only feasible quasi-voluntary prospect.

24 Burch, reference 23, p. 110. **24**

Name Index

Subject Index